CHANGE
AHEAD

How research
and design are
transforming
business
strategy

BIS Publishers
Building Het Sieraad
Postjesweg 1
1057 DT Amsterdam
The Netherlands
T +31 (0)20 515 02 30
F +31 (0)20 515 02 39
bis@bispublishers.com
www.bispublishers.com

ISBN 978 90 6369 398 5

Illustrated by Carola Verschoor
Designed by Boris Rijksen
Copy-edited by John Loughlin

CHANGE AHEAD

How research and design are transforming business strategy

Carola Verschoor

BIS Publishers

Praise for *Change Ahead*

'In today's business world, this book is a must-read for change leaders! The emphasis on research and design is central for emerging new practices, which are needed to sustain every firm's competitive advantage. A plus, the interviews illustrate the aim of this book, and make us come back to the basics when we decide to navigate in turbulent seas!'

Nassim Aissa Belbaly
Professor of Technology and Innovation Management
Montpellier Business School

'A fresh and practical way of looking at business, with an inspirational framework that highlights the human aspect of business.'

Pablo Beramendi
Director of Branding
Google

'Change Ahead is a brilliant masterpiece! The book introduces a fresh perspective of how we should change our mindset about Design, Research, and Strategy and how they are connected in a new model for developing sustainable business. An excellent must-read for anyone who is eager to keep up with the pace of the changing world and respond in a proactive and adequate manner.'

Aneliya Evtimova
Chief Relationship Officer
Future Ideas

'(Herbert) Simon said design is the "transformation of existing conditions into preferred ones". Carola's Change Ahead highlights the catalyst power of our industry to help better design our future. Carola brings both research and design together for those sailors who are feeling a bit lost in this ever-changing sea.'

Patricio Pagani
Executive Director
Infotools

'Change without strategy is luck; strategy without design is faith; design without research is wishful thinking. But by connecting these essential processes we can change the world. It's fantastic to see a beautiful book filled with practical advice and experience from pioneers and experts. This will be a valuable read for anyone making changes based on real human value and on business needs.'

Adam Lawrence
Founding partner WorkPlayExperience
And co-initiator Global Service Jam &
Global GovJam

'To create meaningful change is to understand what really matters. Sail away with Carola Verschoor and get all the necessary answers.'

David Carlson
Design strategist and advisor
And author of Make Design Matter

'Joining ideas, breaking myths, and outlining profiles of contemporary winners, this book shows that there is indeed a way to advance through high transformation conditions as we have nowadays.'

Alejandro Garnica
Independent consultant and Director General
ARIA (Americas Research Industry Alliance)

Kees Elands
Founder / Creative Director
TrendsActive

'The gap between design research and design practice is an ongoing discourse for design management academics. This book provides relevant content about design methods and techniques that could bring the two separated entities together, and have better impact on businesses. I would definitely recommend Change Ahead as a key resource in the reading list for all my Master students.'

Dr. Mersha Aftab
Senior Lecturer in Innovation
Faculty of Arts Design and Social Science
Northumbria University

FOREWORD

Over the last ten years we have seen the traditional ways of doing business give way to the creative empowerment of the people we used to call customers and consumers. New human-centered practices and organizations have formed at the intersection of research, design and business strategy. Carola Verschoor captures and shares this state of flux and confusion in *Change Ahead*. She speaks from experience, having spent the last twenty years in the innovation business. But she also points to the current literature, both academic and commercial, to enrich her discussion of this change.

Carola speaks from the deep intuition that she has gained though many years working as a practioner on the edge of change. This position gives her the ability to speak with clarity about the current situation. It also gives her the perspective to look far out ahead and to help readers who are now attempting to navigate this uncertain future.

Change Ahead describes the kind of mindset and attitude that it will take to succeed in the emerging business environments. This is not a book for beginning designers or researchers who are eager to learn the new tools and methods for human-centered design as applied toward business strategy. There are a number of other resources available for that now. Instead, *Change Ahead* provides orientation to help the reader get on board with the change and learn to enjoy the journey.

The book features short interviews with 42 pioneers and experts who were each asked five simple questions: What is research? What is design? How are they different? How are they simliar? How do you envision the future of research and design within the business context? Their widely divergent responses sometimes reflect the past and at other times give a glimpse of the future.

It's a unique moment in time that we live in now and *Change Ahead* has captured it. It will be interesting to look back ten years from now and see where we have gone on the journey.

Liz Sanders, Ph.D.
Founder of MakeTools
Co-author of *Convivial Toolbox: Generative Research for the Front End of Design*
Associate Professor, Department of Design, The Ohio State University

September 2015

ACKNOWLEDGEMENTS

Change Ahead is for all those who cross oceans, who believe in change as a way of evolving, and who make it a way of life to venture into new places, new topics, and new possibilities with an open heart and an open mind. And also for all of those who accompany us, allowing us to dream big, to open up our sails, and expand our horizons by seeking and creating new opportunities.

Thanks to everyone who joined the conversation and generously contributed their views and expertise. This book, and my own journey as an author, would not have been the same without those inspiring conversations. Special thanks to Kees and Boris for taking the design of this book to a whole new level. And very big thanks to Constant and Emma for believing in this project from the early sketches and visual maps all the way to publication.

DEDICATION

This book is lovingly dedicated to my husband and children, with whom I learn and grow every day.

CONTENTS

1 STRATEGY IN MOTION

2 REDESIGNING RESEARCH

3 RESEARCHING DESIGN

4 SETTING SAIL

5 EMERGING PRACTICES

6 CONVERGING TOWARDS COLLABORATION

7 THE NEXT FRONTIER

8 CHANGE AHEAD

1 STRATEGY
IN MOTION

'The sea, once it casts its spell, holds one in its net of wonder forever.'

- Jacques Cousteau

Strategy in motion

Strategy used to be something business professionals could build in a vacuum, buy from consultants or communicate top-down. That paradigm has been replaced by one in which strategy is collaborative, dynamic, fluid and ongoing.

Strategy gets set in motion as it sails through the turbulent waters of change. It is no longer enough to manage strategic processes. Businesses must integrate their skills adaptively and flexibly to choreograph strategic efforts which will allow them to thrive in a context of chaos, where change is the norm.

Business Sailors

I've been in the business of innovation for over two decades, and having found my way through those uncertain, muddy waters of business renewal I know one thing for sure: it's the attitude that makes the difference. Not just the tools, nor the size of the project, nor the level of budget.

Innovation requires an attitude of curiosity to mix what we know, what we question and what is still to come, to fill the 'space' that lies ahead with new forms and relevant meaning; to do so assertively and with determination, from a shared vision that develops and takes shape throughout the journey, invitingly inspiring others to join in. Much like seafarers who navigate into new dimensions: enjoying

the sense of freedom, the sound of the waves and the feeling of wind through our hair. The sailing team opens the road, enables discovery, facilitates the journey into the unknown and bridges the distance to new shores as they are transformed by the experience.

In the world of business a new breed is emerging. This breed of innovators dares to re-search and re-design what is. They look at the world of possibilities with open minds, dare to search for opportunities and then search some more beyond the constraints of what is known. They integrate, blend, mix, streamline. They interpret and combine and re-create and envision. They guide us together forward in a progressive understanding and collaborative meaning-making which is beyond the obvious, beyond the rational and beyond the known and into the realm of our own, new possibilities and untapped potential.

Ongoing Transformation

As long as we're alive we are transforming. This ongoing transformation is proof of aliveness. When change stops, we are dead. This is the very basis of evolution. Evolution of business is no exception.

Given the degree of complexity and change that surrounds us today, the analogy of our oceans and seas feels appropriate. The Earth's oceans are the origin of life and the realm of continuous change in tides,

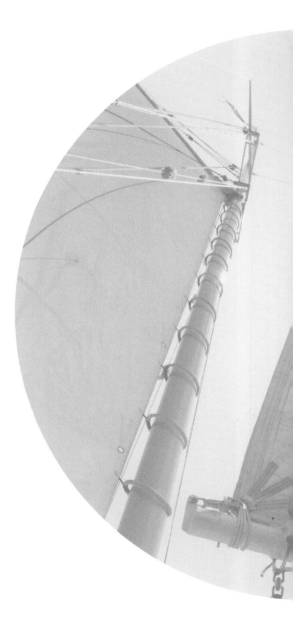

in waves, in winds, in depth and in the life forms that inhabit it.

In business, the strength of these natural forces of change is more felt than ever. Waves of technology, winds of societal change, cycles of economic instability, all make business more difficult than ever before to navigate. So we must learn to navigate. Staying on the shore is not an option.

In order to create meaningful and lasting value, businesses need to embrace the change and the complexity around us. They are an inextricable part of it. There is no point in battling with it, taming it or framing it. Change is ongoing with the chaos and beauty that characterize it, just like the ocean.

Crisis of faith

The business world and large brands are going through a crisis of faith. This crisis is brought about by the users. They are no longer blindly following brands and businesses as a cult. This creates all kinds of ripples, waves and whirlwinds, which in turn affect business.

To maintain its following, -and by extension its profits- business needs to create meaning. This entails gaining an understanding of what is meaningful and being successful in creating meaningful propositions. It implies that businesses journey into the context

-into the full territory- and understand it first hand, in order to flexibly, adaptively, and gradually renew themselves to stay in touch with their users, who are at the core of their business' aliveness and livelihood.

The map is not the territory

Business has traditionally managed itself from within, using different departments or disciplines. It typically kept track of the outside world through the use of analytical tools such as surveys and metrics. However, having all the tools in the world, all the process steps or descriptions and all the models will never explain the full scope of the rapidly changing reality. They are just instruments to help us navigate our journey.

This is, quite simply, because the map is never the territory. Maps are over-simplifications that allow us to fleetingly grasp a bit of understanding. But a map cannot replace the experience of the actual immersion into the territory. Great navigation, therefore, is a much more intuitive task and it is an acquired skill.

Skills are best acquired by experience. So too are skills for navigating business. The territory is best explored by diving into it, immersing into its vastness and emerging from it with new experiences and new insights. This is how humans learn. And how they transform, evolve, and adapt. Human systems are no exception. In this environment of change, conditions have

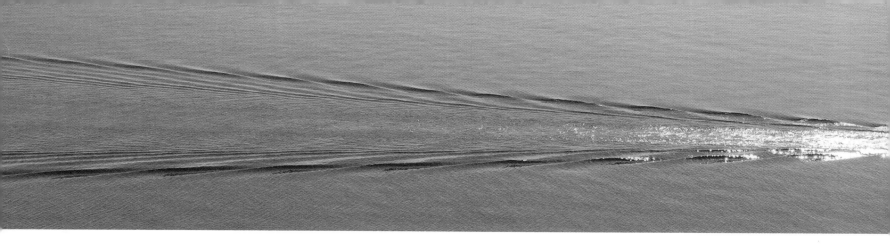

never been better for learning. In the chaos that surrounds us lies the opportunity to deeply engage and truly understand, to shape meaning by connecting what is seemingly fragmented, and to continuously dive into the territory and create new maps, based on new perspectives, new understanding and a sense of adventure.

Integrative thinking

Great navigation cannot only be based on skilful specialists in separate departments within companies. Managing different disciplines and departments separately makes systems inflexible in the face of storms and changing condition. This fragmentation of specialties within the business practice makes businesses ultimately more vulnerable to change and unpredictability. If we are going to embark in new business journeys to renew strategies and create new value we need to look at the existing industrial model of business.

The industrial revolution has undoubtedly allowed a lot of progress. But in this ocean of change, with changing conditions, the traditional instruments of the industrial age are losing relevance. We shouldn't do away with the processes of the industrial age. Those have a place. But they should not, in a changing context, be the only processes businesses use. To navigate into a new paradigm, there is a need for new, emerging processes.

The industrial model is one of planning and predictability which has served us well in getting bigger and scaling up. There is an emerging space beyond the fact-based, linear systems and controlled environments of the industrial paradigm. That is the space where intuition comes in. Not as a uninformed or impulsive, facts-dismissive activity.

Businesses have gone to tremendous efforts to minimize uncertainty, transforming organizations into controlled systems: measuring and readjusting as necessary to make sure they stay on track. In the liquid world of the ocean, readjusting the course, testing new approaches and embracing our humanity are all key elements of an ongoing process. Business needs to be connected and integrated with its natural environment, inspired by a strong purpose and vision and able to move with the waves. This means daring to take the plunge into discovery while not solely relying on rationality.

A quick internet query[1] on the word 'rational' defines it as:
1. "Behaviour guided more by conscious reasoning than by experience, and not adversely affected by emotions.
2. Thinking process that employs logical, objective, and systematic methods in reaching a conclusion or solving a problem."

In the industrial model, businesses had a rational and linear approach to strategy-making. Directors would set a vision and define strategic priorities. The title of 'director' has to do with directing the process, after all.

The role of the director was thus to decide what needed to be done and to manage the organization in towards achieving it. That has changed because these processes are too slow in an ever-changing world, because they lead to a lack of adaptability and because putting the conclusion first by deciding the outcome ahead of the implementation beats the whole purpose. Strategy and innovation are not roles or departments: they are aptitudes in a journey of discovery.

This is where intuitive, experiential processes come in. Intuition is an integrative, selective, whole-brain, and imminently human ability. It is a necessary addition to business over and above linearity and rationality. Intuition allows us to create value by creating meaningful business in a more organic fashion without disregarding the fact. Rather, intuition places the facts in a systemic context. Its value lies in crafting a vision, loading it with meaning, and bringing it to life.

As the context changes, businesses must become more versatile, more creative, and less directive. Managing uncertainty, unpredictability, and complexity is something we are equipped for as humans. This human ability to hold two contradicting thoughts and to deal with paradoxes is nicely linked to the domain of business in Roger L. Martin's book The Opposable Mind[2]. FastCompany[3] comments on Martin's book: "F. Scott Fitzgerald once wrote that one sign of a 'first-rate intelligence" is the ability 'to hold two opposing ideas in mind at the same time and still retain the ability to function.' According to Roger Martin, a sure sign of a first-rate business intelligence is the ability to recognize two diametrically opposing ideas and meld them into a new model that is superior to either."

The ever-changing context is continuously throwing these kinds of paradoxal challenges to business. Dealing with this as a business by having experts and specialists each address

part of the problem is not enough. Addressing the problems only rationally is not enough. We need to up the game of business by integrating skills and by relying on all of our human capacities not just our rational skills.

A sailor who ventures out into sea would never expect conditions to be stable throughout the journey. The sailor would also rely not only on one part of his abilities nor on his own abilities alone, he would literally put 'all hands on deck' to do whatever it takes to have a successful journey. Business must also learn to rely on all of the capacities and skills of its teams, using those talents as appropriate within changing conditions.

Like navigating open waters, applying those skills is purpose driven: the creation of meaning serves as a guiding principle for teams to self-organize, to bring in what is necessary, to rely on one another to do what it takes at each moment when facing all kinds of different conditions.

Meaningfulness

Bringing meaning to life is what research and design do in the best of circumstances. Research helps us understand what matters. Design helps us create meaningful products and services for users. Meaningfulness is a subjective concept: what is meaningful is defined by the user, not by the business. The value of both research and design lies herein: they are both in direct relation to the user.

However, research and design skills have not been traditionally integral to business. In the past, research and design have not always been invited to the strategy table. They were called in whenever information was needed or whenever propositions needed to take shape. In this traditional view research served to provide answers to questions and design served to make things work or make them aesthetically pleasing.

Yet both these disciplines can have a powerful effect in true, deep and meaningful value creation. They are new practices that need to be integrated quickly and effectively into business in order to survive in this interconnected world. Generating meaningfulness is the ultimate way to create sustainable business: which is relevant, connected, and engaging, and thus profitable.

In order to be integrated into business as full strategic partners at the strategy table, research and design need to take a new form within the business context, and not just be relegated to their functional areas. This takes a form that is similar to the world of users. It is collaborative and integrative, and it makes the most use of the unique, individual skills of each discipline with the common goal of enhancing business value and relevance. And it does so in a time and space where these disciplines are changing too. Businesses that are able to revisit how they integrate these disciplines will not only have a competitive advantage. It is my conviction that they will gain entirely new vantage points that will enrich their value creation process.

This, however, will require a change of mindset. A resetting of business priorities.

A Re-Think, Re-Search and Re-Design of the ways of working. This is why the focus of this book is at the intersection of research, design and business strategy. This is an emerging area of practice within business, with still very little consensus with regards to terminology or definitions. Essentially it is the explorative and strategy-making work that businesses do in order to shape their future and sustain their profit.

Companies can no longer expect strategic processes to be annual exercises. The rate of change has accelerated. The cycles are shorter. Strategy and strategic renewal are ongoing activities. Losing sight of the context and its waves of change is dangerous, it disconnects businesses from their environments and makes them reactive instead of purpose driven. Strategic renewal is a crucial cycle: businesses are not only managed, they need to be navigated so that they can aim to fulfil their purpose in ways that are meaningful and relevant for their context.

WAVES OF BUSINESS EVOLUTION

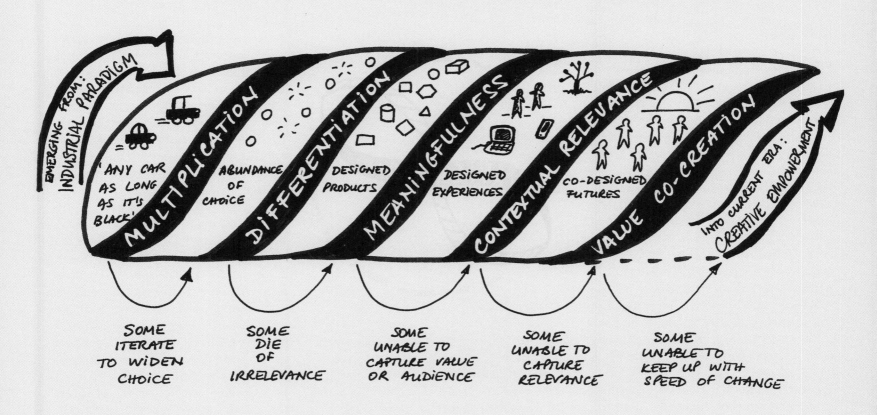

EMERGING FROM: INDUSTRIAL PARADIGM

MULTIPLICATION — "ANY CAR AS LONG AS IT'S BLACK"

DIFFERENTIATION — ABUNDANCE OF CHOICE · DESIGNED PRODUCTS

MEANINGFULNESS — DESIGNED EXPERIENCES

CONTEXTUAL RELEVANCE — CO-DESIGNED FUTURES

VALUE CO-CREATION

INTO CURRENT ERA: CREATIVE EMPOWERMENT

SOME ITERATE TO WIDEN CHOICE

SOME DIE OF IRRELEVANCE

SOME UNABLE TO CAPTURE VALUE OR AUDIENCE

SOME UNABLE TO CAPTURE RELEVANCE

SOME UNABLE TO KEEP UP WITH SPEED OF CHANGE

Shifting tides

So what has changed? And why is business as usual no longer working? Tides have shifted in a gradual process and we are now reaching the point where the waves are following one another at a higher speed. We cannot ignore the change. What started as a subtle transformation is now in full fledge, transforming our context.

The paradigm shift involves a movement away from the industrial era and into a new era of creative empowerment. This did not happen overnight, though it did happen fast, through expansive waves of business consciousness. I have drawn this as a series of waves, as with every new wave a new level of understanding led businesses to take new steps in how to generate value and relevance that would allow them evolve further.

Let's go back to the early twentieth century. One of the most cited dogmas of early Industrialism is Henry Ford's statement that clients could have: "Any car as long as it is black". He is believed to have said that in 1909 in reference to the 'Model T', which was a miracle of assembly line manufacturing at that time.

The success of the Model T was an inspiration to many, who iterated the model in order to widen choice. This led to what I call the multiplication wave. The increased use of assembly line manufacturing led to an abundance of

choice, coming from those production lines. But the thinking was in terms of engineering the products, manufacturing the products and perfecting the products without much consideration for the user. In those times if you could produce, you would find a market. Saturation had not yet become an issue.

The next wave was the differentiation wave. Abundance of choice was not sufficient to ensure sustainable demand streams, and some products died of irrelevance. Clearly, designed products offered a solution to this issue. The wave of differentiation was still very product driven, however with much more fundament to guide the alternative choices.

Some products were able to charm audiences by their uniqueness and edginess, yet many were unable to capture value or develop an audience. Business survival is cruel: these products died of meaninglessness.

This led to the third wave; a quest for meaningfulness. Business dedicated itself to the design of experiences. Aided by the digital revolution which made it easier to connect with the interests of people. Meaning-making led brands to adopt an attitude, create impactful campaigns and seek ways to convey their values to create affinity with their users. However, many forgot that meaningfulness is not something you inject. It is formed by joint beliefs. Some propositions and brands thus died of irrelevance.

We are now in the middle of a wave in which inclusion and collaboration with users are becoming increasingly ingrained practices. This is good, as it is leading to new forms of value expression. In this wave, contextual relevance reigns. Nonetheless, it will entail a difference in speed between different user groups, different geographies, different levels of awareness in each sub-context. This happens when the sparks of connection all take place at different levels. As we will explore throughout the chapters of this book, research, design, and strategy are uniquely positioned for the next wave, a wave of business engagement and integration.

That next wave, which is emerging already will be characterized by journeys of discovery and by the integrative power of business. Here, the paradigm is one of navigating change and the skills and mindsets necessary to embark in that voyage. I call this business navigation.

Journeys of discovery

In his book 'Fixing the game' Roger L. Martin[4] compellingly argues that "We must shift the focus of companies back to the customer and away from shareholder value. In other words, we must turn our attention back to the real market and away from the expectations market. This shift necessitates a fundamental change in our prevailing theory of the firm. The current theory holds that the singular goal of the corporation should be shareholder value maximization. Instead, companies should place customers at the centre of the firm and focus on delighting them, while earning an acceptable return for shareholders."

Much has been written and debated on user-centricity. I would propose that as an additional step, to bring these ideas into practice, the real shift is in how we understand concepts as 'company' and 'venture'.. First, I would be delighted if we could see a 'company' as a group of people. This is dramatically different to the economics definition of a legal entity with limited liability, established with the purpose of profit maximization. A company,

after all, isn't the building it operates in nor its charter of registration at the Chamber of Commerce. It is the people in it.

Importantly, thinking of a 'company' as group of people who come together to generate value entails breaking away with the us-versus-them view of the firm's or entity's relationship to the users. We are all people. And value is so much more than solely monetary gain. Monetary gain is the result of value generation. For money to be exchanged, value needs to be generated. Quite simple. The opposite is not necessarily true: value can be generated and given away or exchanged for other forms of value as we are seeing with the rise of new peer-to-peer systems. This choice is increasingly being made, leading to a redefinition of 'company'.

The second shift involves the concept of venture. The main value linked to venture in business is the entrepreneurial venturing into the unknown. Venturing involves risk taking. It involves passion. Through the years it has lost its meaning as businesses have sought the safety of venture capitalists and the make-believe certainty of their expectations and projections. We need to reconnect business with adventure, which is all about experience, about the journey into the unknown and about creating things together. It is not reckless nor futile. It is expansive, generative and full of possibility.

COMPANY, REDEFINED:

FROM VENTURE TO ADVENTURE

Research, design, and strategy

Both research and design within business practice stem from an industrialist context. They have been subject to a separatist view of their expertise. With a changing context and in the era of creative empowerment, it is time to join forces and integrate research and design in the processes that shape strategy and renew business.

With each wave in the evolution of business, the roles of research and design have changed, too, from being areas of specialisation to being functional departments, and now have less defined roles of exploration, co-creation, and facilitation of change. This evolution is increasingly visible in business today.

These are great times for research and design. The broader business community is changing substantially, including non-researchers and non-designers who wish to embrace curiosity, exploration and creativity. The different functional departments are now embracing skills beyond those which were once particular to their specific domain.

One obvious reason for wanting to integrate research and design into business strategy and business renewal, is that research and design are closest to the user. Another, more important reason has to do with the analytic and synthetic ability both research and design have.

This makes them indispensable in the current ocean of change. They can be the key contributors to business strategy and play an instrumental role towards more adaptive business models. They can do so because of their capacity to bridge different worlds, to create understanding and to integrate emerging concepts into meaningful propositions.

Business strategy itself is also taking new shapes. It used to be a process of planning, analyzing, and defining action plans. Nowadays, while the ink of your strategic plan is drying, the plan is already obsolete. Rational explanations on how to drive businesses forward, fact-based plans, and orchestrated tactics are inflexible. The more complex emerging model is a lot more organic. This means that the context in which business operates and the reality it is a part of interact quickly. And so we require not just systemic thinkers but also systemic changers, guides, and doers.

Research and design are both an integral part of the necessary mechanism of shaping and integrating learning through successive approximations. Research allows businesses to learn from the environment and the users. To map out what is most relevant for people and ultimately more useful for business. Design enables the step into making and delivering on the strategic intent by making the creative thinking and insight development processes explicit, and thus shared, cooperative and co-creative. The key word that emerges is engagement. Research and design can help engage business as it sails into new horizons and expands into new domains.

What characterizes the mindset of both research and design is that they open up perspectives. This mindset embraces growth and possibility. This is its strength and the source of the ability to connect and engage. It is flexible, not rigid. It aims to learn, not to impose. It is both very smart and highly adaptable. This mindset allows us to bridge the gap between the ever-changing sea of context and the ever-adapting journey of business.

The outcome of applying this mindset is what I call creative insight. A space of purposeful understanding and relevant creativity, where new practices are still shaping and the future of business is emerging. As research and design blend together in order to create value, we will see more business teams integrating these skills. In order to do that, we need to take a look at what research and design can bring and whence that has emerged.

Closing the gap with the context

While both research and design have been around for a long time, they have been fairly isolated from business making, partly because of their pre-defined mandates: 'to inform' and 'to make', respectively; partly because they have been unable to appropriately convey the value they bring to business; and finally, because business has gotten on quite well without fully integrating research and design.

The need for the skills offered by research and design is greater than ever. It is time to truly understand what they each could bring, to explore the different ways in which they can be integrated into the heart of business.

Lets look at the shifting paradigms at the different stages of the business evolution cycles. If we go back in time to the era of Henry Ford, design and research were both functions of business. Each with a defined and clear mandate: research informs, design makes.

As the wave of multiplication emerged, the roles shifted slightly to make room for iterations: research started looking at the user groups as different segments with different characteristics and design began to apply creativity in order to iterate possibilities as well as create design. The result of this is that options multiplied and choice became more prevalent.

With the wave of differentiation, again the roles of research and design shifted within the functional areas. Research now not only described the user segments but dove deeper into understanding needs and wants, drivers and barriers. Design's role also extended, from purely creating form and alternatives into delivering solutions that took into account the problem at hand not just the solution briefed by management. The results of this were designed products: that is, products and services catered to the intended audience in order to capture value through relevance and affinity.

With business's need to capture value, the next wave led to contextual relevance as products and services extended their territory into making experiences. Research and design were still encapsulated in their functional roles but increasingly working in cross-functional teams in which research helped explore the context and design co-created solutions with those in the context: the users.

Having learnt that user-centricity is one aspect of strategy and innovation, businesses have moved into a broader stakeholder involvement in the search for new forms of value expression. In so doing, employees, suppliers, clients, and users are all part of a large co-design team that co-creates the joint future we all want to be in. As we move into the era of creative empowerment, design and research work in tandem in order to facilitate and co-design strategy.

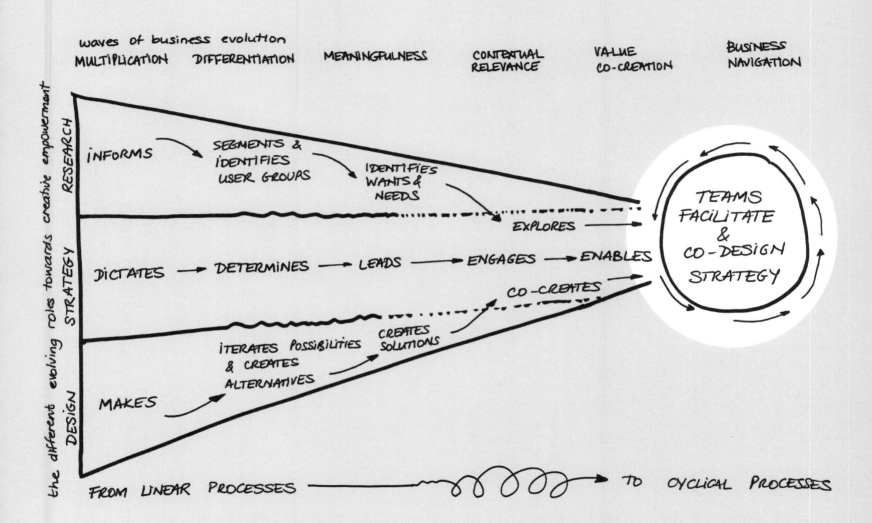

waves of business evolution

MULTIPLICATION   DIFFERENTIATION   MEANINGFULNESS   CONTEXTUAL RELEVANCE   VALUE CO-CREATION   BUSINESS NAVIGATION

the different evolving roles towards creative empowerment

RESEARCH
INFORMS → SEGMENTS & IDENTIFIES USER GROUPS → IDENTIFIES WANTS & NEEDS → EXPLORES

TEAMS FACILITATE & CO-DESIGN STRATEGY

STRATEGY
DICTATES → DETERMINES → LEADS → ENGAGES → ENABLES → CO-CREATES

DESIGN
MAKES → ITERATES POSSIBILITIES & CREATES ALTERNATIVES → CREATES SOLUTIONS

FROM LINEAR PROCESSES ———————— TO CYCLICAL PROCESSES

Why re-design research?

Research can take many forms. It lies at the basis of creation, for it is fed by curiosity as a human trait and by our innate capacity to see patterns and connect dots that lead us to new understanding. The Oxford Dictionary[5] describes it as "The systematic investigation into and study of materials and sources in order to establish facts and reach new conclusions".

Within a business strategy context, we are usually pointed in the direction of what is called market research. According to the ICC/ESOMAR[6] International Code on Market and Social Research: "Market research, which includes social and opinion research, is the systematic gathering and interpretation of information about individuals or organisations using the statistical and analytical methods and techniques of the applied sciences to gain insight or support decision making."

We need market research if we are going to create businesses and propositions that are of value to the users that compose the 'market'.

The problem, however: is that the 'informant' is a part of neither the problem definition nor the decision-making process. Additionally, the 'informant' is too often involved downstream of the decision-making -in most cases, still- to check, to validate, or to confirm what senior management and strategy develops consider to be most plausible.

It is time to reconsider this. Research is not about answers! Research is about questions: it is investigative, explorative, curious, hypothesis-probing and direction-seeking.

We need to re-design the form research takes within business, if we want research to allow us to bridge the gap between business and the world of users, helping to make business more relevant and adaptable.

Why re-search design?

There are many and varied definitions of what design is. The disciplines within the design spectrum vary from the engineering-based practices such as industrial design to the more visual-arts based practices such as graphic design. There is some agreement, nonetheless, on Herbert Simon's (1916-2001) definition as a good one. According to Simon[7], design is the "transformation of existing conditions into preferred ones."

In other words, design is a fundamental process of problem solving, in order to create, express, and shape new, practical solutions.

The problem, however, is that design requires taking a plunge, sometimes making assumptions, sometimes using creative skills. This makes it a bit 'scary' because it feels isolated and unpredictable. Additionally, design for business has evolved and changed rapidly in the last decade. It is time to review what design can do to create business value. This is why we need to re-search design.

Creative Insight

Business is increasingly becoming a dynamic model between organizations/brands and their users. This requires a high level of adaptability, adding layers of meaning to the core values of the business itself, seamlessly integrating the business with its context, yet maintaining the unique attributes that define it.

In the continuous process of value creation there are three essential phases that can be outlined: understanding, creation and making. It is especially interesting to look at the link-ing-pin between understanding the context and making a business come alive through its products and services. Right in the middle is creative insight, linking research and design as strategy-making abilities.

Creative insight is the alchemic point where the understanding of what matters to the user and how one can create relevance is trans-formed into business propositions. These do not need to be breakthrough, game-changing or disruptive. They must be meaningful. The creative endeavour of infusing meaning into products and services is thus the direct result of truly understanding and distilling what matters to others, all while having the vision and tools to shape it in ways that are unique to a given business or brand.

This is where strategy, research and design meet. This is where the user insight gets weaved into the very heart of business. It is instrumental to creating meaningful business: not based on gimmicks, models, or tools but on true understanding. This makes businesses sustainable through time: being engaged with their users, relevant, resilient, and flexible.

This book both re-searches what is required for this new model, and re-designs what that model could look like providing resources to implement these practices as well as show-casing different ways in which pioneers and experts in this field are evolving their practices across the globe.

Emerging Understanding and Emerging Practices

Transformation is always gradual. If we are ob-servant we can anticipate what is coming next by looking at what emerges. To gain both a better understanding and an experience-based view of what is emerging I have interviewed both 'experts' and 'pioneers' at the intersection of strategy, design, and research.

Importantly, each of them works across disciplines and in this way is a connector. We can learn from them about what has been happening, what the connections are that they are seeing develop and how the

understanding of their practices in strategy, research, and design is changing.

To illustrate the intersection of these expertise areas I have triangulated the disciplines and positioned them on an intuitive map. In the middle are the business sailors who, regardless of their primary expertise, connect research, strategy, and design.

Some 'experts' are scholars, some are published authors, and others are recognized opinion leaders of their discipline. The 'pioneers' are practitioners who are shaping business strategy in new ways. They are all business sailors venturing into the unknown and discovering new ways of thinking and doing that will enrich the business practice. We can learn about what drives them, what works and what doesn't and what they have learned and accomplished along the way.

Taking into consideration William Gibson's words, "The future is already here, it is just un-evenly distributed"[8], I interviewed people from different locations across the globe. In this way, they are not selected based on any sample criteria, but rather because of their willingness to change the way things are done and because of their openness to contribute to their views and experiences.

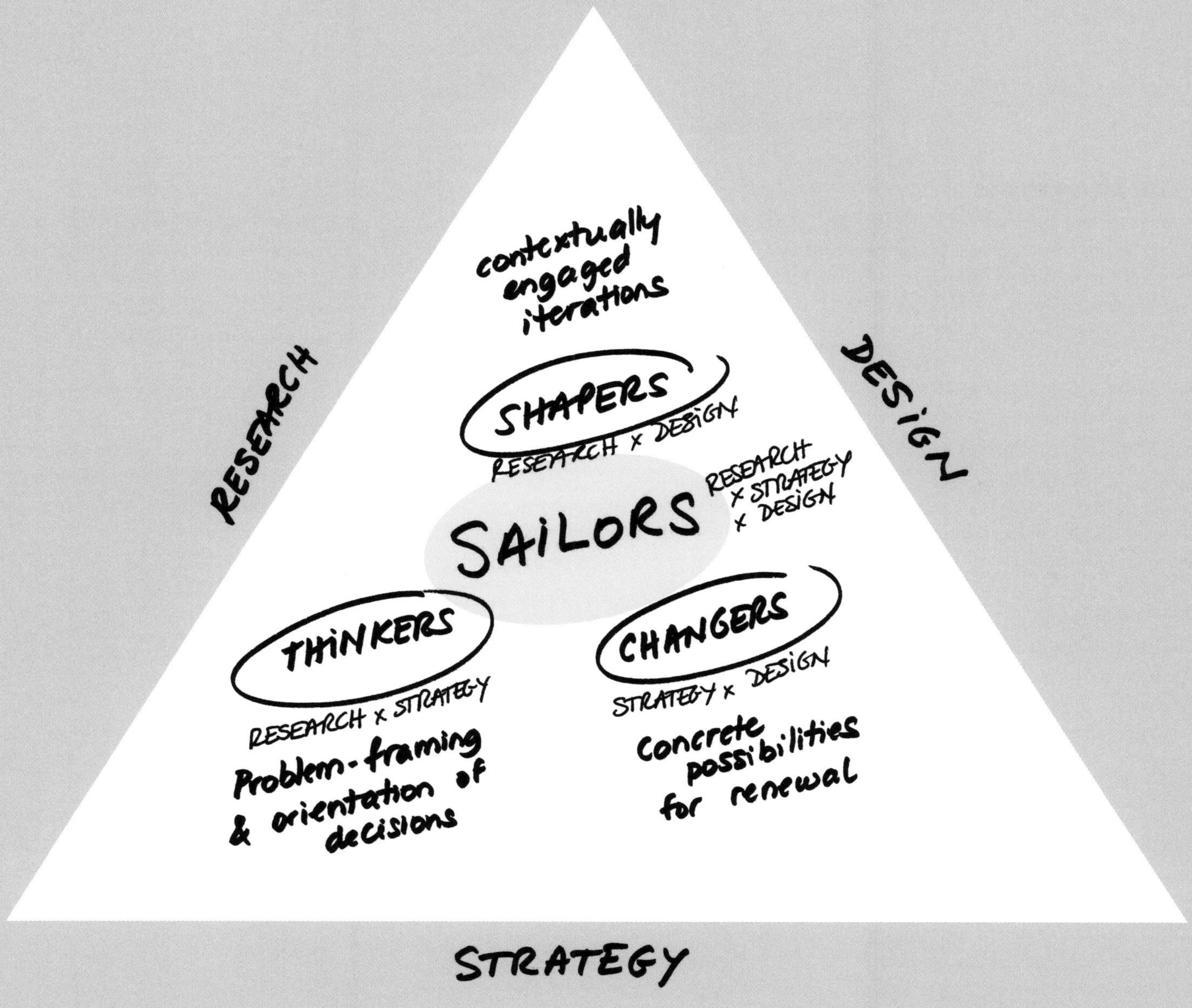

RESEARCH

DESIGN

contextually
engaged
iterations

SHAPERS
RESEARCH × DESIGN

SAILORS
RESEARCH
× STRATEGY
× DESIGN

THINKERS
RESEARCH × STRATEGY
Problem-framing
& orientation of
decisions

CHANGERS
STRATEGY × DESIGN
Concrete
possibilities
for renewal

STRATEGY

Sailing together into new horizons

The twentieth century 'hero' image of a lone ranger galloping into the horizon is up for revision. We need ad-venturous companies, with teams of sailors that navigate the business into a journey of meaningful value creation.

For businesses to be truly adaptable they need a learning attitude and a connection with the context. This is something that needs to be carried by everyone in the business. It is about people, not processes. As Peter Drucker[9] famously said "Culture eats strategy for breakfast".

I have broken these elements of culture open, resulting in fourteen attitudes that form company culture and more specifically successful teams. They will be discussed in detail later in the book, as I hope they will help contribute to replace the C-suite mentality of looking to the hierarchy of organizations for answers and approvals with a C-attitude for integrating meaningfulness to the heart of business.

The work is never done. Context changes, as do tides. We need to be prepared. Not only by our formal education or our tools, because who knows what our jobs will look like years from now. But also by our abilities and talents. These are our best bet in coping with continuous change. They are not often taught in school, as schools still operate mostly under the principles of the industrial era. These skills are learnt and developed in life. If we nurture them and give them room to grow, they can be ultimately integrated into business culture.

Navigating through this book

Change Ahead is a starting point, a way of creating awareness and opening up conversations to enable new connections of skills and attitudes and to bridge different practices and thoughts that are emerging at the forefront of new forms of value creation in business. This book introduces a new hybrid, business sailors, and a new model to sail together with our teams.

It is not possible to know exactly what the future holds. What is clear, however, is that within a world that constantly changes, businesses can change how they work, how they engage with others and how they interact with the ongoing change around them.

So I invite you to navigate this book with curiosity, with an open mind, and looking for ways to bring the skills, attitudes and abilities of research and design into the realm of strategy and business renewal. What will emerge is not purely research, nor purely design, nor purely strategy but a blend of these. Things are changing; purist definitions and clear-cut roles are a thing of the past. As we work together to create meaning, boundaries blur and skills merge to help us navigate the uncertain and unpredictable waters of change with renewed spirits, a sense of adventure, and the determination that comes from being in great company.

2 REDESIGNING RESEARCH

*'Now, Voyager,
sail thou forth, to
seek and find.'*

- Walt Whitman

On Research

Research is often seen as the art of providing answers. While that is the end result of great research, the essence of research is the art of questioning. Great research takes nothing for granted, asks new questions to open new un-explored domains, and questions the answers given to deepen the understanding through more questions.

'Finding answers' only touches the surface of the research activity. If any answer will do, if we are only seeking information, then research is very simple. Anyone could be a researcher in those terms. People are always ready to give you answers, tips and tricks, ideas, and even whole stories if you just open the conversation.

I'll give you a guarantee: if you ask a question you will get an answer. Once you have an-swers you can compile those into information. Great, but not all answers are relevant, or valid, or for that matter even informative.

The essence of research is to find, by listen-ing, by probing, by diving into the unknown without clarity as to what the end result of the search will be. It implies going with the flow of what is happening in people's real lives, without a pre-determined goal or agenda. This requires an open mind, a curious stance, sus-pending one's judgment in order to really listen and see things as they are, an ability to keep inquiring even when it is not yet clear where things are headed, and the essential ability to interpret and understand what one has found, making it useful and accessible as a source of knowledge and inspiration.

Navigating by the stars

In our need for certainty we may have over-re-lied on models that explain reality. Research is always an approximation; by definition it is not reality itself. Research is designed to provide direction, much like a compass aims to point us north so that we may orient ourselves and move forward with a sense of certainty. We seek to explore and understand so that we can find our way decisively and with determination.

The North on our planet is actually imprecise. Compasses and grids would have us think that it is an exact location or point which can be precisely measured and determined. Yet what the North actually is, is the surface of our round planet that points in the direction of the astronomical north and thus as our planet ro-tates it changes position slightly. The magnetic north gives us a good enough approximation which, when applied as a convention has us all more or less pointing in the same direction. Much like a compass, which points to magnetic north not the true north, research is merely a way of interpreting reality. It is a way of look-ing at reality through agreed conventions of what we understand to be true, which works mostly quite well, but loses accuracy when the reality becomes more ambiguous.

To get the right bearings it is much better to be in the territory and look at the stars, because that is what is real and what is happening in real time. Looking at a compass is, like re-search, a model of reality.

Our forefathers navigated by the stars. In this method, the North Star, known as Polaris, -or for those in the Southern hemisphere, the Southern Cross- is the point of reference. So when these stars are visible, and when sailors and voyagers interact with them from the reality of their journey on either hemisphere, they provide the best and 'truest' way of find-ing one's way. This is not due to their accuracy because while they refer to the astronomical north and south respectively they are not per-fect. The reason they are so reliable is because they do not create the impression that they are perfect nor precise -which is also the case for excellent research- and most importantly, because we interact with them continuously to find our way , making dynamic use of the information they provide without losing sight of the actual territory we navigate.

More than one reference, more than one sailor

The fleeting nature of certainty and clarity while navigating the ocean is the reason why experienced sailors use different sources to inform their decisions. From compasses and stars to weather conditions to wind force to real-time feedback on the tension of the sails and ropes. The research equivalent of this is data triangulation. Any expert researcher will tell you that this is one of the biggest sources of insight when conducting research in order to understand when to probe further and when to move on to the next question.

Another aspect of great research that is often overlooked or understated is that by the mere fact of being interpretative, research is subjective. In its search for 'objective' truth, research has lost touch with the human scale and sought for ways to eliminate researcher bias (the bias that takes place by the fact that a researcher is interacting with the subject). While to a degree we need to be mindful of the effect of interventions, it is impossible to remove the human aspect out of the interaction. Research is about many truths and emerging patterns that stem from looking at those diverse truths, so acknowledging and embracing subjectivity actually strengthens it by allowing us to compare and contrast views with other researchers. Just like the best yachts are steered by the efforts of a whole team of sailors, so is research much richer, insightful, and textured when there are several researchers working together, each with their own subjectivity. Such subjectivity is an inevitable human trait given by the fact that we cannot all see all of reality all of the time, but when multiple subjectivities are taken together we can work towards completing a fuller picture and a deeper understanding.

As reality becomes complex, truth becomes elusive because there are so many parallel versions of the 'truth'. This means that no single source of information is entirely valid; rather, several sources of information may provide a pixelated, mosaic-like interpretation of what is.

An ocean of non-linearity

Causalities in our world are now networked, rather than linear. We are all together adrift in a sea of change. In my view that leaves us with the inspiring prospect of becoming purposeful, rather than panicky. Of being proactive, rather than defensive. Of being curious, rather than rigid. Of being adaptive, rather than conservative.

In this non-linear world where cause and effect intermingle and intertwine, weaving all kinds of new connections, there lies the potential for transformation. In this post-industrialist, creatively empowered world we are part of a system much bigger than any business system and the characteristics of this system are non-linear. The combination of turbulence and new connections might just be ideal for businesses who want to make a lasting difference.

While the different systems in which we operate are diverse, they can be categorized. David Snowden[1] has developed a framework for categorizing the different types of contexts in which we interact under the name of *Cynefin*. Cynefin is a Welsh word that means 'habitat', referring to our context.

Snowden identifies five situations in which we can find ourselves depending on the causalities within the system: (a) obvious, in which everybody can see how cause and effect are connected and all we need to do is sense our way through; (b) complicated, when cause and effect are less clear but can be analysed and mapped out and we can apply our existing practice to understand what to do; (c) complex, which is when in hindsight we can see what the cause and effect were that lead to a situation but that within the situation itself we cannot do anything except experiment and respond to the context through emerging practices; (d) chaotic, which is when things occur randomly without clear causality and the way to respond is adaptive, through new practices that are context specific and thus cannot be defined in advance; and finally (e) disorder, which is total unpredictability and thus a situation in which people stick to what they know and retreat away from the situation with as little as possible action.

The situations or types of contexts explained by David Snowden in his Cynefin framework invite us to reflect on our approaches before embarking into projects of any kind. I quite like the similarity this model has with the sea. What I especially appreciate of Snowden's model is the fact that it is based on sensemaking, the ability to look at an ambiguous or volatile situation and understand its implications in order to make decisions. Sensemaking has everything to do with great research.

This is important because it entails zooming out before diving in. It entails, in research terms, questioning the question based on the context. This is a crucial aspect of how we are going to understand a situation that is part of a complex and multi-layered reality.

It also includes a key concept of sufficiency, that is, reaching the point in which you know enough about the context in order to act upon that understanding.

The distinction that Snowden makes between five contexts or conditions can be applied to the analogy of the sea:

- Obvious or simple are low hazard or calm conditions. Whereas the sea is never fully predictable nor obvious, these are the base conditions in which everybody has the same level of understanding of what is going on and how to act within this context.
- Complicated are medium hazard conditions with light surf and currents. This condition requires a better thought-out approach in responding to the conditions, for example by bringing in experts.
- Complex are seas with high hazard or rough conditions. A complex situation requires caution and adequate pre-orientation.
- Chaos does not mean that there is no order, but there is some kind of activity either in the weather, in the water, or both, which is unpredictable. Like in a storm, there are moments of high unpredictability and moments of relative calm that switch at different intervals making the whole very difficult to understand and master.

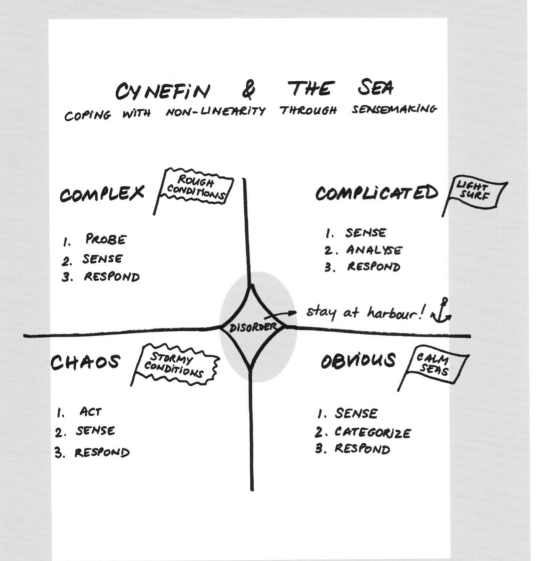

CYNEFIN & THE SEA
COPING WITH NON-LINEARITY THROUGH SENSEMAKING

COMPLEX [ROUGH CONDITIONS]

1. PROBE
2. SENSE
3. RESPOND

COMPLICATED [LIGHT SURF]

1. SENSE
2. ANALYSE
3. RESPOND

DISORDER → stay at harbour! ⚓

CHAOS [STORMY CONDITIONS]

1. ACT
2. SENSE
3. RESPOND

OBVIOUS [CALM SEAS]

1. SENSE
2. CATEGORIZE
3. RESPOND

- Disorder is equivalent to a situation in which the sea is closed to public use. This is when ships stay in the harbour and lay anchor.

This approach to contexts is excellent for appreciating the non-linear relations that increasingly are part of our systems in a networked and interconnected world. Embracing non-linearity has the advantage of allowing us to cope through sensemaking. If we were to continue with a rigid, linear approach: linearity might hit us hard and recovering from the confrontation would be costly, energy consuming, and slow versus a more proactive approach in which we make sense of the contextual situation, taking our bearings and then acting accordingly.

Until now, within the industrial model we have made the assumption that phenomena could be understood scientifically. At the basis of research lies the scientific method. Analyzing and categorizing findings is of course possible under certain conditions, when the context is obvious, and even when it is complicated, these are excellent methods. Yet in more turbulent waters it loses strength versus a more empirical approach.

Sensemaking

So what does this mean for research in a business context? Not every approach is appropriate in every situation and thus approaching research from 'tools and methodologies' would be too disengaged and would assume we can keep doing things the same way we've always done them. In a sea of change that is simply not enough, because different situations require different responses to successfully navigate them. Snowden has looked at the implications of the context on the most effective approaches in each the context to be most effective.

It is important to note that it is not always necessary to do things in new and different ways. But by the same token, it is no longer enough to do things the way we always have done. Renewal in our methods must accompany renewal in the context, which is now more turbulent and ongoing than ever before.

So what are the strategies for sensemaking? When conditions are obvious or simple, problems are well known and the solutions they require exist already. We need to look around, sense, categorize, and respond: this means that we can know what to do and apply best practices that have already been developed in similar situations.

When conditions become complicated, as we look around and sense, we also have to be able to interpret what is going on through analysis. This may require involving experts or people with a deeper understanding to feed our analysis with understanding on how to best respond. Snowden calls this approach good practices, that is, practices based on assessing the situation that require expert knowledge to determine the appropriate course of action.

These first two levels are relatively well known and easy to cope with by using the right tools and systems. But as conditions become complex, even beginning to understand the problem requitres experimentation. There are questions that will appear in the process that you don't even know you'll have when you get started. It makes little sense to start by looking at the situation. It is necessary to introduce experiments and probe in order to start mapping out what works and what doesn't and why. The emerging solution will seem obvious in hindsight but it cannot be analyzed or categorized beforehand. Iteration is key to this approach: experimentation allows knowledge to be gathered, interpreted, and evaluated in order to try again and by approximation develop emergent practices that can lead to a solution. At this level, research starts becoming more experimental/empirical and less scientific, though the documentation and learning process is very structured.

And then there is of course chaos. While not all people are likely to enter the sea in

"In a sea of change, different situations require different responses."

these challenging and chaotic conditions, it is likely that it might catch you unaware or too far off shore that you might have to face it. Here the best approach is to act, sense, and respond. This means that in order to get out of chaos you need to immerse into it and swim your way out. Here, research needs to become collaborative in order to shape solutions through interventions learning what works and what doesn't in the midst of ongoing change.

Finally, there is the level of Snowden's disorder. It is so unpredictable that people chose to stay in their comfort zone and not enter the waters. When there is disorder it becomes imperative to go back into one of the domains of order. Re-search is here in the ultimate position to bring a new order by making clear what is known and what is unknown and embarking in a search for new understanding that will bring new order somewhere along the continuum described above from simple to chaotic.

Gary Klein[2] defines sensemaking as follows: "Sensemaking is the ability or attempt to make sense of an ambiguous situation. More exactly, sensemaking is the process of creating situational awareness and understanding in situations of high complexity or uncertainty in order to make decisions. It is a motivated, continuous effort to understand connections (which can be among people, places, and events) in order to anticipate their trajectories and act effectively." The ability to make connections is what defines great creativity and great research. It is about seeing new things in new ways through a healthy balance of art and science in order to act in new, effective ways that will impact the context positively. Sense-making is the ultimate ability for navigating through these transient and whimsical times.

Navigating through change

The science of knowledge gathering and validation is a science of the precise. The art of understanding the context and becoming effective within it is linked to sensemaking. When the context moves fast, current affairs become torrential like a current. It changes and mutates before our eyes in ways we cannot always predict or foresee.

We live in a VUCA world: it is volatile, uncertain, complex, and ambiguous. The term VUCA is originally a military acronym from the nineteen-nineties. Its adoption within the business vocabulary is one manifestation of how deep the realization of the effect our changing context has on business success.

In a VUCA world, we are limited by anything we think we know for sure as it blinds us to what is possible. Imagine for a moment that we believed in the myth that the Earth is a flat square and rests on turtles. Then, confirmation bias (the tendency to observe the world as evidence that confirms what we already know or believe) makes us relate all observations back to that certainty. And it all makes perfect sense for a while. Until it doesn't.

In this context, in which reality is more fluid and erratic than ever before, the challenge for research becomes how to portray something that continuously moves.

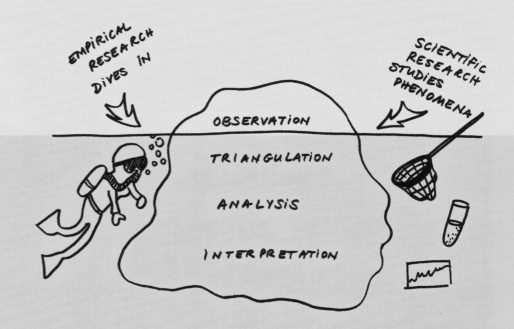

Just one vantage point, or even a handful of sources is not enough. Business is surrounded by seas of information and it becomes overwhelming to deal with the amount of –often contradictory- information available. In this context, research potentially loses its authority by being too rigid and thus needs to reinvent its own meaning. So how to approach research: as an art or as a science?

To deal with this sea of change from a scientific perspective requires isolating phenomena, because we need to frame what we need to understand and investigate to have a clear point of departure for our research. This is possible, but it is perhaps too static and siloed to allow us to navigate the context in appropriately.

Conducting research scientifically involves the following steps:
• Asking a question, defining what it is that research seeks to answer or understand
• Formulating a hypothesis, stating what potentially could be the answer to the research question
• Testing the hypothesis through experiments
• Recording the results of the experiment
• Analyzing the results and comparing them versus the hypothesis
• Drawing a conclusion about what the answer to the research question is (the hypothesis or otherwise)

Researching from an empirical perspective requires diving in and, per definition, losing sight of the shore, because we need to get up close in order to immerse in the context and experience it from within. This is probably not enough if conducted intermittently. Every immersion constitutes one snapshot and thus cannot fully reflect what is ongoing.

Conducting research empirically involves these steps:
• Observing different situations, and reflecting upon them while looking for saliency, surprises, new information, and anything that characterizes them
• Identifying patterns and relationships based on the observed characteristics
• Generalizing those patterns into overarching explanations of the situations and phenomena observed
• Generating potential scenarios based on what is possible, plausible, probable, and preferable
• Using these scenarios as tools for decision-making, by drawing conclusions on the implications of each scenario

A combination of art and science could potentially provide us with understanding of emerging patterns, of the seas of possibility, and of our potential role within the waves of change. Like experienced sailors, connected researchers could help businesses understand when to go with the flow, when to play with the wind -even if it feels counterintuitive- by adjusting the sails, and when to take out the oars and push for a destination to shape strategy through focused efforts.

The reason research plays an important role is simple yet powerful: factual knowledge can only be gathered based on the past. But decisions are all about the future. Research potentially helps bridge the gap between what we know today and the effect our decisions will have in shaping the future. While this is not solely the task of research, it is research that helps create the basis for understanding, to get our bearings, to look out at sea and interpret the existing conditions and their implications.

Good researchers are able to look at the emerging reality beyond the constructs and scientific models, with a gut-level understanding that today searching for 'truth' is impossible. Truth has been multiplied into billions of sub-cells, every actor in the context holds potentially a different version, a different perspective of the truth. So looking for understanding involves looking for meaning. For it is meaning that shapes people's lives, as people signify meaning through their own daily realities, their own truths as they elevate what is important to them. This requires research to rise to the challenge of being both an art and a science: unlocking meaning and impacting the number of possibilities to design new futures in the ongoing current.

"Research is about a quest for questions, driven by curiosity."

Knowledge does not equal understanding

Research that only delivered answers is a thing of the past. Answers do not necessarily mean better or more relevant understanding. They generate an illusion of understanding through knowledge which can be quite limiting when developing business strategy. When it comes to shaping the future of business through strategic thinking, the things we know will always be less than the things we do not know.

There will always be a space for market intelligence. That is data intensive information that helps us with the basic mapping out of our conditions. It is the most fundamental understanding of what can be known, quantified, and analysed for anyone to know where they stand and how they compare to other variables. This information is the same for all and there are specialist data gatherers and statisticians that help us with these 'answers'. This includes demographic data, transactional data, digital footprints, and such. While this information is valuable, it is only a start. It shows us what can be known, it usually provides information and seldom provides explanation. And in so doing reveals that there are many unknowns too.

The quest for questions

Research is about a quest. A quest for questions, which is driven by curiosity. Not a quest for knowledge driven by a need for certainty. The industrial paradigm has shifted and our new paradigm is no longer one in which pre-defined plans can be executed without dynamic adaptation and flexibility.

Knowledge has become highly democratized making it grow exponentially. The individual versions of knowledge are thus potentially infinite. This means that nothing is truly knowable in its totality. So in a business context, what you get to know is never the full picture because that would simply take too long to be of any immediate use.

The quest for questions is defined by a drive to explore, to recognize, and to learn, not simply to inform. Researchers become explorer guides who look outside, enjoying the process and letting it unfold. Insight is less of a eureka experience. It is a progressive realization as layer upon layer of dynamic knowledge is uncovered. Researchers adapt to the conditions, as do expert sailors, and act upon the emerging conditions pivoting the course, meandering their way towards richer understanding through adaptive inquiry and nimble approaches. New questions arise from the original questions, and questions are asked more frequently, probing. Researchers play with the dynamics and participate in the changing context to develop progressive understanding, seeking to understand enough to make sense of the context rather than seeking to know it all and decipher it all accurately.

Waves of knowing

What we will find in today's world is that the very nature of knowledge is changing. Sensemaking is a progressive set of realizations, waves of knowing that pile up leading to a new hypothesis to describe reality. There is no certainty; quite frankly there never was. We thought we had certainty because we had systems that did a good job at explaining reality and the dynamics of reality were less mercurial and volatile, so those systems did their work for a while.

The need for certainty within the industrial era stems from the fear of not knowing and the risk of getting it wrong. Of course that has high costs and affects the success of a business. Yet it assumes that knowing with certainty is possible. In this era of creative empowerment, uncertainty is the rule, which, from a creative point of view is fabulous because there are so many more possibilities for making new combinations when things aren't fixed or dogmatic. In this setting, research becomes the enabler for making new connections. Research becomes the preparation of the creative work in an explorative sense from an appreciative perspective, where systematic searching is less about thoroughness and more about completing the picture, understanding the territory in which companies will intervene or interact.

We are moving away from a business world in which information was power, to a business world where interconnectedness and understanding are the keys to meaningfulness and relevance. Researchers of all kinds are the potential connectors between businesses and the outside world, channelling inspiration, progressively building insight and continuously scanning the world for opportunities to create meaning.

Redesigning Research

In this shift towards interconnectedness and understanding it is time to revisit research. From an industrial point of view research has been mandated with the intelligent and smart skills of providing information for making better decisions. This is a very limited view of research and implies that research is downstream from strategy to validate the chosen course or merely a purveyor of information not a part of the strategic discussions.

Research can take many forms. It lies at the basis of creation, for it is fed by curiosity as a human trait and by our innate capacity to see patterns and connect dots that lead us to new understanding. The Oxford English Dictionary[3] describes it as "The systematic investigation into and study of materials and sources in order to establish facts and reach new conclusions".

We need different kinds of research if we are going to create businesses and propositions that are of value to the users that compose the 'market'. The problem, however is that as part of the legacy from the industrial model the 'informant' is not part of the decision-making process. We need to re-design the form research takes within business, if research is going to work for business and subsist as a discipline.

Redesigning research involves embracing the quest for questions. It means admitting all that we do not know, even more so than confirming what we do know. Much like business needs to reconnect with its sense of adventure, research needs to redesign itself in order to get back to its very essence: the search for meaning. This starts by admitting that research will never provide the perfect answers, nor come up with the perfect questions nor deliver a perfect representation of reality. It starts by going back to the human scale, the human level, and the human connection.

Human-centred, responsive research

Research needs to centre around people. This may sound redundant because much of the research work done, be it market research, academic research, or design research, is done to better understand people. And yet it is based on scientific models that abstract us from people. The rise of complexity in our world is making it very difficult to map out situations through research. This makes it imperative for researchers to redesign themselves and their work, not only by their approach and techniques, which have become indirect and distanced from reality, but also through the types of interaction which need to become more fluid and more dynamic and less researcher led.

Just look at the language that businesses frequently use: 'consumers', 'respondents', 'participants', 'users', 'customers' are all terms that refer to people. Yet by abstracting the human element an us-versus-them tension arises. It may be a well-intended one: in order to service clients better. But it causes empathy to fly out the window. Thinking of massive numbers of 'clients' is anything but personal.

The rise of social science-based, qualitative research points to the need to regain touch. The interpretative capacity of research becomes one of its core qualities: to see and document what is going on, but especially to create explanations and a language that gives meaning to the emerging reality, exposingthe full iceberg to support a better navigation of the tumultuous seas.

The levels of the iceberg in terms of human-centred research include
• observations at surface level: What is happening?
• triangulation of sources: What else is happening? Where else is it happening? How else is it happening?
• analysis of the observations: What are the recurring themes? What patterns emerge?
• interpretation of the themes: What are the underlying drivers and mental models that are behind these themes and patterns? Why are people acting in certain ways? Which emotions, beliefs or values guide their behaviour?

By looking at all these levels more in depth, we see the whole iceberg come into view as a system. By zooming out, research allows us to integrate the human perspective into strategy making. Research becomes not just info-bits but explanations in narrative form, that describe and explain what is going on both at the surface level and beneath the surface, making information available and accessible as well as dynamic. Once the whole system is in view it becomes easier to see future implications and thus make decisions based on different scenarios. This is where the art and science of research meet.

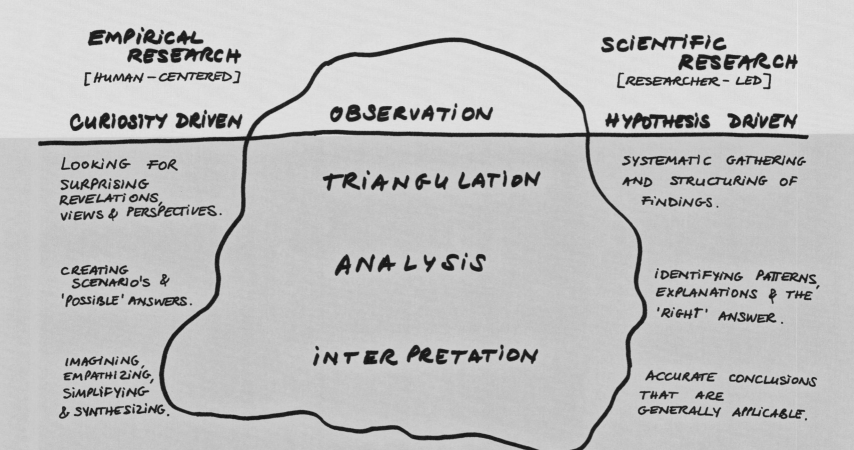

RESPONSIVE RESEARCH IS BOTH ART & SCIENCE

EMPIRICAL RESEARCH
[HUMAN – CENTERED]

SCIENTIFIC RESEARCH
[RESEARCHER – LED]

CURIOSITY DRIVEN

OBSERVATION

HYPOTHESIS DRIVEN

Looking for surprising revelations, views & perspectives.

TRIANGULATION

Systematic gathering and structuring of findings.

Creating scenario's & 'possible' answers.

ANALYSIS

Identifying patterns, explanations & the 'right' answer.

Imagining, empathizing, simplifying & synthesizing.

INTERPRETATION

Accurate conclusions that are generally applicable.

When people are at the heart of research, the methodologies are a set of tools to support inquiry. The prime goal of research becomes understanding people, and thus the selection of methods is responsive to the context. And so research draws from a multiplicity of methods and techniques in order to serve its goal of revealing the whole iceberg.

Choices need not be either/or, yet instead can follow the logic of diving deeper and deeper to seek meaning -sometimes scientifically, sometimes empirically, and sometimes in a combination of both, responding to the context and the possibilities that emerge as understanding progresses. Responsive research follows the steps of observation, triangulation, analysis, and interpretation:

• Where observation can be either 'scientific' or researcher led, looking to systematically gather information or be 'empirical', driven by curiosity and thus human-centric based on what happens in the real world;

• Triangulation can be 'scientific' by structuring the findings methodically, or 'empirical' by looking for surprising revelations, comparing views and perspectives and looking to inspire by contrasting findings;

• Analysis can be 'scientific' by looking for patterns and valid explanations, searching for the right answer and the highest possible level of certainty or it can be 'empirical' by challenging and prospecting, creating scenarios of possible explanations and posing new questions as they arise;

• And finally, interpretation can be 'scientific' by providing accuracy, courses of action focused on what business can do, looking for scientific rigour, making the conclusions generally applicable and more abstract, or 'empirical' by imagining future scenarios, empathizing with what could happen to the user, simplifying and synthesizing the findings into concrete situations.

Whether research is conducted as an art or a science or both will depend on various factors ranging from the industry, to the company culture, to the level of change to the loyalty of the users or the strength of the brand. We should not take anything for granted, it is important that research remains responsive, flexible, and is ready to put the tools and techniques necessary to make the most practical and significant contribution to business strategy.

The scientific approach is valuable because it helps to extract layers of meaning, the empirical approach is valuable because it helps to immerse oneself into the context to bring meaning to life and a combination of both is ideal because it brings the world of decision-making and the context together in a more dynamic and integrated way, enhancing understanding.

The possibilities to combine them are endless and therein lies the strength of responsive research: it helps reveal unexplored combinations which might just be a new source of competitive advantage or increased interconnection with the users. Responsive research is about what is meaningful and relevant beyond the surface. It is smart and inquisitive. It gets to the heart of the matter, revealing the most essential understanding of people and contexts by adapting tools and methods expertly and dynamically to complete the multi-layered and multi-faceted picture of what is going on.

The degree of responsiveness and flexibility is not linked to the number of tools and methodologies available. It is defined by the level and quality of experience, the open mindset, the ability to learn and the ability to integrate the perspectives of the research team.

"The prime goal of research is understanding people."

Theory versus practice

There is a well-known expression that I cite frequently: "In theory, theory and practice are the same. In practice they are not". This also holds true in the business domain. Strategy is nothing but intent put on paper, which is the 'theory' of what will be put into action. However, putting strategy into action is an entirely different matter.

Coming from an industrial paradigm, strategy used to be an obscure science of defining a plan somewhere in a meeting room bringing in all kinds of information and argumentation, but ultimately an isolated endeavour. In our creatively empowered world, strategy conducted in a vacuum is doomed to fail in practice, simply because practice and theory are never the same in practice.

And yet, because we are still in transition all different kinds of research and strategy models pervade at the intersection of theory and practice. Lets consider for a moment what the implications of 'theory' and 'practice' are within the business world at the crossroads of strategy and research, which is where strategy development takes place within business.

Theory, in this case, relates to the process of strategy definition. It is a thought process, in which possibilities for the future of the business are considered. The modes in which it operates are either deductive or inductive, although some entrepreneurial, more disruptive companies also use abductive thinking to develop their strategy. We will come to that in more detail later, in the chapter on design.

Deductive strategy seeks to confirm a strategic angle or point of view by iterating the manifestation of that strategy in practice. The deductive mode involves a top-down approach: in the case of strategy it refers roughly to the process of starting with a vision, following with a mission, values, strategic goals, and strategic plans.

Inductive strategy involves an orchestrated effort around specific initiatives, all of which add up in some form or other to the overall strategy. The inductive mode involves a bottom-up approach and is action-biased: in the case of strategy it is about the process of ideating different kinds of actions and repeating or enlarging those based on their success. It is about setting out experiments and driving strategy based on what works. Once you know what works, you can generalize and create other similar actions that will help grow your business. Strategy emerges from the internal coherence of those multiple efforts.

Practice relates to the field in which strategy is developed and which needs to be understood and explained by research in order to support the strategic planning process. Is it acontextual, where a researcher is sent out into the field to find answers that will inform strategy in an abstract and indirect way? Or is it contextual, where user-centricity leads the researcher into new, unknown territories in order to learn and understand?

Research and strategy interact at the crossroads of theory and practice. Industry has traditionally assessed the interaction of research and strategy in simulation and out of context. Businesses linked their need for research to their need to develop guiding principles for strategy based on information. But, increasingly, businesses consider the interaction of strategy and research in a real-life, context-immersive fashion to get real-time, applicable, and timely feedback in a more continuous way, which proactively feeds strategic thinking with ongoing, explorative research.

This shift in the practical aspect of research for strategic practicability is visible in the rise of qualitative and explorative techniques which are gaining the preference of most businesses to understand the markets they operate in, in more dynamic and textured ways.

Whenever research is acontextual you'll find that its main purpose is to evaluate and validate by asking questions. Its field of study is existing worlds, which are understood to the degree that one would either know what to ask (quantitative) or whom to ask (both quantitative and qualitative) in the search for answers.

In acontextual studies, when strategy formulation is deductive (top right quadrant), a hypothesis is formulated in strategic terms and can thus be validated. In this quadrant we thus find surveys, analytics ,and big data. The role of research is to catalogue proven or confirmed phenomena to confirm the chosen strategic course.

When strategy formulation is inductive, acontextual research can be used to map and storify existing patterns (bottom right quadrant), for example through the use of focus-groups, online communities or in-depth interviews.

In this case, we would know what topics to discuss and which imagery we want to elicit based on the generalizable strategic principle we are looking for.

Increasingly, though, businesses have come to realize that acontextual research cannot be a source of competitive advantage. Because it is based on what is known or knowable, and in this day and age the likelihood that acontextual research will provide information any different from that which your competitors are also buying is very low. So it is imperative to immerse yourself into the context, to look for the emerging cultures, for the hidden clues, for the associated behaviours, and all the different elements that emerge and can be discovered by engaging with the context directly.

In contextual or immersive research, when strategy is deductive (top left quadrant), the purpose is to understand relevant interactions between the defined strategy and the world of the user. This includes observational tools such as videos, photos, and field notes made in the context. It involves immersive explorations and safaris, co-creation with consumers and contextual inquiry tools. What defines this type of research is that it is focused on confirming how the strategy might work when applied into practice.

When strategy is inductive and research is contextual or immersive, the purpose of re-search is to understand and describe emerging behaviours. In this quadrant (bottom left), the unknowns are larger than the knowns. Research is seeking for new questions, as well as for surprises and creative triggers than may be generalizable into a strategic direction. Tools include ethnographic research, mobile diaries, and context mapping.

At any point in time a business team can perform research within various quadrants of the chart, based on the desired outcome. While acontextual studies are informative, contextual studies are exploratory and both have a role to fulfil in helping to shape strategic choices.

SEEKS TO
CONFIRM
THEORY

DEDUCTIVE

UNDERSTAND
RELEVANT
INTERACTIONS

CATALOGUE
PHENOMENA &
VALIDATE
HYPOTHESES

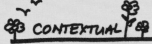

CONTEXTUAL

SEEKS SURPRISES
& NEW QUESTIONS

A-CONTEXTUAL

SEEKS ANSWERS

UNDERSTAND &
DESCRIBE EMERGING
BEHAVIOURS

MAP OUT &
STORIFY
PATTERNS

SEEKS TO
GENERALIZE
THROUGH
PRACTICE

INDUCTIVE

Explorative, generative, evaluative

Research comes in many forms. My aim here is certainly not a categorization of research types and methods. Categorizing research carries the implicit idea that research can be used in a prescriptive way, that there is a 'right' tool for every research question. I consider that to be too simplistic. The expertise of research lies not in the tools but in the quality and drive of the researcher to rise above the tools and see them as elements supporting the process of inquiry. However, some basic clarification is required before we can look at the ways in which research can be instrumental to business and to design.

Lets bring research down to four types: academic research, market research, research and development, and design research.
• Academic research is done by academic institutions with the purpose of publishing findings as a contribution to a broader base of knowledge and can provide a strong backbone to business decision-making. It provides a scientific fundament and validity to the findings in ways that objectify the information as valuable.
• Market research is research conducted by business, often through third parties, in order to gather intelligence and facts about the market or to support business decision-making, from more strategic to more operational.
• Research and development involves the fundamental activity of scoping out alternatives for new product and service development by investigating the technology and knowledge available and applying it to the development of future propositions.
• And finally, design research is research conducted to inform, provide feedback, and to validate the creative process of generating concrete products, services, or business solutions.

Some authors like to classify research as quantitative and qualitative. This is an easy way out, because in actual business practice the method is less important than the purpose. Research methods and techniques should be selected based on what one is aiming to achieve and not on the kind of information obtained. Roughly speaking quantitative research is used to measure, monitor and describe existing phenomena. It is numbers-based and quantifiable. Qualitative research is used to explain why consumers behave the way they do and what guides those behaviours. It is inquisitive and interpretative.

What really matters is not the technique but the outcome. The best forms of research are a combination of art and science, with more complexity than simple labels of methods and techniques can handle. Are researchers looking for facts? Those can be obtained both quantitatively and qualitatively. Are researchers looking for a narrative? It is possible to build stories through quantitative and through qualitative studies. The important element thus is what is research aiming to do? Will it help business explore possibilities? Will it help business generate ideas? Will it support business in validating and evaluating strategic initiatives?

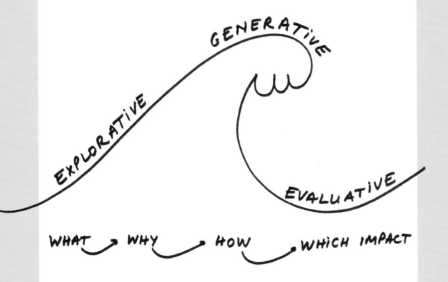

THE RESEARCH WAVE

GENERATIVE

EXPLORATIVE

EVALUATIVE

WHAT → WHY → HOW → WHICH IMPACT

The versatility of research can be seen as a wave, gaining momentum from what to why to how in the cycles of strategic understanding and development and then reflecting back to the effect of the actions. Like waves, the beginnings and endings integrate fluidly and seamlessly. Gone are the times of annual strategic planning: it is now an ongoing wave of exploration, generation, and validation.

The impulse of this wave, its inner motivation is learning; an eagerness to understand and apply the understanding in order to learn more, thereby elevating the understanding to new levels that raise new questions and propel the learning even further. This impulse in itself is interesting, but not enough to have a lasting effect on business. For research to be purposeful to business it needs to focus on the result not just on the process.

Outcome-driven research

When research is driven by outcome, the methodologies and tools become part of the skillset of the researcher to be used in a discretionary way through his or her expertise. This is quite a contrast to the prescriptive nature with which most research is still done within businesses.

As research progresses and evolves it moves away from tools and methodologies as main drivers, into research as a process of learning and engaging and then further into outcome-driven research where it delivers tangible results to business and co-shapes strategy.

Nonetheless, still the bulk of research budgets are used to confirm what businesses already know, often times far beyond the point of theoretical saturation.

Theoretical saturation refers to the point, mainly in qualitative research, at which more data will not lead to more information related to the research questions. Additional data, more studies and more information will not deliver new conclusions or new combinations. It is the point at which the patterns in the data start repeating themselves.

As we saw at the crossroads of theory and practice, there is an outward-oriented, generative movement in the search for new information. Beyond that the wave towards an increased connection with the context leads into new ways of searching. Research becomes more immersive, because people are experts of their own experience.

Businesses that dare to break the cycle of looking to confirm what they know and dive into the unknown can bring an enhanced dynamic into their strategic process because the process of insight gathering is never final and always progressing. The boundaries of what research is stretch out into newer fields, from the inevitable understanding that practice (as opposed to theory) is complicated, complex, layered and nuanced.

This means that the research approach also has to have those nuances, advancing from simple observation and documentation to analyzing and interpreting what is observed and documented, from just looking to truly seeing, from asking to probing, from making hypotheses to wondering about which theories might emerge from the collected data, from acontextual interviewing to contextual understanding, from being an outside expert to being a responsive researcher.

The roles of research for strategy-making

The implication of putting the research approach above the method is that we need to understand how research can inform strategy in meaningful ways. Research rises above being a 'study' and actually becomes a process.

On top of its basic role of informing, research can also inspire strategy-making and rather than just generate knowledge through individual interventions (static pictures as it were), it becomes dynamic and ongoing to provide continuous sources of learning (delivering a movie or a series of episodes rather than separate pictures).

What is research bringing to the table? Which roles does it fulfil? What is the outcome or result it aims to provide in order to add value to business?
- Documentary research is research that looks to the outside world and developments within society and aims to learn from what is happening by documenting social phenomena. Its value is in explaining what is happening and staying informed of current affairs. It is mainly descriptive, though it involves some level of interpretation.
- Narrative research is research that looks at people's lives through the lens of their stories. It focuses on what people say they do, which then translates into patterns and stories based on the information provided. Its value is in getting the language, anecdotes, and ideas at the source. It is mainly descriptive from a first person perspective and allows researchers to gain access into a mindset different to their own and generate empathy with different groups of people.
- Testimonial research is the kind of research that looks at people's actual behaviours.

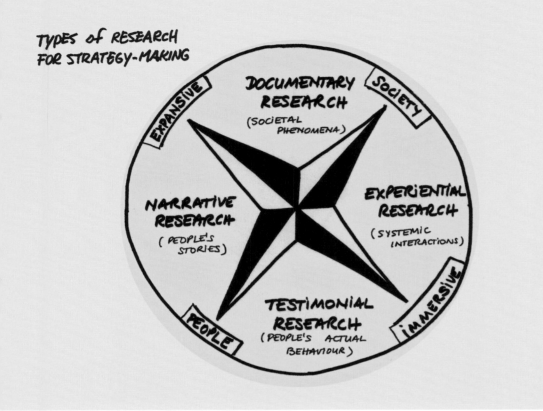

TYPES of RESEARCH FOR STRATEGY-MAKING

DOCUMENTARY RESEARCH (SOCIETAL PHENOMENA)

EXPERIENTIAL RESEARCH (SYSTEMIC INTERACTIONS)

NARRATIVE RESEARCH (PEOPLE'S STORIES)

TESTIMONIAL RESEARCH (PEOPLE'S ACTUAL BEHAVIOUR)

EXPANSIVE · SOCIETY · IMMERSIVE · PEOPLE

The approach is defined by the type of outcome required and thus the type of effort and mind-set needed. Within the context of business, the applications of research are broad, from market research to research and development activities and to design research in its many forms. What changes respective of the desired outcome is which tools are used and how they are used.

The roles of research are not mutually exclusive; circumstances and contexts vary and thus may require different types of approaches, successively or in parallel. Research is increasingly becoming situational in order to adapt to the needs of business and the changes in the environment. Businesses are seeing that with an increased contextual complexity, diving too deep into research can be counterproductive. That is, the point of theoretical saturation is reached and the needs instead are for momentum and for the business to interact with the context through shorter cycles.

This takes the analysis beyond the discourse of how people say they do things and dives right into what they are actually doing. It is immersive and curious, looking at individuals up close to understand their whole process through the activities that manifest as people go about their lives. By seeking the testimony, we actually get to better understand what people are doing and probe deeper into why this might be so.

• Experiential research is research in which the researcher himself bears witness to behaviour. It involves quick prototyping and systemic interactions, taking research to the co-creative realm. If it were simply observational it would be documentary research as described above. What defines experiential research is that the researcher is part of the subjective experience. This kind of research requires a team of researchers so that several perspectives can be gathered to understand the different levels of the experience.

All of these approaches can use either qualitative or quantitative tools and methods.

WEST ANTARKTIS

Jason-L.ᵈ
19. I. 1902
Frannäs
18. X. 1902
Wetter-I.
Foyn-L.ᵈ

K. Enttäuschung
Scott-B.
terrasse
Richthof.
Tal
Pendleton-B.
Graham-

Biscoe 1830

Sandwich-Inseln
(1775 v. Cook entd.)
Traverse I.s
Cumberl.-B.
Clerke-I.s
Montague I.
Bristol I.
Süd-Georgien
(1675 v. de la Roche entd.)
Südl. Thule
Shag Rocks

Sawadowskij-I (vulk.)
Wisokoi I.
Saunders-I. (vulk.?)

Cook 1775
Bellingshausen 1820
Scotia 1904
Biscoe

Ross 1843
Biscoe 1830
Packeis 1843
Südlich
Bellingsh.
I. 1820

Pt. Stanley
Burdwood Bank

ÜD-RIKA
Neujahrs-I.
Le Maire
Staaten-I.
Feuerland
K. Hoorn
Ushuaia

Laurie-I.
Süd-Orkney-I.
Coronation-I.
Powell I.
Inaccess.

Bellinghausen
I. 1820

Coats-Land
(1904 v. Bruce en
Südlichster v. d. Sco
erreichter Punkt,

Caird-Küste
v. Shackleto
Jan. 1915

Süd-Shetland-I.
Joinville-I.
Hope-I.
West-Antarktis

Loubet-L.
(1904 v. Charcot entd.)
Adelaide-I.
Fallieres-L.ᵈ
(1909 v. Charcot entd.)

Südl. v. d. Francais
(Charcot) erreicht Pkt. 1904

Alexander I-L.ᵈ
(1821 v. Bellingshn. entd.)
Charcot-L.ᵈ
(1910 v. Charcot entd.)

Südl. v. Morell
erreicht Pkt. III. 1823

Ross, III. 1843

Weddell-Meer

Südl. v. Weddell erreicht Pkt.
20. II. 1823

Herzog-Ernst-B.

Prinzregent-Luitpold-Land
(1912 v. Filchner entd.)
Südl. v. d. Deutschl. erreicht Pkt., 31. I. 1912

Filchner Barriere

Südlichster v. Larsen erreichter
Punkt, 6. XII. 1893

Beagle-Kan.
Magalhaes-Str.
D. Ramirez-I.

K. Oskar II. L.ᵈ (1893 v. Larsen entd.)

ANTARK

GET

Friction versus Traction

Essentially, research aims to uncover what business can do in order to provide value to people's lives and thus extract value from the market. This is why researchers are mandated to search for insights that businesses can exploit through value addition.

Because the term 'insight' has been so over-stretched and over-used it has lost its impact. So let's define it here as the deep understanding of the human truths that people identify with and the reasons why they matter. You get to the insight level by asking 'why?' Gaining insights is a process of discovery, either when observing phenomena or when observing people: discovering why things happen the way they do and why people behave the way they do. Insight is about realization. It is not just an observation, because an insight should be actionable. When the insight is revealed it changes how we look at the situation. This realization that something can be done or needs to be done to improve the situation by putting it in synch with the underlying human truths is at the core of what an insight enables. The lever for actionability is often referred to as a 'friction' or a problem. If there is nothing being perceived as a friction, then nothing is wrong and no intervention is required.

I like this definition by Adrian Ho, partner at Zeus Jones Minneapolis, which I found online[4],

'To me an insight is any piece of information or knowledge that reshapes how we see a situation. To be useful, it has to reshape our perception so that we can see opportunities that weren't visible before.'

Once the friction becomes visible it is critical to do something about it. This is an ongoing, iterative process because once there is a solution to an insight it becomes obvious in hindsight and new insights emerge. The delivery of a solution leads to 'traction'. Traction is all about making a connection, by understanding that people are experts of their own experience. Research, and design as we will see in the next chapter, are enabling experts in this process. They both work together and shape the process, which is led by strategy through a vision of what needs to happen and why. Strategy provides direction and through the uncovering of the friction via research, plus the creation of traction by design, it all meshes and interweaves into one common unfolding story in which strategic direction connects with market opportunity.

It is a constant wave of learning in which thinking and doing, reflecting and interacting, immersing and emerging continuously intertwine while the gap between the business and its market decreases through better understanding and empathy.

Scenario planning and creative exploration

As strategy becomes a more iterative process of reflection and action, we come to the creative core of business: its engine of inspiration. Of course it is possible to shape strategy purely from a creative impulse, some entrepreneurs do nothing else. But that leaves a lot of strategy-making to chance and may mean overlooking opportunities that are within reach.

So lets look at the implications of research for strategy-making. Research allows business to consider the full range of options available. By exploring and immersing in the context it uncovers and reveals what is going on and what can be done about it. This is what business school scenario planning is all about. In the light of the proactive roles of research and design within business it becomes a process of creating opportunities. This is the essence of any creative process: to make new connections, to see what was hidden in plain sight and not seen by others, to play with the different combinations to create new, inspiring, meaningful things.

"Research is a practice in understanding, curiosity, and discovery."

Thus, when you bring research and design into the mix, strategy becomes about creative exploration. Involving research and design later in the process can lead to good results in the execution, though these results will not be as long lasting simply because the waves of change and complexity of the market are going to reposition the activities as soon as they manifest. In order to develop the initiatives in a more integrated manner, research and design need to be part of that planning process. They can do so by feeding and informing strategy in short, ongoing cycles to make it fluid and flexible and resilient, while also supporting strategy downstream. This makes it possible to integrate initiatives by creating and validating throughout the process as a continuous wave of progressive learning and development.

Get lost

In the first volume of *The Lord of the Rings, The Fellowship of the Ring,* J.R.R. Tolkien writes "Not all those who wander are lost'" I believe researchers need to make this their mantra again. There is a huge, untapped value in getting lost. Namely: re-discovery. It is time for research to regain its independence and freedom of spirit. Merely answering questions to inform business does no service to business.

Research needs to embrace the quest for questions by daring to reframe the question. Albert Einstein famously said: "If I had an hour to solve a problem and my life depended on the solution, I would spend the first fifty-five minutes determining the proper question to ask, for once I know the proper question, I could solve the problem in less than five minutes." Reframing as a tool is very common in creative disciplines, for it allows you to shift perspectives and gain a deeper understanding of the underlying issues.

In her book *InGenius: A Crash Course on Creativity*[5], Tina Seelig elaborates on the importance of reframing problems in business. She states that all companies need to reframe continuously in order to survive as the market and available technologies change. This entails thoroughly understanding the context as well as the company's (potential) role within it. Seelig states: "Being able to connect and combine non-obvious ideas and objects is essential for innovation and a key part of the creative process. Along with your ability to reframe problems, it engages your imagination. Essentially you need to be able to reorganize and rearrange the things you know and the resources you have in order to come up with brand new ideas."

Research is a practice in understanding, curiosity, and discovery. We need to relearn to look at the world with our minds, our hearts, and our eyes truly open to possibility, to re-enter the space of interaction between business, brands and people from new perspectives.

Research redesigned

What does redesigned research look like? I believe that the new researcher is a facilitator who enables communication and connection. The new researcher embraces the fact that there is a degree of subjectivity through interpretation and dares to go beyond the obvious to develop meaning from which businesses can create solutions and grow sustainably. New research integrates 'seeing the truth' through observations and answering the 'what' questions with 'sensing the truth' through interpretations and asking 'why'.

It is like learning a new language. Learning the rules of grammar is not enough; even if you studied grammar to the point of knowing it perfectly, it is not the only factor that defines how well you communicate. Native speakers don't learn the grammatical rules for their own languages until they are in formal education, because grammar plays a role in formal use of the language, but not necessarily in communication and fluidity. Consider this: if you learn grammar first, without context, it can actually act as an impediment to fluency. You might not dare to speak for fear of getting the grammatical structures wrong. Language gains meaning in the context of use, and this is more important to understanding than technicalities or mechanical aspects of language use. This is a great example of how theory and practice are truly different in practice. Herein lies the opportunity to improve the output of research.

New researchers have the compass at hand, the stars and sun as key points for navigating the context and the ability to reframe the issues in their ongoing quest for questions. New researchers know that there is a need to understand before you can explain, there is a need to question before you can answer, and there is a need to contextualize before you can generalize.

The new researcher does not work alone. As part of a team, researchers bring in perspectives, possibilities, and scenarios to help business teams be more resilient to change and ultimately sail more smoothly. The researcher as navigator reminds us that the map is not the territory and that our sense of direction needs to be constantly contrasted against the changing sea of context.

RESEARCH REDESIGNED

RESEARCHERS AS INTERPRETERS WHO NAVIGATE THE CONTEXT, REFRAME ISSUES, AND BRIDGE THEORY AND PRACTICE IN A CONTINUOUS QUEST FOR QUESTIONS.

3 RESEARCHING DESIGN

'I need the sea,
because it
teaches me.'

- Pablo Neruda

On Design

There are many and varied definitions of what design is. There is some agreement, nonetheless, on Herbert Simon's[1] definition being a good one. According to Simon, design is the "transformation of existing conditions into preferred ones."

In other words, design is a fundamental process of problem solving, in order to create, express, and shape new, practical solutions.

Design is often misunderstood and seen simply as the design of form. While most design disciplines have an element of harmony and aesthetics, that is not the essence of design. Design is about creation: shaping and forming by probing, questioning, and experimenting. Like research, it is also focussed on questions, but with a bias towards action. It does not stay 'in' the question: it moves with each answer to create new questions, and explores by doing while it learns by adapting. This creative act may or may not lead to tangible outcomes and form. It is a mindset and an attitude to think in possibilities.

Design in business

Several authors have attempted to explain the different levels of design applied to business. The Danish Design Centre conducted research under Danish companies in 2003 and 2007, using a model called The Design Ladder to represent where companies stood in terms of the application of design practices in management[2]. They categorized them as follows:
- no use of design,
- design as style,
- design as process, and
- design as a strategy.

In situations in which design was not explicitly used, it was attributed to lack of awareness. This is stage zero, where there is no design present in the culture of an organization, either manifest or intended.

The first level of awareness starts with design as a function to style or form. This is stage one, in which the relevance of design is only appreciated in terms of style and is left to the 'creatives' who design products, services, or touchpoints.

The second stage of design involves seeing design as a process or a method that can be used to solve discrete problems or to guide the development process using tools and techniques from the design discipline. On this level, design is integrated into the process as a means to drive change. Principles and guidelines play a key role, almost on a mechanical level: if you follow these rules then you will be 'designing' the solutions through a set of consecutive steps. However, design is not the final result, and it cannot be, because in this stage it is not the design skills that are put into practice but the systematic steps of a process that is empty of design meaning. The focus here is in design as a method, not a designerly mindset.

Finally, when organizations embrace design fully they raise it to the strategic level. In the third stage, the design skills, mindset, processes and tools all converge into the organizational culture allowing it to be more adaptable and agile. Design as strategy is a key driver for innovation and growth, bringing organizations closer to their users, encouraging knowledge transfer, and enabling businesses to develop human-centred strategies for sustainable growth. The design mindset becomes an ingrained part of the company culture and there is a synergy between business objectives and the design strategy to create the company's desired future.

Companies that are higher in the design ladder are more adaptive to change and less affected by the tidal changes in the context. They steer the organization from a strategic intent while remaining adaptive to their environment. The strategic intent is key to determining the course of the company and the design role is to guide choices, supporting the chosen strategic direction in an outcome-driven manner to put the abstract strategic thinking in motion through concrete initiatives.

Steering in ever-changing conditions

The starting point of design is today more confuse than ever before; it is complex and dynamic. Thus, for the tangible aspect of design to be effective, the understanding that precedes making needs to be more thorough. Understanding provides a foundation in terms of what matters to the users in their context. It is not enough just to make. Today's design efforts are only successful if adopted by users. Not understanding the user means risking the adoption, effectively missing the boat.

Attributing the steering wheel of the sailboat to design might be provocative but it is also a way of raising awareness of the formative role of design. Design shapes the actual course of organizations; it defines what truly matters through its interaction with the market and its tangibility. This is something that is accomplished by doing, by venturing into the waters and which is much more action oriented than being the captain of a ship (strategy) looking at the situation from a cabin. It demands skills that are unique to design and that confirm the essence of design as a problem solving discipline.

There cannot be two captains on a ship. On our sailboat, let's be clear: the captain is strategy. Strategy's two main supports are research (the compass that suggests true north and the ability to read the context continuously -as presented in the previous chapter) and design

(the steering wheel and the engaged and flexible capacity to steer in the context in order to reach the desired outcome).

Design at the steering wheel brings a series of unique capabilities to the table. These include aspects that are linked to the design mindset (not just the specific design skills of 'making') and which are very inspiring to the whole business team and stakeholders. These design-based skills include
• Visual thinking
• Creativity
• Human-centricity
• Conceptualization
• Bias to action
• Prototyping
• Iteration and learning
• Collaboration and team work
The list could be longer and more detailed, yet in my experience this covers the essence of what design brings to the table and helps clarify why these are 'steering' skills that can be used flexibly to make the strategic intent real and tangible and engaged with the user.

Lets look at each in a bit of detail:
• Visual thinking is a human ability and designers tend to prefer it because it allows them to create a shareable overview of the issues and make the discussions explicit. It also works better. Approximately 65 percent of people are visual learners and the human brain processes visual information sixty thousand times faster

than it does text. Truly, a picture speaks more than a thousand words. As the world becomes increasingly complex and people are overwhelmed by information, visual thinking is a tool to provide synthesis. On his website, Dave Gray[3] puts it succinctly: "Visual thinking is a way to organize your thoughts and improve your ability to think and communicate. It's a way to expand your range and capacity by going beyond the linear world of the written word, list and spreadsheet, and entering the non-linear world of complex spatial relationships, networks, maps and diagrams."

• Creativity is another human ability that is not unique to design. Yet it is essential to design, because design is about creating possibilities. In order to design it is necessary to apply creativity to existing conditions or problems and emerge with new solutions. Design makes new combinations, creates alternatives and delivers applied creativity in the form of possible solutions. As Rob Curedale [4]simply states: "Design is creativity with strategy". In other words, design is a focused creative effort to deliver relevant outcomes.

• Human-centricity is what differentiates design as a discipline within business. Unlike any other discipline it is directly concerned with the end user. Design is the point of contact with the end user because whatever value is added by business and by design is measured in terms of the value for the user. This then

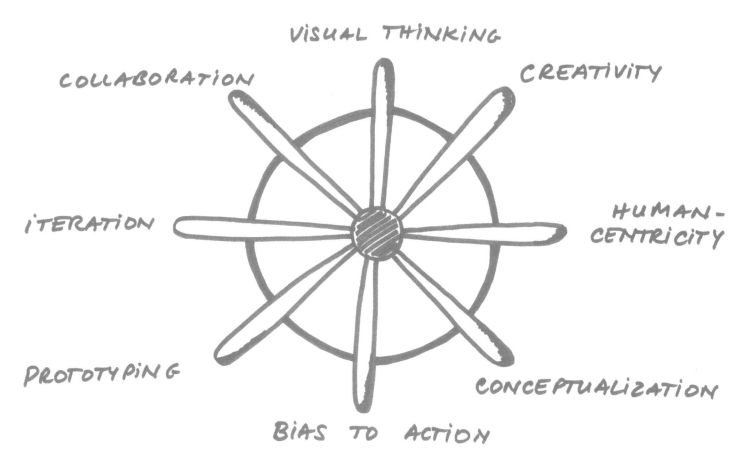

VISUAL THINKING

COLLABORATION

CREATIVITY

ITERATION

HUMAN-CENTRICITY

PROTOTYPING

CONCEPTUALIZATION

BIAS TO ACTION

might lead to a transfer in economic value, but only if there is some kind of value that is experienced by the user. This means that design starts and ends with the user. Design is for people. And these people have their own wants, needs, perceptions, and motivations. Human-centricity is about the ability to integrate human characteristics into business strategy. These characteristics include things like empathy, realizing that people are experts of their own experience, contextual immersion, and anything that allows the designer to see people as people with their natural human imperfection.

• Conceptualization: somewhere between the strategic intent and the realization of ideas is the moment where ideas start taking shape. This entails the ability to understand the problem, frame it, and develop initial conceptual directions for exploration. Because the design process is iterative, designers are perfectly comfortable with not having all the details ironed out from the beginning. That is not necessary. The conceptualization skills allow designers to outline what the areas of exploration are about without limiting the number or quality of potential solutions.

• Bias to action: this element points to the action-based aspect of design. Rather than wait for conditions to be perfect and discuss details on a theoretical level, designers prefer to act and interact in order to gain feedback and learn through the impact of their actions or interventions. This is both at the research/ explorative level where the designer prefers to immerse himself and interact in the context of the user in the more tangible level of prototype generation and confrontation with users. The term bias-to-action is attributed to Indira Gandhi, India's former prime minister, who said "Have a bias toward action—let's see something happen now. You can break that big plan into small steps and take the first step right away."

• Prototyping: a prototype is an early version of a thing. By making your idea materialize, you are able to see what works, what doesn't, what is missing, what needs to be adapted, and how the user might engage with it. It allows you to put something out there so you may have a conversation about its impact and its implications. It is a crucial tool for learning that bridges the bias to action with the iterative capacity of design. Prototypes are tangible and, as such, action-oriented: they offer something with which to involve others and they raise a lot of questions, making the designer evolve answers into later prototypes through applied creative skills. Probably most importantly, when ideas become prototypes, assumptions need to become explicit and thus they allow for a thorough think-through of what is actually being done, what value is being provided, and which choices are being made during the ideation process.

• Iteration and learning: the basic premise that we are always learning as we create is the cornerstone of iteration. Because design can cope with complex situations and non-linearity it requires iteration as a basic element in its process. At any given point in time you may have overlooked something or not fully appreciated its effect on the whole. According to Wikipedia[5]: "Iteration is the act of repeating a process with the aim of approaching a desired goal, target or result. Each repetition of the process is also called an 'iteration', and the results of one iteration are used as the starting point for the next iteration." Iteration is a cyclical loop by which systematic learning takes place: first understand, then ideate, then prototype, then refine, then prototype, then refine, etc., until the prototype feels ready for production. And even once a product or service is produced and launched, iteration can keep taking place in the form of improvements. It is the most effective way to learn and stay in touch with the context

• Collaboration and team work: perhaps because of the vastness of the design discipline in its fields of specialization, which ranges from the arts to engineering, from interaction design to experiential design, it is essential to understand that it takes a team to deliver great design at any and every level. Firstly not everyone sees things in the same way, so more people will bring in more perspectives. Secondly, not everyone has the same skills, so more people will bring more means to tackle the issue. Designers do not work alone, they work in teams because this enriches themselves, the process and the end result.

With these amazing skills it is no coincidence that design is at the steering wheel. It can be a key contributor to making strategy happen, by elevating the entrepreneurial culture, empowering the teams, re-connecting people with their innate creativity, curiosity, and playfulness. There are many new and different ways in which design might help by being more integrated into business practice.

Adaptive Design

Strategy makers are tasked with a captainship role of charting the course of an organization into the future. Increasingly, this is becoming more of a collaborative task rather than a directive task. Within the industrial paradigm, this process was mainly linear. It involved a series of steps from analyzing the conditions, making choices to enhance chances of success and revenue maximization, and strategic reviews and planning cycles to monitor progress and viability. However, as the context becomes more complex and dynamic, the planning cycles of businesses are too slow to keep up with the changing conditions and they get out of synch with the pace of change in the context.

Design is adaptive and as such is the ideal partner to strategy-making in this era of creative empowerment. Because design is exactly at the interface of intent and execution, it is the translator of strategy into reality and it has a pivotal role in flexibly making use of contextual opportunities to deliver business success through designed solutions.

The degree of adaptability of design is determined by both a design mindset and by design processes and methods. The design mindset is crucial because it entails relying on one's skills without pushing them to the front. Knowing that depending on the circumstances, an assessment of the circumstances will lead to the choice of a tool or set of tools and not the other way round. This is important because it is, in the business context, the most misunderstood aspect of design.

The design processes and methods are a multitude of templates, tools, and guidelines that serve the process of understanding and synthesis that characterizes any design exploration. They are not limited to the disciplines of design and can include anything from social sciences, to art, to engineering. What characterizes the use of these tools in the context of design is that they are outcome driven: that is, the tools are used with an end in mind, be it to learn, create, evaluate, or whatever is necessary at a given point in the design process.

The adaptability of design is anything but linear and as such can feel very uncomfortable in a business setting. It is impossible to know upfront where the design process will take the team. However, it is outcome driven because it has as its main purpose the creation of user value. Design is not only expressive, it aims to create something of value to the user, and therein lies its strength in supporting businesses.

The wave of adaptive design is cyclical and ongoing, starting with an open mind that allows the designer to question the question and revise the assumptions. What is really happening? How does it affect the problem? Is there another problem behind the problem? What is the perspective of the user? With this open mind, the designer almost inadvertently immerses herself into the world of the user. This process is both art and science. It involves empathy towards the user and the ability to switch perspective, to see the world through someone else's eyes. And it also involves creative interventions, as the most reliable tool to understand the effect of design on any given context, by probing, by confronting with prototypes and by iterating. The designer incorporates the lessons learned into the next prototype and into the next question while the understanding of what the possible solutions could be progresses. Finally, the wave of adaptive design is evaluative: What was the effect? What can still be improved? What could we do better or differently next time? All of these efforts are pulled forward by the eagerness to enhance, improve, or better tailor solutions to the user of any product or service for a better user experience.

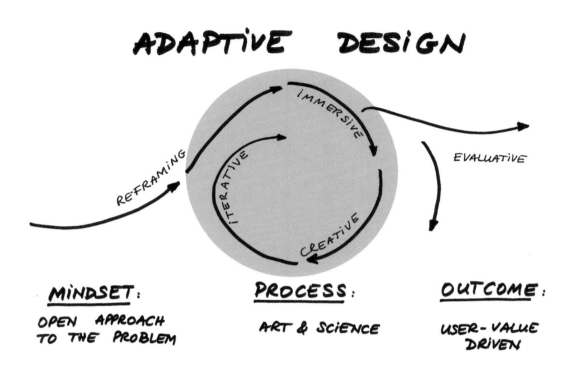

ADAPTIVE DESIGN

REFRAMING

ITERATIVE

IMMERSIVE

CREATIVE

EVALUATIVE

MINDSET:
OPEN APPROACH
TO THE PROBLEM

PROCESS:
ART & SCIENCE

OUTCOME:
USER-VALUE
DRIVEN

The art of not-knowing

Mostly when you design, you are designing for someone else. This makes it a very difficult process, because by definition you are not someone else. A mindset of curiosity and openness are therefore mandatory to good design. A designer knows that the waters being sailed are unknown and unpredictable. This is what makes it fascinating. It is truly an adventure, and the key to it is to just get started.

Not-knowing or not having the full scope of information in view has never been more current an issue. We are surrounded and overwhelmed by information to the point it is potentially paralyzing. The ability to observe and understand information within its context is crucial. The immersive nature of design gives a framework of meaning to the information and makes it significant instead of bewildering. Design does not aim for accuracy or rigour or completeness of

information. It looks for relevance, from the perspective of the user.

The first phase in this search for relevance is to diverge. In order to consider different strategies and positioning options, these options need to be generated. They are embedded in a context of things that are going on, continuously, around us. At this stage, design is concerned with understanding and analyzing in order to create choices.

The second phase is to converge, that is, to make choices. This is a process of synthesis and involves choosing what to let go and what to keep and build upon further.

These two phases of diverging and converging are present in any creative endeavour. Most models for creative thinking and design include these two phases in one form or another. What is important here is not so much the process but what is pulling it forward, which in the context of business involves the creation of user value. Considering the user as a muse for exploring the world and making choices is a skill set central to design within business.

Converging and diverging, that is, exploring and synthesizing, are key elements in dealing with the unknown. But for this to work in business, design needs to make its contribution more explicit, both in terms of new thinking as well as in terms of new solutions.

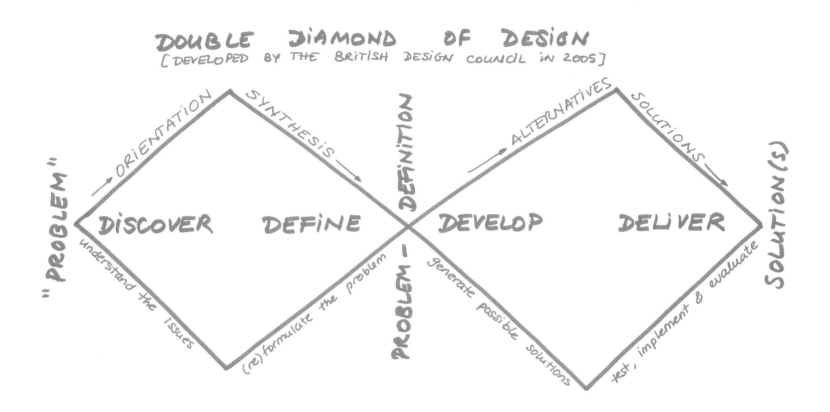

DOUBLE DIAMOND OF DESIGN
[DEVELOPED BY THE BRITISH DESIGN COUNCIL IN 2005]

"PROBLEM"

ORIENTATION

SYNTHESIS

DISCOVER   DEFINE

understand the issues

(re)formulate the problem

DEFINITION

PROBLEM

DEVELOP   DELIVER

ALTERNATIVES

SOLUTIONS

generate possible solutions

test, implement & evaluate

SOLUTION(S)

The Double Diamond of Design

Through in-house research, the British Design Council generated the Double Diamond of Design[6] model in 2005. This model differentiates four steps in the design process: discover, define, develop and deliver; making a double loop of diverging and converging.

The reason that there are two 'diamonds' in this model is that a differentiation is made between the planning stage and the implementation stage. Both require diverging and converging, though the approaches and tools are slightly different as the process of design moves from intent to realization.

The first activity, diverging, involves discovery of (latent) user needs. In this phase, all kinds of research tools are used. These vary widely from more formal tools of market and user research to more informal tools such as team meetings, observations, and desk research. What is important is the outcome sought:

namely orientation, not the tools. In this stage, the perspective is widened as much as possible in order to get inspiration and new ideas that help identify what the challenge is. It involves the interpretation of information in order to understand what it might mean for the organizational strategy and the projects to be initiated.

The second activity, converging, is the definition of the project. During the Define phase, taking as input the inspiration and ideas from the Discover phase, during the Define phase the teams analyze and synthesize the information into a project charter with planned steps, activities and tasks for project development. The team reconsiders the initially formulated problem and reframes it as necessary to create clarity with regards to the work to be done and the issue requiring a solution. In this phase, teams understand, prioritize and organize the project taking into consideration any gaps and opportunities ahead of the actual project work. It includes the refining of the scope and reach of the project to ensure it fits with the strategic intent and success rate in terms of user value.

The third step in the Double Diamond of Design is the Develop stage. Based on the defined project mandate, the designers, together with the different departments in the team, start developing alternatives for implementation. This includes the use of creative skills and techniques for ideation such as visualization, scenarios and prototyping. It also is the most multi-disciplinary phase in any project because this phase seeks to find different approaches to the challenge identified in the previous phases. It integrates all kinds of expertise to solve problems and does so in an open, engaging manner through visual tools so that the progress is visible to all. Here, the role of design to create studio conditions for creative problem solving is instrumental to the adaptability of the whole team: the ability to 'read' the information and play into it from different functionalities and expertise areas is key.

The fourth and final step is Deliver. This is where it all comes together and where the new product or service is generated out of the prototype that emerges out of the iterations during development. For the deliver phase to be a success, the generated result needs to address the challenges identified in the discovery phase and defined within the scope of the project during the Define phase. In design, action and reflection are part of an ongoing continuum. So in this phase, the execution of the idea is not the final step. The evaluation and feedback are equally important as they contribute to the organizational resilience and expertise for future projects.

The Double Diamond Model has proven effective to many business practitioners and is increasingly gaining use, following the publication of the 'Eleven Lessons Study' by the British Design Council in 2007. In that study[7] the British Design Council showed that leading companies were able to better respond to common business challenge through design, with the following conclusions:
"• Good design makes products more competitive. It keeps production costs down but allows higher prices in the shops
• Good design keeps users happy, making them come back again and encouraging them to recommend things to their friends
• Design applies the power of the brand. A strong brand identity encourages customers to trust existing products and to try new ones"
All of these are good reasons for design to become a valuable partner to business.

Researching Design

Design requires taking a plunge, sometimes making assumptions, sometimes using creative skills. This makes it a bit 'scary' because it feels isolated and unpredictable in the context of business. Additionally, design for business has evolved and changed rapidly in the last decade. By re-searching design we can better understand the vectors of change and how these can be used for business value creation.

Design is traditionally a makers' profession. The disciplines that fall under the realm of design either come from the arts, like graphic design, from engineering, like industrial design or from technology like interaction design. The term makers covers the creation of solutions in all kinds of levels and forms, ranging from the more tangible aspects of graphic design to the more abstract design of experience via service design for example.

In his book *Change by Design*[8], Tim Brown famously differentiates design doing from design thinking. Design doing refers to the applied design skills that the designer utilizes to develop a solution or design an experience based on a predefined briefing. However, there is more to design than just the activities carried out: there is a blueprint to how a designer thinks which is what we call design thinking and which precedes design doing. Brown goes on to say: "The natural evolution from design doing to design thinking reflects the growing

recognition on the part of today's business leaders that design has become too important to be left to designers." This sets the stage for the democratization of design and the potential risk this carries.

The other, more positive, side of the coin is of course that design as a discipline bridges the thinking and the doing, which is something that businesses need in order to stay competitive. It is not enough to set out a strategy, no matter how well planned. Businesses must implement the ideas well and in time if they want to be successful, which is why designerly skills are in such high demand with business people. As business leaders know all too well, "You can have brilliant ideas, but if you can't get them across, your ideas won't get you anywhere."[9]

When re-searching design back to its origins as a discipline, we see that it has several building blocks or levels and that a lot of these skills were traditionally learnt through apprenticeship, studio hours, and essentially putting in the time. The reason is that design skills are very difficult to transfer in classroom conditions and that there are no prescriptive rules on how to apply these skills. In a way, learning to design from a book would be analogous to learning to sail on dry land. You might get to know all the theories and even some lovely examples, but it is not until you are on the water that those skills are proven.

As a consequence, design was pigeon-holed into the realm of doing, leaving it at the bottom steps of the Design Ladder presented earlier in this chapter: either non aware or simply as an aesthetic function. This is not how designers see the world, though it is how much of the world sees designers.

The way designers see the world is much more nuanced. Design is a way of viewing things and of scoping out potential ways to improve existing conditions. In that sense it is much more about thinking than about doing, more than what it is usually thought to be from outside the design disciplines. In any case, as any experienced designer will tell you, design requires reflection in order to engage in focused action.

Now that the rest of the world is catching up to the designer's positive view, and as problems have become difficult to solve with traditional skills we can revisit the areas of application for design. Rising above the level of doing and into the higher orders of design.

Design emergence

Over time design emerged by expanding its own boundaries into what is still emerging and changing today. Professor Richard Buchanan[10], contributed greatly to our understanding of the design discipline through his Four Orders of Design model.

He looks at the emergence of the different fields within design, not so much as specific disciplines but as what he calls 'areas of invention'. that is, spaces in time in which through the application of design skills, the level of awareness around what design can do grew beyond the boundaries of what was known into a next level of application.

The first order of design is the simplest way of looking at design, as quite simply the graphic skills to visualize information in a way that is useful to the audience. This can range from communication, signage, and presentations to packaging graphics. But very soon, designers realize that their intervention has an impact, an effect on others. That it leads somewhere because their visuals mobilize people to want to do something based on what they see and learn, there is a movement towards action and intervention. They want to do something.

This leads into the second order of design which is the creation of products or objects. Typically this is the objective of industrial design, which concerns itself with the creation of artefacts. Yet objects do not exist in a vacuum; they have an effect on the user and on the context leading to a need to understand the total experience and evolving into the next order of design.

The third order of design is about interaction. It is the level at which we see that the creative process is inextricably related to the user and that there is an experiential element -which is strictly personal- to any use of design be it as a product, a service, an experience,or a piece of technology. The newer disciplines of design expand into this area through human-centricity and user experience design. But that is not enough, because this sets things in motion in the broader system. Everything is interconnected and dynamic, and an intervention is never isolated from the whole system.

The fourth order of design is therefore the systemic layer, and here is where the element of culture and society becomes mixed in with design. We as humans cannot see ourselves as disconnected from the whole. All human systems, ecosystems and environments are eventually interconnected in one way or another. This is relevant in that we need to understand the users in that light: as people, not as 'others'. Design has a role to play here because design serves people so that they may improve their condition. This can be very superficial and glitzy but it doesn't have to be. Primarily, design improves the human condition. And that makes design uniquely positioned to help us tackle the wicked problems and social issues from healthcare to educational design, from cities to cultures in order to help shape a better future. This is where design thinking, design as a mindset, comes in.

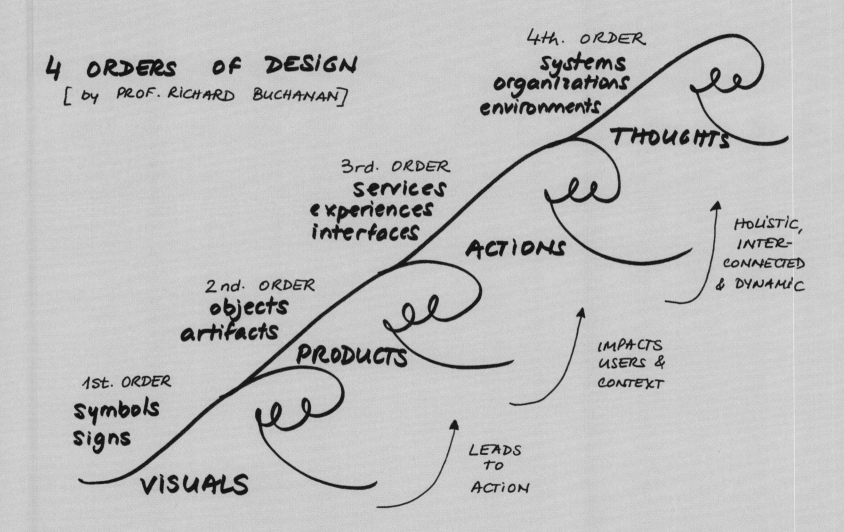

4 ORDERS OF DESIGN
[by PROF. RICHARD BUCHANAN]

1st. ORDER
symbols
signs
VISUALS

2nd. ORDER
objects
artifacts
PRODUCTS

3rd. ORDER
services
experiences
interfaces
ACTIONS

4th. ORDER
systems
organizations
environments
THOUGHTS

LEADS TO ACTION

IMPACTS USERS & CONTEXT

HOLISTIC, INTER-CONNECTED & DYNAMIC

Transformative Journeys

One ripple of change can lead to a minor wave, but all together, within the dynamics of change, evolution, growth, insight, cycles… they become a lot of waves. Together they form a tumultuous ocean that needs to be navigated. Staying safe at shore is like standing still -not an option. So businesses must navigate, which is an intuitive task as much as it is an acquired skill. All the tools in the world, all the process steps and all the how-to's or descriptions are not what makes a good sailor. Experience does. This is how humans learn, how they transform and how they evolve.

Within design, transformation and change are accepted conditions. Design is about transformation and change in two fundamental elements: time and matter. Design aims to move us from the current state to a new state, causing us to change in time and to become a different version of ourselves through the intervention of design. Design changes us by changing our degree of comfort. It does so by manifesting 'matter'. And it does so by giving us access to new insights through experience or by occupying a physical or mental space that required attention.

This is why I like the idea of design as a verb. Beyond all the disciplinary labels, functionalities, ladders and orders of design, design implies movement and transformation. However, it is important to signal that the shift that design produces is not necessarily one linked to artefacts, objects or interfaces.

Increasingly, through the rise of behavioural economics as a discipline -one that has helped us understand that people are less rational than we assumed they were- we are coming to appreciate the indirectness of design. By indirectness I mean that design is not just tangible or instrumental and that design is always contextual. Within a rational appreciation of consumers, it would be okay to analyse phenomena removed from the context. However, since we are "feeling machines that think, not thinking machines that feel" as Antonio Damasio[11] cleverly formulated, we are linked to the intuitive aspects of the context in everything we do.

Thus, thinking of design as an intervention to generate change based on observations would be too simplistic. Design is as much concerned with the intangible aspects as it is with the tangible interfaces. On one level it is highly immersive and highly contextual, because it is focussed on action and on what happens. On another level it is highly empathic and very human because it covers the intangible aspects of the experience; what people desire and what they value.

Quoting Steward Brand in *The Clock of the Long Now:* "This present moment used to be the unimaginable future'" But design applies imagination, leveraging the intangible aspects and creating a new future that is very concrete and interactive.

Imagine the 'D' of design at the hull of the sailboat. The water that is touched by the bow (the front of the sailboat) is different to the water that emerges from the stern (the back of the sailboat), generating a new and different wave by the passing of the sailboat. The 'flow' can be defined in terms of the current state and its attributes, while the 'transformation' manifests consequences and value emerging through the act of sailing and leading to a new state. The keel and rudder of the sailboat, which are linked to the steering wheel, are symbolic in this case for the design interventions. This is where design acts as a verb: flexibly, adaptively, and dynamically. Once design solutions are generated, new waves are formed that affect the dynamic of the interaction so that designers can learn from them and adjust the course. The process is highly interactive, ongoing and cyclical. It is also hugely experiential: there is a lot of dynamic exchange and contact.

Each of the steps in this transformative process is directly linked to the user: design only has relevance and value when linked to the user and the environment. The framing of the design problem at the front of the process integrates the user perspective: Why does this matter? Why is there an issue? This insight is then applied to the generation of alternative,

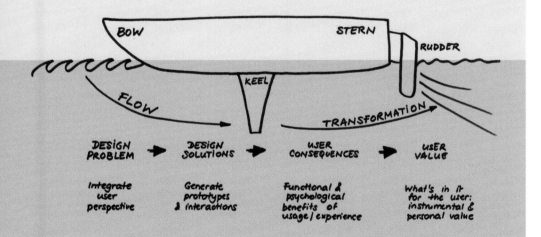

DESIGN AS A VERB.

BOW | STERN | RUDDER
FLOW | KEEL | TRANSFORMATION

DESIGN PROBLEM → DESIGN SOLUTIONS → USER CONSEQUENCES → USER VALUE

Integrate user perspective | Generate prototypes & interactions | Functional & psychological benefits of usage/experience | What's in it for the user: instrumental & personal value

possible solutions that are tested in context to learn about their effect and steered as appropriate (which is where the keel plays a role to keep the sailboat on its course while interacting with the environment). These design solutions affect the perception of the user who experiences consequences both at the functional and psychological levels and then extracts value or utility from those consequences, valuing the design by his own personal experience and individual measures.

Moving from a latent need to value is an experiential process not a cognitive process. We are increasingly aware of the limits of our cognition and the implications this has for business. As Nobel-prize winner Daniel Kahneman[12] points out, "Our comforting conviction that the world makes sense rests on a secure foundation: our almost unlimited ability to ignore our ignorance." Design is able to break through that clutter in that it takes nothing for granted and does not seek explanations solely by asking questions but rather looks for reactions by probing and prototyping.

Creating waves, affecting the context

Central to the immersive and transforming nature of design is the idea of dynamic equilibrium. Dynamic equilibrium can be defined as a "changing yet finely-balanced condition (like that of a tightrope walker) which requires continuous adjustments in order to maintain its present or stable state."[13] This means that design as the interface between business and its key constituents is the space where impact is created. The abilities to interact with complexity, to create solutions through understanding of the context, to have empathy with the user and to master creative skills are what make design particularly relevant today.

The conditions that design is able to create in order to steer business towards its strategic 'North' go beyond the applied skills of design and include
• Iteration and Learning
• Studio conditions
• Continuous Morphing
• Abductive reasoning
• Human Centricity
Each of these constitutes part of the design mindset, and is the part of design that (as per Tim Brown's quote earlier in this chapter) "is too important to be left to the designers."

Iteration and learning

One of the essential drivers of design is improvement of the human condition. Humans are continuously evolving, and by definition so is design. In practice this translates to an evolving appreciation of the truth, where insight is a progressive state never a permanent one. This impermanence of insight links to dynamic equilibrium: the job of design is never final.

In business this means that any proposition or brand, any company or culture is also never final and is always a work in progress. This creates an openness of mind and spirit both in the internal interactions of teams as in the interactions with external stakeholders and users: we are always learning so that we may grow and improve.

The central tool in design is the prototype. As such, the prototype is an attempt to understand and learn by doing. It makes the gaps in reasoning and assumption explicit through making. When you make something, it becomes an opportunity to learn how to make it better. And it depersonalizes the discussion, making it about functionality, benefit and value (ie the top layers of the means end chain) not about the quality of the thinking.

Studio Conditions

The word studio comes from the Latin *studium*, which has to do with learning. *Studium's* meaning suggests creating the conditions to learn and to strive to develop understanding. It evolved through use into 'studio' as in the workspace or atelier of an artist, a space in which there is room for experimentation and learning, room for getting acquainted with a subject in relative safety and with dedication to the task.

Within schools of design, learning to work in studio conditions is essential to honing the skills of design, because essentially, design is something you learn by doing and studios are ideal for experiential learning. But also, they tend to be shared spaces where you can learn from others too.

One of the things that I find particularly fascinating about design practices within studio conditions is that the thinking is expressive. When you walk into design spaces, information and thinking is visible in varying states of completion all around you. From walls and whiteboards, to tables and work surfaces. This opens more space for creative thinking, idea sharing, cross-fertilization of expertise and discovery.

Continuous morphing

In *The End of Competitive Advantage* Rita Gunther McGrath[14] suggests that companies have been after a holy grail: competitive advantage. This defined their thinking and doing to the extent that the common belief was that you could obtain competitive advantage, secure it and milk it for profit. This fallacy led companies to believe that it was possible to secure a competitive advantage as a static concept and that it was possible to protect it from others.

Companies have been confronted with the facts that change causes the source of competitive advantage to shift or even disappear and that barricading the source of competitive advantage does not keep it safe from becoming outdated or surpassed by better alternatives. The idea then is to let go of this business concept of sustainable competitive advantage and to start thinking in new terms: an ongoing, morphing strategy that shapes and blends with the environmental complexities and a continuous, systematic revision of the resources and the opportunities to shape the strategic ambition as you go.

As Pablo Picasso nicely worded, "Action is the foundational key to all success". Design has the ability to morph and change by doing; it is strategy in motion and it is intention in action. These concepts are new to the business establishment, and their adoption might enable businesses to better adapt to the environmental complexities that have deemed industrial thinking old fashioned.

Abductive Reasoning

In the previous chapter of research we looked at deductive and inductive processes in strategy development. These forms of reasoning originate from science, where inductive and deductive reasoning are both seen as valid ways of reaching conclusions.

As we've seen already, inductive reasoning is bottom-up logic which is evidence-based and involves generalizing findings and particular instances into an overarching conclusion. Deductive reasoning uses top-down logic and is based on a general premise or theory which leads to specific conclusions by narrowing down the scope from the general theory to its particular manifestations.

A third approach is abductive reasoning, which is a more informal yet valid approach of inferring conclusions based on data and observation. Instead of looking for more accuracy, more detail or more examples to support a hypothesis, abductive reasoning takes the most probable explanation as the leading one.

The relevance of abductive reasoning within design is clear: within the dynamic equilibrium, abductive reason is one more element in which the most probable, most likely and most sound explanation is assumed to be true until proven otherwise. The strength of abductive reasoning within this frame of mind is that it is not final, rather it allows designers to continue to learn, iterate and develop without having to wait for perfect conditions to be met in hypothesis formulation and data gathering. Thus it makes teams agile and adaptive while making the most of the information available.

CHANGE.

CHANGE
AGAIN.

AND
AGAIN.

Human centricity

Earlier versions of the human-insight driven approach are well documented in theories like the means-end chain[15] and the jobs-to-be-done framework[16]. These theories were important contributors to the realization that product and service design were not just about the objects designed but about the utility derived by the user through the experience of use. Said differently, value is in the eyes of the beholder.

The transformative power of design lies in the fact that a situation in which design intervenes is changed forever. Adding the human dimension to this, implies understanding that a user is not necessarily looking for objects but is especially looking for benefits that ensue from using those objects or having those experiences.

In economic terms this is the concept of utility: something is of value to the degree it delivers usefulness and satisfaction to the person who buys it and/or uses it. The means-end chain is a first step in human-centricity while the jobs-to-be-done framework allowed for a pragmatic view of what mattered to the user: 'The jobs-to-be-done framework is a tool for evaluating the circumstances that arise in customers' lives. Customers rarely make buying decisions around what the 'average' customer in their category may do — but they often buy things because they find themselves with a problem they would like to solve. With an

understanding of the 'job' for which customers find themselves 'hiring' a product or service, companies can more accurately develop and market products well-tailored to what customers are already trying to do."[17]

This way of looking at things allowed designers to look up from their workspaces, studios and drawing tables and start looking into another world: the world of the user. This is a world that designers have learned to uncover with each project by understanding not only what it is that should be designed, but also, importantly, what it does for the users and how it makes them feel. Design therefore has to signify something to someone, by becoming a means to an end.

Today, one of the basic premises of design is that people are experts of their own experience. This opens an opportunity to learn from them in order to better help them through design. This shifts design away from an artful form or expression or an instrumental means of solving problems and towards a means to deliver value for people.

The designers' toolkit is vast, yet the relevance of those tools is determined by the user. In their *Human Centred Design Toolkit*[18], IDEO summarizes: 'Why do human centred design? Because it can help your organization connect better with the people you serve. It can transform data into actionable ideas. It can help

you to see new opportunities. It can help to increase the speed and effectiveness of creating new solutions.'

Human centricity is a key mindset because it puts the power where it belongs: with the user. Throughout the process of design it allows us to empathize with the user by continuously bringing in her perspective and asking whether the activities teams engage in will deliver something desirable to her. Additionally, it infuses the projects with a sense of purpose which is not only linked to the strategic intent but also to the outside world.

These five attitudes start in the domain of design but would do well being applied to the broader company culture. They are equally relevant to other areas of business, enabling learning, sharing, visualization, and the evolution and morphing of ideas on an ongoing basis and with an open mind. It is partly thanks to the value of these skills that design thinking has become such a welcome expertise in companies.

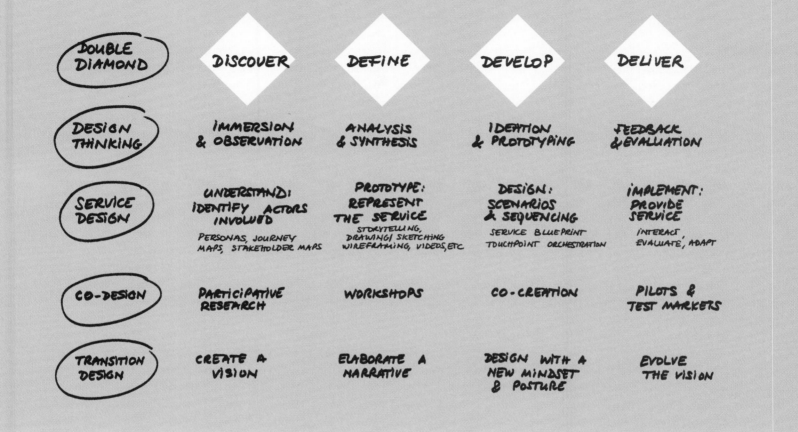

	DISCOVER	DEFINE	DEVELOP	DELIVER
DOUBLE DIAMOND				
DESIGN THINKING	IMMERSION & OBSERVATION	ANALYSIS & SYNTHESIS	IDEATION & PROTOTYPING	FEEDBACK & EVALUATION
SERVICE DESIGN	UNDERSTAND: IDENTIFY ACTORS INVOLVED — PERSONAS, JOURNEY MAPS, STAKEHOLDER MAPS	PROTOTYPE: REPRESENT THE SERVICE — STORYTELLING, DRAWING/ SKETCHING WIREFRAMING, VIDEOS, ETC	DESIGN: SCENARIOS & SEQUENCING — SERVICE BLUEPRINT TOUCHPOINT ORCHESTRATION	IMPLEMENT: PROVIDE SERVICE — INTERACT, EVALUATE, ADAPT
CO-DESIGN	PARTICIPATIVE RESEARCH	WORKSHOPS	CO-CREATION	PILOTS & TEST MARKETS
TRANSITION DESIGN	CREATE A VISION	ELABORATE A NARRATIVE	DESIGN WITH A NEW MINDSET & POSTURE	EVOLVE THE VISION

Design sub-modalities

Ask different people about what design practice involves and you are likely to get a larger number of answers than the number of people you asked. Design is an evolving discipline and an area of practice and as such includes various sub-modalities. These include

- Design Thinking
- Co-design
- Service Design
- Transition Design

There is a fluidity in these definitions that needs to be highlighted. What we understand to be 'design thinking', 'service design', 'co-design' or 'transition design' today will effectively morph, evolve and transition as we develop new language, new tools and new views to explain design practice in all its manifestations within the business context.

Each of these sub-modalities is a different manifestation of the basic design process illustrated with the Double Diamond of Design. Because they come from different backgrounds and needs, they have taken different forms. Let's explore them briefly here.

Design Thinking

Design thinking has made its entry into business practice and is here to stay. Wikipedia lists the following definition[19] for it: "Design Thinking is a methodology for practical, creative resolution of problems or issues that looks for an improved future result. It is the essential ability to combine empathy, creativity and rationality to meet user needs and drive business success. Unlike analytical thinking, design thinking is a creative process based around the 'building up' of ideas. There are no judgments early on in design thinking. This eliminates the fear of failure and encourages maximum input and participation in the ideation and prototype phases. Outside the box thinking is encouraged in these earlier processes since this can often lead to creative solutions."

I prefer the more compact definition by Charles Burnette[20], who says design thinking is "a process of creative and critical thinking that allows information and ideas to be organized, decisions to be made, situations to be improved and knowledge to be gained."

Design thinking makes 'thinking like a designer' available to non-designers, making designerly approaches accessible to other disciplines as never before. Given that the design disciplines are so broad, ranging from art to engineering, there has been a bit of mystery about what design is when seen from the outside. Design thinking unifies the patterns of thought and processes for applied creativity, making them available at conceptual level to others outside of design. Design thinking does not replace design, but makes the unique approach of designers to problem solving more broadly available.

As a framework, design thinking empowers people and teams to approach the world with a sense of curiosity and openness, an eagerness to learn and discover and a willingness to apply those lessons to create new things, conditions or experiences.

In this era of creative empowerment, this is hugely liberating, hugely empowering and very human. Tim Brown of IDEO says: "Design thinking is a human-centred approach to innovation that draws from the designer's toolkit to integrate the needs of people, the possibilities of technology, and the requirements for business success."

Several different models have appeared for design thinking, all of them stemming in one way or other from the basic design process as portrayed by the Double Diamond of Design: discover, define, develop and deliver. For design thinking, the phases of those models boil down to the following process phases: immersion and observation, analysis and synthesis, ideation and prototyping, feedback and evaluation. Importantly, these phases are cyclical. That means that while they may be phases in a given project, they constitute an ongoing cycle of strategic planning and as such they help shape the future of a business.

Immersion and observation concern understanding what is going on in the context. It looks for ways to extract the stories of what is the existing world and what the potential issues are with which design could help.

Analysis and synthesis are the consolidation of what was observed objectively into conclusions of what might be the case and what emerging patterns are possible explanations and starting points for idea generation.

Ideation and prototyping are close to scenario planning. For the generation of prototypes, one could consider strategic scenarios:
• what is possible (ie what might happen)
• what is plausible (ie what could happen)
• what is probable (ie what is likely to happen)
• what is preferable (ie what do we want to happen)
For each of these scenarios, alternative prototypes can be generated: turning design into a foresight tool through creativity. Being able to play with scenarios in a very concrete manner becomes the ideal tool for business: it is fast, it gives a sense of control, and it is easy to assess in terms of strategic fit. No wonder that design thinking is being adopted by business.

"Think like a designer."

Importantly, in this phase concept development makes tangible what the design solutions might be. Prototypes help materialize the ideas. Though the name 'design thinking' implies thinking, this phase is all about doing thorough iterating prototypes.

Feedback and evaluation constitute an iterative phase that allows for ideas and protoypes to be improved. It does not prove the idea, but rather signals how it can be made better. It includes tools like customer co-creation to incorporate new insights into the developed solution, things we could not have known upfront but that could enrich or improve the final outcome. Finally this phase provides insights from evaluation that can be brought into the beginning of the next cycle as we immerse into a new challenge.

In her book *Designing for Growth*, Jeanne Liedtka[21] calls these phases
• What is? (immersion and observation)
• What if? (analysis and synthesis)
• What wows? (ideation and prototyping)
• What works? (feedback and evaluation)

These are nice, simple questions that contain the essence of what is being done in each step. However, as she warns in her book: design thinking is not a series of steps in a process. It is experiential. Liedtka says, "Incorporating design thinking into your search for growth is going to take some practice on your part. Most companies, however well intentioned and excited about innovation, aren't P&G and Google. They still don't 'get it'. Chances are yours is one of those. All kinds of obstacles will probably be thrown your way while you are being asked to find profitable new growth opportunities. "That is very true, design thinking as design-doing take practice and experience. While it offers an excellent process and guidelines, it is not just following such guidelines blindly that will guarantee success. That is more dependant on what going through the process does for the business and the team: like sailing the sea, the process transforms you through the journey itself.

One of the main reasons why incorporating design thinking into business practice is very difficult is that from the industrial paradigm, business fosters individuality and competition.

Functional areas and separate departments all compete for resources and budget in a competitive, expertise-driven and isolated manner. As you are probably inferring from this the result is that there are many captains wanting to steer the ship based on their separate views. Large corporations even have job titles to signal that, like divisional director or senior vice-president.

This may have worked in other times and contexts but is quickly becoming outdated in a highly networked and rapidly changing world. The flexibility and resilience of organizations becomes compromised when value creation is subdivided into tactical drivers.

Businesses need coordination and coherence among departments, so that they can create value and unify towards a common goal and from a common and shared vision to meet the challenge at hand. It becomes mandatory to clarify the intent, to share a common purpose, and then to visualize and facilitate the strategic process, the decision-making steps, as well as to design the process, to allocate resources, and share the load of the implementation work. This requires a skill set beyond the process of design thinking and its different steps. It requires facilitation and communication, which starts by understanding that multiple disciplines working together deliver much better results than when they work separately.

Service Design

Service design entails establishing a common language to enable multi-disciplinary collaboration. It started out of a need to design services collaboratively and builds on the philosophy of design thinking. Obviously, the design of services requires a lot more communication and collaboration than does the design of products. A lot of what is developed and created in services is intangible and every moment and point of contact with the user is unique.

In the early '90s, design theorist Prof. Dr. Michael Erlhoff introduced the concept of 'service design' as a discipline to be taught at the International School for Design in Cologne, Germany. This was quite unique because service design had arisen from design practice and was now being incorporated to an academic curriculum. The implication of this is that service design is an empirical discipline rather than a methodology or a set of models.

As the British Design Council defines it: "Service design is all about making the service you deliver useful, usable, efficient, effective and desirable." What business wouldn't want that?

I see service design as being much broader in scope than the design of services. It has bridged a gap between design and business unlike any other sub-modality of design. This is because, traditionally, the marketing departments within organizations handled the design of services, and as things became more complex the business teams started adopting elements of the design culture and embracing the designerly ways of developing propositions.

As any seasoned marketing professional knows, what people buy is linked to the benefits they experience from using a product or a service. This has caused the service component of many propositions to be the main differentiator. Technology is no longer as expensive as it once was, and it evolves fast. Because the difference is made increasingly through services. Which is why service design has gained much terrain in business: it is imminently practical and it relates directly to the creation of user value.

And value is increasingly defined by the service component of any proposition. The lines between products and services is blurring in the experience economy. In most industrialized countries, services account for about seventy percent of the GDP. Service design understands this and takes human centricity and user experience to a new level by integrating it with business practice.

Some authors argue that design thinking and service design are essentially the same: a customer-centric focus to design and the introduction of design tools into the value creation process. In *This is Service Design Thinking*, a book featuring twenty three authors from the global service design community, Marc Stickdorn defines the five principles of service design:
"1. User centred: services should be experienced through the customer's eyes.
2. Co-creative: all stakeholders should be included in the service design process.
3. Sequencing: all stakeholders should be visualized in a sequence of interrelated actions.
4. Evidencing: intangible services should be visualized in terms of tangible artefacts.
5. Holistic: the entire environment of a service should be considered." [21]

Indeed there are many similarities between design thinking and service design. Because service design aims to orchestrate services, which are complex and networked systems in which there is ongoing interaction and fluidity, it has huge applicability to the issues businesses are facing in a changing, complex world.

The increasing importance of services as experiential components and the increasing need for coordination and teamwork to make brands and business agile in a complex context have raised service design to a strategic level. As this quote of Lao Tzu perfectly summarizes: "'If you do not change direction, you may end up where you are heading." Service design increases the awareness and the engagement needed to steer business through collaboration and teamwork, in a turbulent context. It is iterative and uses the intelligence of the whole team to understand whether the choices made along the way are leading towards the strategic intent and adding value where it matters.

The great contribution of service design is linked to the facilitation and collaborative aspects of the design process, engaging teams in focused communication and co-designing strategy implementation.

Whereas design thinking concerns user-centric processes that lead teams towards an outcome through a series of steps, service design looks at connections, relationships, and stakeholder engagement. It takes the hands-on approach of design thinking into the intangible realm of experience and focuses on the coordination and collaboration of the team to deliver value. It seeks opportunities for innovation not only as 'solutions' but also as improvements at every stage of the delivery of an experience.

The steps involved in service design are also linked to the design process, as portrayed by the Double Diamond of Design. The way they are applied is more practical and more fluid, in broad terms involving the following phases:
• Understanding: an initial phase in which the team identifies the actors involved and the context in which they interact. There are several tools to aid this step, including stakeholder maps, personas, and customer journey maps.
• Prototyping: this is the essence of service design because by representing the service through visual and prototyping tools, the team can best explore different scenarios and alternatives for service delivery. Service design entails making process manifest and interactions tangible so that they can be orchestrated or redesigned to meet user needs. Tools for prototyping come from a variety of disciplines, all aimed at representing the service in order to consider and build alternatives. Tools include drawing/sketching, role-playing, wireframing, video making and storytelling, among others.
• Designing: this phase involves generating a service blueprint and orchestrating touch points. This is where the script of how the service will be delivered is generated, what needs to be done, in which sequence and by whom. Because of the previous steps this involves not only design skills but also a thorough understanding of the user and the ability to choreograph and organize the total service.
• Implementing: a service is always a work in progress and thus every interaction with the user, once the service is implemented is an opportunity to adapt and learn, making use of the feedback loop to inform the understanding of the overall process.
As with all sub-modalities of design, service design is cyclical and iterative in nature.

Co-design

Co-design as a practice is directly related to applying the human-centric philosophy of design thinking with its tools and processes and integrating the connective, relational aspect that service design brings to the table. It is about designing 'with' rather than 'for' people, in order to create shared value.

Co-design involves engaging different people to work together towards a solution by understanding the different perspectives and experiences of people around a given issue, brand, product, or service. 'People' includes all those involved, not just the user, but also the business teams and supplier teams who are part of delivering the experiences.

As a practice co-design originated from business's need to involve users in the creative process: 'The practice of co-design allows users to become an active part of the creative development of a product by interacting directly with design and research teams. It is grounded in the belief that all people are creative and that users, as experts of their own experiences, bring different points of view that inform design and innovation direction. Co-design is a method that can be used in all stages of the design process, but especially in the ideation or concepting phases. Partnering with users ensures their inclusion in knowledge development, idea generation, and concept development on products whose ultimate goal is to best serve these same users."[23]

Collaborative innovation is the core of co-design, letting each collaborator in the design process bring in his or her expertise to elevate the number of opportunities of the total group. Researchers are experts in understanding people and their motivations and drivers, Designers are experts in translating user needs into workable and working solutions and Users are experts of their own experience. By engaging these different forms of expertise in a participatory fashion, solutions address real problems and deliver real benefits, while giving the team a real sense of purpose throughout the process.

In co-design everyone is assumed to be creative, though not everyone is a designer. As Liz Sanders and Pieter-Jan Stappers point out in *Convivial Toolbox*, "In a co-design process [...] the roles change: the person who will eventually be served through the design process is given the position of 'experts of their own experience', and plays a role in knowledge development, idea generation and concept development. In generating insights, the researcher supports the 'expert of his/her experience' by providing tools for ideation because design skills are very important in the development of the tools. The designer continues to play a critical role in giving form to the ideas."[24]

This way of working is very different from the hierarchical, departmental structures of many large organizations in which functional areas each do a part of the work separately. It reflects a new model, in which participation and collaboration engage people to deliver because they can add value from their own expertise and because they are passionate about the purpose of the project. Work methods that are innate to design disciplines, but fairly new to the field of business -if the business team is ready to engage in the adventure- can have a transformative effect on the culture of individuality, silos and meetings, changing it for good and making the whole process of strategy generation and implementation more purposeful and more organic.

Again the phases of co-design stem from the basic design process of discover, define, develop and deliver. Because of its participatory nature, all of these phases involve collaboration with the community outside the company. The lines of designer and user become blurred, and it not only sees people as experts of their own experiences but as empowered individuals who participate in shaping their world and their future. The phases of co-design are similar to those of the other sub-modalities of design but characterized by the joint collaboration with users:

• Participative research: user research in which generative tools are used to learn alongside the participant. These involve viewing and interpreting the world through their eyes. Tools that can be used include storyboarding, ethnographic research or mobile ethnography tools, photo-based or video-based journaling,

"Co-design is about designing 'with' rather than 'for' people in order to create shared value."

or context mapping among others. The collection of data takes place together with the participant, who is actively involved in the research process.

• Interpretative workshops: while using tools and techniques from the design and/or research expertise, to conduct analysis and draw conclusions, there is a dialogue with the participant in the process. This can involve all kinds of workshops, from sharing feedback, to exhibiting findings, to using more expressive or intuitive means of capturing the essence of what was learnt. It necessitates the openness to keep asking: Is this what we understood? Does it make sense to you? How would you define it? The use of generative and projective techniques to help the participant imagine alternatives is crucial to the workshop element. The design team is a facilitator not a shaper of this process.

• Co-creation: like the generation of conclusions, the generation of solutions is also collaborative. Designers provide interactive prototypes to engage in a series of iterations with the user to co-shape what the solutions could be. The designers translate the needs into solutions and probe through co-creation what the user experience is. Users interact through their usage, hacks and ideas for improvement until there is a solution that meets the requirements and needs jointly identified in the previous phases.

• Pilots and test markets: to promote continued learning, the delivery phase includes experimentation through pilots and beta versions, and possibly smaller markets for testing and fine-tuning the solution before the final implementation.

Co-design is participatory and collective, and through this engagement in all stages of the cycle, learning is ongoing. Users work alongside the design teams and develop progressive insight into the possibilities by seeing the designers at work. The level of empowerment increases for all, as the users articulate their needs and experiences directly and the designers can apply creative thinking to the generation of solutions that are relevant and engaging, obtaining direct feedback for their efforts.

Transition Design

The rise in complexity, uncertainty and world-problems like climate change, obesity, population growth, poverty, pollution and urban concentration, presents new design challenges. The reason these challenges are design challenges and not challenges for designers is that they require problem-solving on a very large scale. We need all kinds of talent, all kinds of views and all hands on deck to navigate ourselves into a sustainable future.

Challenges of this size affect business, society and our very livelihood as a species on Earth. Enter, Transition Design. Transition Design "is a new term that the [Carnegie Mellon] School of Design is introducing to refer to design-enabled, system level change. Transition Design involves working at multiple levels of scale, over time so that social, economic and technological systems co-evolve toward more sustainable futures. Transition Designers combine the tools and processes of design with new understandings of living systems, innovation diffusion, and community organizing. The result is a capacity to identify the leverage points for reconceiving lifestyles

and the infrastructures that resource them. You cannot design a transition to start; rather, systems begin to transition, and when they do, they afford designers the opportunity to create preferable states."[25]

Designers are no longer alone; non-designers have joined to help solve the biggest problems of our time. Nor do they work in isolation, because the effect of their solutions encompasses new areas that are interconnected and which contribute to both the problem and the solution.

Transition design addresses the role of designers as stewards of the transition. Design skills are skills for transformation and for the creation of new and better conditions. Terry Irwin, Gideon Kossoff and Cameron Tonkinwise of The Carnegie Mellon School of Design are the main proponents of transition design. I believe that this way of looking at design will have a massive effect on how business plays a role within society in the coming decades.

Business has always been interlinked with society. Now, in the era of creative empowerment, society's constituents -citizens, families, groups and associations- all want to participate in the process of designing the ecology we all live in. Or, as the late Wubbo Ockels (Dutch astronaut and physicist) said, "We are all astronauts of spaceship Earth."

On top of that, as a result of the continued crisis of faith in businesses and the world financial crisis, business is also in transition. New, more integrative models are arising in the form of start-ups that grow at the speed of light (like Google and Facebook), multiply exponentially through new channels (like the internet, peer-to-peer platforms, and local businesses) and a whole list of things that are emerging and happening right now that we couldn't have foreseen a couple of years ago. This means that business needs to develop new skills and embrace change in adaptive ways. This is where business can learn from transition design.

The four characteristics of transition design are strategic in nature because they serve to transition from the current state into the future state: Transition design charts a course by creating a vision in the form of a future-oriented narrative, which serves to inspire and streamline the transition, Transition design elaborates alternatives in the form of theories of change, by understanding and explaining the dynamics of change through new knowledge and referencing other disciplines outside of design, Transition design has a systems-oriented, ecological worldview, with a mindset and posture that enable multi-disciplinary collaboration, Transition design will lead to the emergence of new ways of designing.

This is an emerging field of design and we cannot know what it might bring. Nonetheless it is inspiring because it acknowledges that while we are all sailing out into the unknown, we can co-develop and shape the world around us through a conscious effort of turning our imagination to the long term and narrating our own process to get there.

Joining hands, minds, and hearts

Sailing into the future is as fascinating as it is inevitable. Change is the natural state of anything that is alive. We live on a planet that is alive and we are part of that living system. Understanding that there are no static, linear models that can control the cyclicality and unpredictability of our context is a key skill in this new world. Connecting the sub-modalities of design will help us in the next steps we need to take as citizens of this beautiful planet: joining hands through creative approaches, joining minds through communication, joining hearts through purpose, and collaborating in designerly ways to create a better future.

Design thinking bridges the gap between thinking and doing, providing a conceptual framework and a mindset. It introduces non-designers into the ways designers think: understanding and framing problems, applying creativity with a strong bias to action, generating options through prototyping, and learning by doing.

Service design helps frame initiatives through tools like service blueprints and journey maps that allow the team to see the whole system at work, not just the individual parts. The team can therefore better address ambiguity and uncertainty by clarifying the challenges throughout the development process. There are no holy-houses or wrong questions: the goal is to understand together what the challenge is and solving it together instead of leaving the difficult bits to other departments. Through service design, teams work multi-functionally to clarify the issues and tackle the challenges in a responsive manner.

Co-design makes collaboration and participation the default, allowing us to learn and create collectively as a team by incorporating different areas of expertise to enrich the understanding and allowing different perspectives to emerge and blend throughout the development process.

Transition design regards the future; it helps us realize that there is one common future that we are all a part of. As we shift away from an industrial model and into a creative empowerment model we will also gain more awareness of the system we are all a part of, the impact of our actions on it and the role we can play in it to design sustainable futures for the longer term. This is a transition that also needs to take place in business, which is so interweaved with society's key constituents (citizens, groups, associations, etc.) and which has to take on the challenges that come from being a part of a bigger, organic system. It provides an opportunity not to engage only from a profit maximization perspective in which our hands and our minds create value that can be expressed economically. Value has many more forms when we are willing to also engage our hearts; progress is not only measured in profit terms, it has everything to do with people and with our broader ecosystem. There is a role for business in that space too.

DESIGN REVISITED

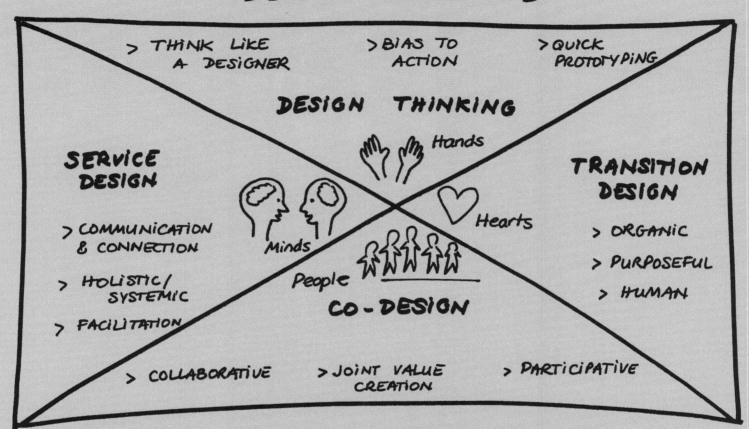

> THINK LIKE A DESIGNER   > BIAS TO ACTION   > QUICK PROTOTYPING

DESIGN THINKING

Hands

Hearts

Minds

SERVICE DESIGN

> COMMUNICATION & CONNECTION

> HOLISTIC/ SYSTEMIC

> FACILITATION

TRANSITION DESIGN

> ORGANIC

> PURPOSEFUL

> HUMAN

People

CO-DESIGN

> COLLABORATIVE   > JOINT VALUE CREATION   > PARTICIPATIVE

DESIGN = CONNECTING THE DOTS IN NEW WAYS TO ENHANCE VALUE FOR EVERYONE INVOLVED.

Oceans of opportunity

IBM generated a report in 2010 called *Capitalising on Complexity*[26]. It conducted interviews with leading CEOs worldwide and concluded that while rising complexity is unavoidable in today's world and while they themselves seriously doubt their ability to cope with that complexity, the way companies respond to it can be a game changer.

IBM's Global CEO study goes on to conclude that incremental changes are not enough to keep at pace with the complexity around us. The four main conclusions of the study were that
a/ "Today's complexity is only expected to rise and more than half of CEOs doubt their ability to manage it"
b/ "Creativity is the most important leadership quality, according to CEOs"
c/ "The most successful organisations co-create products and services with customers, and integrate customers into core processes"
d/ "Better performers manage complexity on behalf of their organizations, customers and partners".

The way to capitalize on complexity, according to the IBM study is to build operational dexterity, embody creative leadership, and reinvent customer relationships. "The effects of rising complexity call for CEOs and their teams to lead with bold creativity, connect with customers in imaginative ways and design their operations for speed and flexibility to position their organizations for twenty-first century success", it concludes.

We have looked at design in this chapter across its different levels. As we saw with the design ladder model, it all starts with awareness. Recognizing that design as a tool can help improve conditions, from form to strategy is a key starting point. The steering wheel of design has showed us that the skills of designers can be used in a multiplicity of ways and that they are flexible enough to adapt to the conditions of complexity and turbulence. Then we dove into the process of the double-diamond and the different levels of application or orders of design. Finally we looked at the key attitudes of design. Looking at design through

the lens of business and the complex problems that business will need to tackle in the twenty-first century, it is clear that design is being revisited in order to emerge as a mindset for growth and innovation that businesses cannot go without and to be embraced as a right-hand partner to business strategy that will help navigate the unknown and shape future opportunities.

Design is uniquely positioned to help business. By doing what designers do best: understand problems, recognize opportunities and solutions, iterate those solutions and evolving them so that they add value and appropriately address the problem. The tools are being democratized: via the processes and methodologies of design thinking, the facilitation skills of service design and the awareness of transition design.

Because design itself is evolving and changing it does not have off-the-shelf answers. But it does offer new ways of approaching complexity and elevating business creativity to make

"Business is increasingly designing strategy in a context of change."

business more resilient and adaptive in the process of strategy renewal. It helps converge the mental processes of thinking and planning with the creative processes of doing and making, by bringing non-designers into the process and unlocking everybody's creative potential.

Brand consultants Wolff Olins' 2015 report[27], *Impossible and Now: How Leaders are Creating the Uncorporation* describes how CEOs are reacting to the changing, turbulent context, "Leaders, in response, are learning to be less the visionary, less the sage, less the objective-setter, and more the shaper, the connector, the questioner. And yet at times, they also need to intervene, to insist, to control. It's a fluid role, its shape not yet clear.'"And they go on to quote Marty Neumeier[28]: "If design thinking is about moving from an existing situation to a better one, then the CEO is designer-in-chief."

Sooner or later that might happen, as business is increasingly designing strategy in a context of change. Above all, this signals the importance of a creative mindset and a realization that the hierarchical, industrialist model has started to give way to a collaborative, human and more organic model of creative empowerment. More than ever, people are starting to embrace the power of their innate creative abilities, embracing their limitations by daring to embark in an adventure of discovery knowing that, as English actor and comedian John Cleese so brilliantly expresses it, *"When you're being creative nothing is wrong."*

Design Revisited

Design is no longer only concerned with making, it has evolved into a mindset. Businesses and people are more than ever interconnected as co-shapers of our world than ever before. People do not accept that businesses unilaterally define for them how they lead their lives and what they can chose. This era of dialogue and integration means that businesses are becoming living, breathing ecosystems and not just capitalistic entities playing a zero-sum game. This calls for a more systemic approach to business, not just with systemic thinkers but also with systemic changers, systemic guides, and systemic doers.

We are moving from rational explanation to an ever more complex emerging model which is organic and which is based on a more holistic understanding of the different realities and perspectives that live alongside each other within the total system.

Design provides a mechanism for shaping and integrating learning by successive approximations of what might work. It allows us to make thought processes explicit and thus shared, out in the open, and co-creative. It requires an open mindset and the acceptance that there is always a customer experience whether or not companies have planned a customer experience strategy. Design looks at the interaction and the interface with the consumer and breaks the experience down into its components: social, emotional, and transactional. Design maps it and understands it through the eyes of the user and plans and designs it in line with the strategic intent. Design brings the human lens.

As Buckminster Fuller brilliantly summarized: "You never change things by fighting the existing reality. To change something, build a new model that makes the existing one obsolete." Design thinking brings in the perspective of the user to a place where it had been lost. Companies had been looking for competitive edge, for speed and control, for scalability. And they may have just forgotten who they were doing it all for in the end.

Design in this day and age is linked to the ability of understanding and building the story of people and brands and businesses as it unfolds. It starts with paying attention to the individual stories out in the world and it develops through the creative ability to connect the dots in new ways to deliver new value. That is design, revisited: connecting the dots in new ways in order to enhance value for everyone involved. Designing and co-designing our systems together so that we are all better off through better understanding, better tailored solutions and better experiences.

4 SETTING SAIL

*'It is the set of
the sails, not the
direction of the wind
that determines
which way we
will go.'*

–Jim Rohn

What sailing has to do with strategy

Strategy is more than ever about a journey. It involves the process of determining what the direction of a business will be and following through accordingly, having the ability to understand the context and the business' role in it. Linear models of strategy, as they were traditionally taught in business schools will no longer work. Strategy requires teamwork, and 'adjusting the sails' in an ongoing engagement with the context.

Time has changed, literally. In the *2015 Customer Experience Outlook* report by Kerry Bodine and Doberman[1], Fred Leichter of Fidelity Investments re-introduces the concept of time, which we have taken for granted as a sequential succession of events. He says: 'The Ancient Greeks had two ways of keeping time. The first method, and the one that caught on, was chronos time, quantified by the passage of seconds, days and years – always in equal measure. Today's successful organizations have become very good at managing chronos time. They create project plans that span weeks and months, deliver the things that are 'in scope' for a given number of days, and factor person-hours into calculations of corporate costs and margins. In chronos time, every paddle stroke moves an organization forward at the same rate. The Greeks' second method of keeping time was called kairos time, measured the passage of opportunities. Unlike chronos time, kairos time is not flat, steady or sequential. Instead, it undulates. Surfers know kairos time well, waiting patiently in the right place for a wave and then seizing the right moment to accelerate."

The implications of this for strategy are clear: embracing fluidity and non-linearity will pay dividends. Much like in sailing, embracing fluidity does not mean letting go of every aspect of planning nor disregarding the overarching vision. Seasoned sailors, like expert strategists are determined, self-aware and realistic. They also are sensible enough to know that weather and wind are not to be controlled and that no matter how good the plan is, it will be tried and tested by the act of sailing itself. This makes sailors context-aware while they are driven towards results, whether the aim is to sail a great regatta, a pleasurable sailing trip, or to simply arrive at harbour safe with the joy of having mastered the sail. Embracing non-linearity entails a holistic approach in which the different aspects are connected and re-connected through responsive research and adaptive design in order to arrive successfully at the envisioned destination.

It also requires using the time at harbour wisely: learning new skills; making sure the ship and sails are in good condition; exchanging thoughts, ideas and stories with other sailors; spending time understanding the context; and practicing patience and resilience when conditions are less favourable.

It is the journey that counts

When it comes to business strategy and innovation, companies embark upon the journey with a clear beginning and with the end in mind. What happens in between the beginning and the end of any strategic journey cannot be foreseen although it is of course possible to plan for it adaptively. This is very different to the model-driven, linear approach to planning that was the norm in industrialist thinking.

Business thinking has traditionally sought structure in models that would help explain reality and define courses of action. From Michael Porter's five forces model to explain the competitive context to process tools for innovation management such as the innovation funnel and tunnel with Robert Cooper's StageGate® methodology, these models are linear and static. They assume implicitly, that there is time to sit back and reflect upon what is happening and how to act upon it. Or else they assume that key performance indicators could be set in advance and serve as a lasting benchmark. Many of the large corporations still maintain annual strategic planning rounds, in which they define plans for a year, that they subsequently implement as planned. It is a nice, predictable, and structured ways of doing things, but it generates a big gap between the business and its context, with the obvious implication that business starts lagging due to a lack of self-actualization, being out of

synch with the context. The reason for this asynchronous development is not only the speed of change, it is also the length of the cycles: if your planning cycle is shorter than the cycle of change, there is room to adapt. On the other hand, if the cycles of change are shorter than the planning cycle, then the planning quickly becomes obsolete.

Because change is so prevalent, so quick, and so unpredictable, there is a need to revise the length of the planning cycles. Smaller, more reflective planning that is integrated to the journey allows for continuous adaptability.

To understand business growth as a journey is to embrace the dynamics of this process. The journey is essentially a process of connection with the context in real-time and a process of problem solving for the generation of value. Alain de Botton[2] succinctly describes the purpose of business: "Every business is at heart an attempt to solve someone else's problem . The bigger and the more urgent the problem, the bigger the opportunity." Therefore, companies start the process of strategy and innovation with a problem and know they want to end with a solution that adds value. The solution is not yet clear at the start of the journey, whether it is a small project, a new proposition or the very essence of what the company stands for. There is only one way forward: an attitude of readiness to change. The company must learn

as it goes, adapt as it learns and maintain an agile, flexible mindset for change.

When strategy, research and design work together they set a dynamic in motion that can fuel the strategic journey through creative insight. This is a progressive and ongoing process that is fed by their interactions with the context, with each other, and with the internal teams. It is both integrative and abductive because it brings ideas and insights together while transforming them into an adaptive plan based on what is best at that particular moment. Creative insight is the process by which the sailboat cuts through the water, it describes the balance between strategic planning and strategy implementation.

The strategic journey is iterative, interactive and interpretative. This is why bringing strategy, research, and design together makes it more agile and flexible. To 'solve' the strategy conundrum of understanding and building almost simultaneously in order to move forward, there are several questions to be answered. These questions will help give a more dynamic and broader perspective to the task at hand, much like it would happen on the deck of a sailboat. Expert sailors would not just ask a question once and assume that the answer is a 'given' from that point onwards. The same is true in the development of creative insight.

The what, why, and how of creative insight

At the intersection of strategy and research is the ability to sense the environment, not just by scanning the landscape at intervals but by staying constantly engaged and scanning the environment continuously. The question that strategy and research aim to answer is, 'What?' In other words: What is going on? And what can we do about it? And what else? It keeps scanning and searching and sensing in order to be in tune to the conditions and signal what matters.

Expert sailors are hybrids: they work independently with unique expertise ,and they work together as members of a team. When research and design work together, the question that arises is 'Why?' as in, Why does it matter to the user? Why should this be part of our strategic journey? Importantly, at this intersection, strategy is in the background whereas research and design assume autonomous roles -employing curiosity and creativity interchangeably- to better explain the context and its changing condition, changing angles, switching perspectives and tirelessly asking why, and ultimately, interpreting the implications of what is being observed and understood by asking, 'Why?.'

Another trait of expert sailors is that they have what designers call a 'beginner's mindset': they maintain an eager attitude of openness and

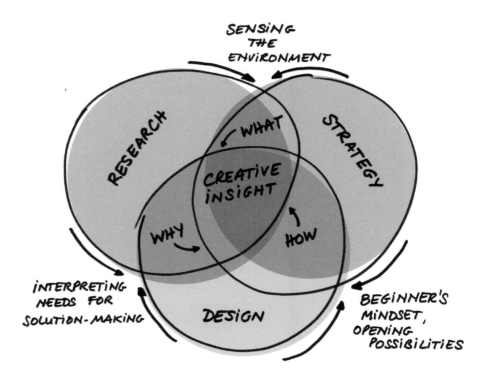

lack of preconceptions in order to understand which opportunities are at hand. A beginner's mindset is free of constraints and sees endless possibilities, taking nothing for granted and nothing as given. Where strategy and design meet the question is, 'How?' How do we make this happen? How do we apply resources?

Where what, why, and how come together is where creative insight is generated. There are no hard and fast rules with regards to which question to ask first, there are no right or wrong ways of navigating and there is no predefined map with navigation guidelines. A lot of what occurs at sea is based on knowledge yet guided by intuition. That intuition develops itself through experience, which is why teamwork and mentorship are so important in these non-linear processes.

Strategy as choreography

In previous chapters we have looked at the directional role of research -navigating with a compass and by looking at the stars as approximations of reality. We have looked at design as the wheel of the ship: steering with the use of the rudder and the keel in an adaptive and versatile interaction with the context leading towards the strategic intent. In this metaphor of a sailboat, the sails represent the twenty-first century, post-industrialist role of strategy. Strategy is the captain of the metaphorical ship, who determines its course by adjusting the sails. This is a pivotal role, a central role, a choreographer's role. It takes into account what is happening and what might be possible, and unifies these into a vision in order to sail onwards.

Strategy should not be linear as the industrial paradigm would have us think; it should be nimble. Strategy involves a series of steps which need to happen in a certain harmonic interaction (like in a choreography) but which can take many forms as they manifest (adjusting the sails to the conditions in order to reach the desired destination) -indeed, like the surrounding surf and waves that are undulating rather than linear. Offering resistance to that movement -always present in the context- by aiming for linearity, means taking on the full force of the surf as it plunges against the intent of the strategic plan.

To choreograph strategy and give it the flexibility it needs in a complex environment, three phases can be identified: strategy development, strategy planning and strategy implementation.

Strategy development is the phase in which options are generated. It involves preparing the journey and involves understanding the territory. As we have seen it includes sensing, exploring, and accepting that information is ambiguous or incomplete and requires analysis and synthesis of the problems and opportunities in order to decide which options are available.

Like expert sailors, business professionals should explore what is possible before deciding what to explore in depth. This is why research is an excellent partner to this phase of strategy. Parallel to this, it is key to develop alternatives to see what works, which is where design plays a key role.

The next step is strategy planning, which is when the decisions are made on which options to pursue. Strategic planning is the charting of the strategic journey and the setting of a destination. In this phase the understanding of the situation is deepened, by gauging reactions in the context, which is where design and prototyping become a learning tool through research, since it allows businesses to gauge reactions in advance of a full-fledged implementation.

It prepares the journey through concrete consideration of alternative scenarios and interprets possible courses of action.

Once the analysis and planning have been done, it is time for strategy implementation. This is the moment for action and involves navigating the territory for real. There is no theory or planning here, this is the pragmatic phase of doing and interacting.

In this phase strategy execution can be improved by testing real experience and getting real feedback which are activities that can be easily achieved through the immersive, hands-on skills of design and the empathic, human aspects of research.

These three phases interact and intertwine with each other in dialogue with the context. Strategy is as much about defining a vision as it is about negotiating a way through the context with evolving understanding, moments of disruption and varying degrees of clarity. The main tools for negotiating in the turbulent environment are the sails and the most important skill is teamwork. Adjusting sails takes vision, determination and more than one person in order to operate fast, securely and adaptively.

- LINEAR MODEL: SEQUENTIAL

ASSESS ⟶ PLAN ⟶ IMPLEMENT AS PLANNED

- CHOREOGRAPHED STRATEGY: NIMBLE & ADAPTIVE

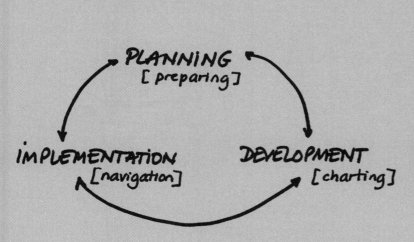

PLANNING
[preparing]

IMPLEMENTATION
[navigation]

DEVELOPMENT
[charting]

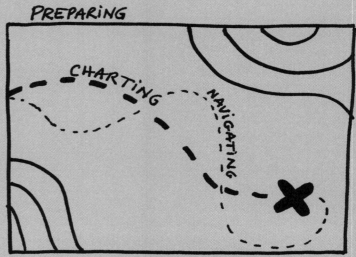

PREPARING

CHARTING

NAVIGATING

Setting S.A.I.L.

The three stages of strategy development as a choreographed effort are all immersive: business cannot be seen as isolated from the environment it acts in. The mere fact that business is contextual implies that it also affects the environment and that the dynamics of that process are what leads to developing meaningful value propositions. Strategy development is an ongoing dialogue with the context, which requires continuous monitoring and scoping (through research) as well as constant steering and intervention (through design).

The use of terminology such as 'navigation' and 'choreography' is not casual; I feel it is the best language to express that strategy is an interactive effort. It necessarily must be flexible in order to succeed. Thus, the mast of the ship represents the backbone of strategic intent. It is supported by the sails, as instrument of strategic adaptability, which catch as much wind from the context as is useful and opportune to reach the desired destination or strategic intent. The depth of the keel (an element of design) gives the sailboat stability, more synergy and thoroughness of involvement with the context. The navigational abilities of research to read the context and assess the most favourable conditions are important for charting the course and keeping a sense of what is emerging and changing in the context.

Sailing becomes an engaged and engaging activity where every member of the crew contributes expertise and perspective. The activities are a concerted, choreographed effort not so much because of the use of a script but because of the dynamic interaction of talent. It is somewhat improvised in that it takes into account the context; yet it is also highly focused in that it aims for a higher strategic purpose or goal.

The activities in the strategic cycle can be brought together under the acronym S.A.I.L., which stands for: Sensing, Analyzing, Inventing and Learning. These activities are ongoing ways in which strategy, with research and design, shape business.

Unlike the models in previous chapters which either originated from research or from design, with the S.A.I.L. model I have attempted to unify research and design as ongoing activities in the research process. Each of these activities involves elements of research and of design, with the aim of shaping strategy in a cyclical and iterative way, without pre-defined processes or answers. It is as much about the mindset as it is about taking the best of both worlds, the worlds of research and of design and bringing them together in a new model for business practice.

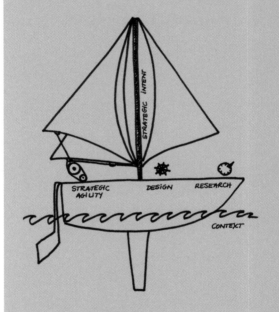

BUSINESS NAVIGATION

Sensing (S)

Sensing is exploring the context in which the business operates with an open mind. The main characteristic of this phase is discovery by being aware that the context is always changing, that learning is an ongoing process. Sensing allows businesses to broaden their understanding so that new connections can be made that reveal new meaning and enhance the organization's ability to create value from new and emerging sources.

This is a diverging activity, broadening the scope of possibility from the very basic understanding that ideas can come from anywhere. The aim is to bring in fresh perspectives from the context into the realm of business creation, to sense where business can make a difference and create value from the perspective of the user.

Analyzing (A)

Where sensing is a diverging activity intended to open up opportunities, analyzing is a converging activity intended to understand what truly matters and where the difference can be made. Analysis applies curiosity and applies imagination, taking the opportunities a step further into scenarios of what could be done. Like Sensing, Analyzing is shaped by thinking. While it is immersive and full of empathy it is not action based. Rahter, it involves planning of what might be done in the next step. Analysis and synthesis engender insights and create

the first hypothesis on which solutions will be generated. These possibilities can lead to transformation and innovation if they are captured by the business proposition in the form of products and services as thinking turns into acting by way of inventing.

Inventing (I)

Inventing or creating is when we cross the line between thinking and doing. It is experiential and it involves redefining the experience by applying what was learnt through sensing and analyzing. It is the most versatile point of strategy and business creation, since it involves understanding the opportunities identified, then applying this insight into prototyping -taking into account the constraints of making

and creating- and finally integrating the solution or invention with a reality that is complex and changing. More often than not invention is about redefinition and reinvention; in other words, invention is making new connections and combinations based on the conclusions of the analysis.

Learning (L)

Once inventions are embedded in the context, the opportunity to learn and gather evidence of how things have been adopted and adapted, how the user has experienced the solution and the degree to which the problem has been answered arises. This is a cyclical element in the process, as the learning process allows for a new round of sensing to unfold so that we can see what the effect is of the actions and which adjustments need to take place to keep strategy in motion.

The S.A.I.L. process is itself a cyclical process that moves us from the current state into a future state. On one hand, it involves the integration of the what, why and how of research, strategy and design in generating creative insight. On the other hand it is the ongoing manifestation of strategy as the sailboat cuts through the water when ideas and inventions are implemented and become embedded. The application of creative insight leads to the new manifestation of what is current and creates room for a process of evolution into new futures.

Cycles of strategic understanding

The strategic process sets the course, research helps us understand the terrain, and design navigates it. The goal is not per se to stay the course per se, but to reach the destination adaptively and fluidly. This involves going through cycles of understanding, cycles that start with the pull of adventure, gain momentum with the swirl of discovery and end with the inspiration of new shores. Strategic renewal is the process that takes place as the cycles of strategic understanding succeed one another.

Whether the cycles of strategy are linked to renewal and reinventing the category in which an organization participates or whether they are oriented to the short-term to refuel and reconnect with the context, they will all go more quickly or more slowly, more exploratively or more thoroughly through the cycle of S.A.I.L. This is a dynamic process of adjusting and readjusting the sails.

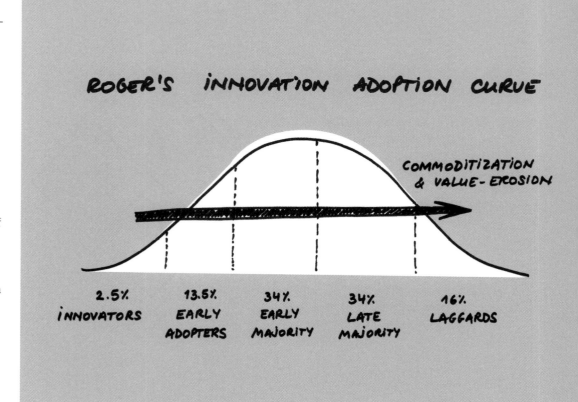

The reason this process is ongoing and continuous is of course that the context changes, which demands readjusting the sails. The changes in the context have to do with the evolution of understanding from the perspective of the user and are best explained by Everett Roger's curve[3]. Rogers argues that there is a diffusion of innovation that over time spreads and changes in value as it is adopted by different people within the population. The rate at which this happens is variable, however; the

direction of diffusion is clear: innovators and early adopters are the ones who lead the way by choosing what is authentically relevant. They are attuned with their own needs and they trigger change. The early majority emulates these choices because they are trendy or new and they want to try them out. They are followed by the early majority; those who are ready to embrace change and adopt it as it becomes visible. They consider their choices based on what is available to them. The next stage is when the

late majority adopts an innovation. The late majority are those who tend to be skeptical of anything new but eventually adopt it because of its prevalence. Finally, the laggards only really accept innovation once it has become mainstream or traditional because everyone else has adopted the innovation already.

As the illustration of Roger's curve shows, percentages can be allocated to represent the size of each of these groups of people in the innovation life cycle. Logically, businesses will want to maximize revenue and thus address the middle of the curve, which represents the largest groups. Roger argues that this is futile, because these people make choices based on what is already available not on what is new as that would be too risky for them. The challenge, then, is how to capture value by taking on the wave from the beginning and sailing with it into the mainstream segments.

The goal of any business is to capture market value by fulfilling a user need effectively. Roger's curve shows us that as people embrace innovations their value starts to erode. In the early phases of adoption innovations capture value due to their novelty as much as due to their ability to fulfill needs. The initial enthusiasm attracts the attention of other businesses that participate in the opportunity and help innovation spread, and as ideas go mainstream, value diminishes because of competition, larger scale and availability. Ideas that are mainstream generally capture less value; as they move into the final phases they get commoditized and become part of the standard. They lose the novelty aspect as new ideas are adopted by innovators that surpass the old paradigms in both novelty and value, and so on. This flow of commoditization versus the waves of innovation is what creates a constant gap between existing business and emerging consumer needs. This is the reason why innovation is so high on the strategic agenda of many businesses.

Generating options

Business strategy has become inextricably linked to innovation due to the speed of change. Those businesses that are able to change ahead, anticipating the future, will be able to make a meaningful difference. Not doing so, means accepting the consequences of being pushed by the current since there will always be change again, and again: making it virtually impossible to become a relevant player in the interaction between context and business as one tumbles under the waves of context instead of sailing them. You either change or are changed, the latter leading to an increased gap between the desired course and the actual course.

Strategy 's main role is to generate options. Business schools have been teaching scenario planning for decades now. The purpose of strategy is to open the sails to catch favourable wind so that more destinations and alternative routes become possible. This is a creative capacity -the creation of opportunities- which is at the very heart of business evolution and growth.

There is a saying in Dutch that roughly translated would be: 'the wharf veers the ship' -the equivalent to 'the tail wags the dog' but metaphorically more appropriate to sailing. What this means in our sailing analogy, is that unless the captain leads with a strategic vision, and design steers with concrete actions that are shaped by sensing the context through research:, then

arriving safely at harbour might be compromised. The sailboat will not be steered towards the wharf but rather will be confronted with the inflexibility of the wharf and 'pushed' or veered into position purely by resistance.

Innovation is what gives business room to manoeuvre and adapt. Innovation is the transient element of strategy that propels business into its future form as it is shaped by research and design. It is the set of initiatives that bridge the gap between business's current form and its future form, helping business sail smoothly into its future state. The continuous pull of the context, as shown by Roger's curve, makes it mandatory for innovation and the art of adjusting sails to be part of business strategy cycles.

As Paddy Harrington[4] explains for *FastCoDesign*: "'Innovation,' the word, was first seen in the 1540s. It comes from the Latin word innovatus, which means 'to renew or change' and is made up of two words: in which means 'into' and novus which means 'new.' So, to innovate is to go into the new."

Sailing is for the positive minded, brave-hearted and optimistic 'builders'. Setting off, going out to sea, is a big step but one that can be seen as the first of many. This is what innovation is about: propelling the business forward by daring to try. Should conditions be too averse, the sailboat can turn back to harbour or set anchor and reflect on the next course of action.

Wind and weather strengthen the team and help build character, an important aspect of resilience in business. And successful sailing trips and explorations make for great stories and a sense of achievement as options are generated and business is extended into new territories and domains.

The art of sailing

Wikipedia defines sailing[5] as "the propulsion of a vehicle and the control of its movement with large (usually fabric) foils called sails. By changing the rigging, rudder, and sometimes the keel or centreboard, a sailor manages the force of the wind on the sails in order to move the vessel relative to its surrounding medium (typically water, but also land and ice) and change its direction and speed. Mastery of the skill requires experience in varying wind and sea conditions, as well as knowledge concerning sailboats themselves and an understanding of one's surroundings."

Understanding the interaction between the context and the business, and managing that gap is key to a successful strategic journey. Wikipedia goes on to say, "The air interacting with the sails of a sailing vessel creates various forces, including reaction forces. If the sails are properly oriented with respect to the wind, then the net force on the sails will move the vessel forward. However, boats propelled by sails cannot sail directly into the wind. They must tack (turn the boat through

"S.A.I.L. integrates ratio and intuition, research and design, now and the future."

the eye of the wind) back and forth in order to progress directly upwind."

Historically, sailing had been critically important to the development of civilization as it allowed people to reach new horizons and interact with different cultures and learn from each voyage. It has allowed us to make new connections between things that were seemingly disconnected, these new connections propelled innovation, growth and progress.

Importantly, as Wikipedia points out, to sail forward a boat cannot sail directly into the wind. It requires managing the different aspects of sailing in order to propel the sailboat in the desired direction. Handling ropes and lines in order to adjust the sails is key to the art

of sailing. It is by adapting the sails to the conditions that the gap between the conditions and the desired direction is bridged, in order to stay the course, albeit indirectly at times.

The art of sailing has evolved from a very physical activity into one in which intelligent systems of ropes and pulleys help sailors be more resilient, flexible and agile, even in the trickiest of conditions. It is still a high contact, high effort sport in which working as a team is crucial to keeping all perspectives, opportunities, and risks in view while adapting to them in real time. Tying knots is part of the repertoire of any sailor, but I am also sure you would agree that it is not because of the knots alone that a sailor is successful at sea.

Learning the ropes

There are many books and models that prescribe tools for different strategic goals. Yet I believe business navigation is better handled by understanding the guiding principles that define each phase of S.A.I.L. and applying them in context than it is by applying a set of tools.

There are no shortcuts to developing and delivering sustainable business value. We must realize that it is not just having read about the tools that makes dynamic business design a matter of process. One of the first lessons in sailing is learning to tie knots, for it is important to have good command of the toolset. Yet there is also a danger in being prescriptive about the use of tools, as it would be to prescribe knots to a sailor. The use of these knots becomes intuitive through practice, it is through using them that they are best understood.

In the same way, to achieve the levels of understanding required to make strategy work and help business gain relevance we need to make the processes explicit.

The following guiding principles represent the things that have worked for me and for my clients in the past, though they do not aim to be complete nor thorough. These principles, like boating knots, are for reference of what is available to adjust the course of business as one would adjust sails.

Nonetheless, the main thing when it comes to evolving understanding is to engage playfully, with curiosity, and not taking anything for granted. With time and use, these principles become part of the intuitive set of ropes that are applied to sailing: a bit like art and a bit like science.

Sailing guidelines

With the use of S.A.I.L. it all comes together: ratio and intuition, research and design, now and the future. There are no limits to the combinations that can be made in the process: sensing is not only researching and inventing is not only designing. The principles provided here aim to integrate and unify the application, while drawing from my own experience as an innovator and business designer.

The reason for providing a synthesis of the principles that frame each phase through this book is that everything is changing and morphing continuously and we need to have a reference to inspire our work as we contribute to business strategy. Ultimately, the relevance to business is proven by the ability to generate value (be it strategic, monetary, social, or of any other kind) that is the very livelihood of organizations.

Thanks to models like Richard Buchanan's Four Orders of Design and through the adoption of design practices by non-designers in the realm of business, the methods of design practice are changing too. Increasingly, it takes interdisciplinary teams of specialists in all kinds of disciplines to tackle problems.

The same is true for research. Whereas research used to be the go-to department for information, now information is overwhelming us all. This means that we all have to become researchers in one way or another, for we must do something with all that information to make it work for us. Again here, interdisciplinary teams are adopting research tools, even though at times the practitioners are not necessarily trained or schooled as researchers.

These guidelines are not static, they will keep changing and evolving. For now, let them serve as a point of reference of where our sailing skills come together and let them be available to all in order to make sailing smoother, more open, and more inspiring than ever before.

Principles for Sensing

1 Observe without filtering

The main principle for sensing is entering the context with a blank slate. This is easier said than done. It is difficult to let go of what one knows! Because often we have taken what we know to be part of what is, and that makes how things might have changed less apparent to us.

Simple rules of thumb as you set out to research the context without interaction with the user include

• Formulate your research question as a journey of exploration, not as a question that could be answered with a yes or a no.

• For user observation: be a fly on the wall! Look at the context, the user, and the situation as if you had just stumbled into it without any prejudice. Listen for what is said and for what is not said. Look at any compensation behaviour by the user: how do they bridge the gap between what needs to be done and what is available for doing it?

• Immersive self-research: consider being a user of your own product or service for a while. Experience can be a great teacher. So get physical. Go where your users are, get in their shoes. Walt Disney kneeled to observe the world through child's eyes.

• If you decide to conduct desk research: remember that for sensing to be complete you will need detailed data (statistics, metrics, digital footprints) as well as thick data (explanations, stories, motivations,

drivers of why people do what they do). Look for complementarity on your data so you can see the full picture.

• Make sure you record your observations objectively. Do not analyse at this stage! Keep an open mind.

2 Engage openly with people

Remember that by being in the role of researcher you automatically introduce bias. Those being interviewed will engage with you as a researcher, so give considerate thought as to how you will engage with them:

• Which approach will you take in your personal interaction with users: Shadowing? Focus groups? Contextual inquiry? Ethnography? Diaries? Context mapping? In depth interviews? Usually to allow for exploration the methodologies used are qualitative. Be aware that even if there is no direct contact with the user, the researcher bias is present. After all, someone has formulated the questions. Consider the benefits of the different techniques available.

• When you interview people, make sure to use open questions that are not suggestive. If you have a topical guide or questionnaire, have someone else look at it first and point out where you might improve. You want to learn from people: so see them as experts and assume a mindset of curiosity and learning.

• Let the interview take its course as the interviewee shares her views with you. Use your topical guideline to help you navigate

the interview but dare to take a sidetrack if you feel it is worth investigating.

• Don't forget that you yourself are a person too, let the human element be present in the interaction.

3 Don't be a pirate

Pirates are archetypically drawn with a patch on one eye. But mastery in sailing requires full vision because using both eyes provides depth. Without depth we cannot have the full picture. Jumping to conclusions during the sensing stage is the equivalent of being a pirate. Once conclusions are drawn, they limit our ability to see the full picture. We will have a tendency to want to confirm what we know.

Avoid being a pirate by

• Re-reading what you've already learnt through past studies. More often than not, big companies have lots of knowledge lying around. There is no need for more research. Look for patterns across available studies and let new questions arise.

• Working together with others as a team: the more pairs of eyes the more textured and rich the picture will be.

• Using different techniques to learn and sense, and triangulate them. The value is in the patterns that emerge. By comparing and contrasting different sources we are able to see more.

• Using whatever you need to generate an objective explanation of what you learn, but be ethical and responsible about it. As we open up the ways of working to non-designers and non-researchers it is important to remember that we work with people for people and that the aim is to add value for the user.

4 Look for insights, not facts

Albert Einstein is quoted to have said "Any fool can know. The point is to understand". Sensemaking is exactly that: making sense. The purpose of gathering insights is to act upon them in order to design meaning. Facts are seldom actionable unless they are understood as insight: what do the facts mean and why should this matter to anyone? To get beyond facts and into insight

• Keep asking why: this will make your results less superficial.

• Dare to interpret what things mean and dare to probe about that interpretation. This is the key to generative research: you learn as you go. Involve the user in your learning process, so that you may learn together.

• Use cultural probes: by doing some thinking ahead of time with regards to what you want to learn, you can imagine more and better ways to collect insights: you can prepare kits for the respondents including colour markers and pens, paper cards to complete, a photo camera for registration, product or service ideas to try out, and games to play that will all help you get insights instead of just getting responses to questions. How people do things can be very insightful. And following up with an short interview as to what happened and why will also help you understand what the drivers and motivations were.

• Create personas: synthesize the archetypical profiles of the users you interacted with into personas, this will allow you to deal with complexity at a human level, in a human dimension. By creating imagery and names for each persona you can keep referring back to them and check what you think might work for them.

• Enough is enough: realize that there is a point of saturation. While research and exploration can be great fun, there is a point where gathering more information and asking more questions is not going to give new insights. Simply accumulating facts will not necessarily deliver more understanding.

From Sensing to Analyzing

The analysis phase involves shifting from thinking in terms of what is and moving towards what could be, taking understanding and insight and mapping out the implications, and reframing the challenge based on the conclusions derived. This generates forward-moving momentum to the process of S.A.I.L. and is generative in that it moves us from what we know for sure to what we start to envision as possible, moving from the world as it is into the future implications of how we understand it.

Each quadrant in the S.A.I.L. framework requires a different attitude as we shift first from 'now' and 'the future', and then from 'thinking' into 'doing'. As we sail forward from Sensing into Analyzing, the mindset is more interpretative and projective. Interpretative because it seeks to decipher what the implications might be of what we have understood in the Sensing phase. Interpretation requires a certain subjective analysis and the capacity to shift the information into potential new futures and contexts. And the mindset becomes projective because it is not applied to the same conditions, but extrapolated and transposed to new situations that are not yet manifest but which could potentially take place. All of these activities are still in the realm of thought, in the realm of analysis.

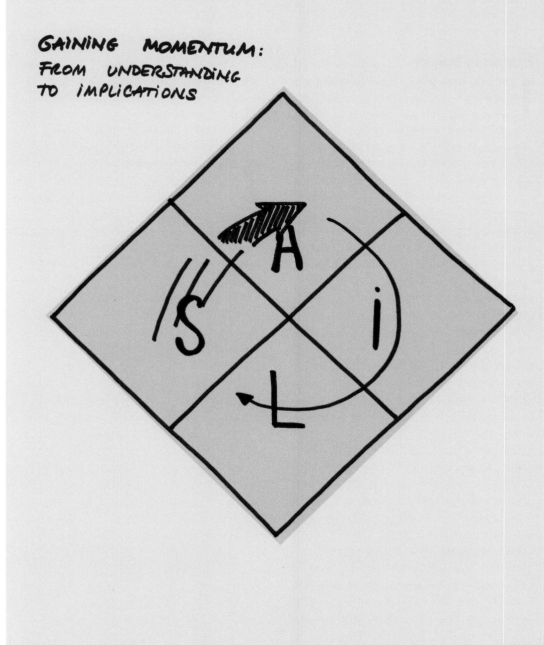

GAINING MOMENTUM: FROM UNDERSTANDING TO IMPLICATIONS

Principles for Analyzing

1 Look for both saliency and completeness

Once you have done your contextual immersion, lay it all out and fill your workspace with it. Most people associate this phase with colourful post-it notes. This is nice and bright, but misses the point, which is patterning and clustering in order to understand what can be done. Some of the things I typically do in this phase include

• Memory Game is similar to the game kids play in which you have a tray with assorted items that players can look at for a few seconds, then it is covered and they need to recall what was on the tray. This is an excellent exercise in saliency. What do you remember? What have you overlooked? Once you have all your materials and lessons gathered from sensemaking, it is a good thing to sit with a blank page and write your analysis of what you saw, heard, felt and did during the previous phase. What you remember says as much as the things that, looking back at your notes after writing what you remember, helps you complete the analysis. This is a great exercise to do as a group: generally people remember some of the same things, some remember different things. Together, they complete an analysis through their interpretation.

• Mind mapping, which is excellent for making the blanks visual. Mind mapping allows you to map out the lessons in all its branches, answering the What question that leads to creative insight. Take a step back and ask yourself,

Is there anything unanswered? What are the things you still would like to know or understand? Go back to sensing if you need more information (completeness) or move into identifying patterns based on what is emerging.

2 Explain it to a foreigner

It is a well-known popular truth that you only ever really understand something once you can explain it to others. Use any kind language that you may need to do so; people who communicate across languages and cultures do that all the time! Consider the following:

• Visualize what you've learnt: draw diagrams, sketches and anything that helps convey the essence of what you've learnt to others. Visualizing levels the playing field so that all are 'talking' in the same ways.

• Have a debate. I am quite fond of World Café's: write your learnings or conclusions from analysis as a series of statements. Have a debate about each in a group. This will put you in a position in which you will have to explain how you came to your conclusion and what your analysis is based on and it is sure to bring you new levels of insight and analysis.

• Walkthrough: take any kinds of props or toys and re-create the situation by walking other people through it. Lego® and Playmobil® figures make great material but you can use virtually anything you have at hand to represent the situation. Get creative in your representation: it will help you uncover new levels in the

analysis and start experimenting with scenarios as you move into the invention phase.

3 Narrate your lessons in story form

Turning the lessons into a story involves interpretation and subjectivity. Traditionally these are 'banned' from research practices that aim to be fact-based and objective. However, people learn from and retain stories much more easily than they do facts or even insights. Narrative involves putting people's insights into broader contexts so that bigger meanings emerge like stories in a story. In order to achieve this in an outcome-driven manner, and to support the strategic cycle, one could

• Create a storyboard: this is a technique that comes from screenwriting. It helps to see the whole and then zoom into the specifics. With the use of drawings and small text prompts, a storyboard can be used to illustrate the story from the perspective of the user. Of course there are more fancy tools like customer journey mapping, but the essence is the same; to put the main actors in motion and understand the interactions that take place as the process unfolds. As you set the journey in a storyboard focus on one possible path through the experience at a time in order not to become overwhelmed or lose focus. You can represent several different paths.

• Story building is also a nice way to bring it all together. As a group you can spin the story based on what you have seen by building on one another's narrative. One person in the team must be responsible for writing the script as it is generated by the team. In the invention phase you can take it a step further and build different scenarios for how the story unfolds.

• Drawing and sprinting. This is a way of creating time boxes to manage the energy of the team so that the stories can emerge rapidly and fluidly. As a team everybody draws the essence of the story from his or her own point of view, say in fifteen minutes, drawing simple stick figures. Then in another period of fifteen minutes, the team does an interactive run-through (a sprint) of the drawings by building the story together. Use 'connecting' language: eg and then..., and then..., and then.... This 'yes, and' mindset is borrowed from improvisational theatre, whose purpose is also to create narratives in the moment.

• Start in the middle: pick the most important point in the interaction between the business and its users, put that in the middle of the storyline and explain to one another in the group what happened before and what happened after. Remember to keep the perspective of the user in mind since a user-centric approach is crucial to creating value and meaningful solutions.

• Cast and crew: this is an alternative to stakeholder mapping. It allows you to take inventory of the most important players in the narrative. The users are the main actors or cast and the business is the facilitator of the process or crew. Make a thorough list of the involved and map out what each brings and what each receives from the interaction as well as the hierarchy in the roles: who has the main role, the supportive role, etc.

4 Reframe the problem

In strategy and innovation, usually the question or problem defined at the beginning of the process is not the real question. This is simply because we cannot know what other perspectives there are until we connect with the context through sensing. During the analysis phase we are confronted with what we have sensed and understood and the patterns that have emerged by analyzing. This means that we are now able to see the issues in a different light, and can reframe the problem by

• Fast-forwarding time: imagining the world without the problem in the future and re-constructing the steps it took us to get there. This is almost child's play, but it is very effective. It helps us to let go of the comfortable constraints of our mindsets of what is today so that we can then see the problem in a different light, which is what reframing is for.

• Scenarios: mapping out potential implications in a future context leads to the generating of alternative scenarios. Scenarios are written or visual recounts of what the challenge actually is, and possible ways of addressing it. In the analysis phase this allows you to consider the potential opportunities and implications of shifting from the present conditions into the future. It is concrete and specific about which solutions need (re-)inventing.

• Make new combinations: looking at the patterns that emerged from your analysis can identify the main explanatory variables. Create a matrix by combining different variables and seeing what emerges in the spaces where the variables cross. Give each quadrant a label to help you categorize and observe whether there are other problems or descriptors than those you had initially seen. Make it simple; use as many matrices as you need to help identify all possible areas of overlap. Sometimes there is more to patterns than meets the eye. By forcing the connections and looking more closely, or from a different perspective, you can better understand whether there are issues or opportunities you may not have spotted otherwise.

From Analyzing to Inventing

The position of the 'I' for Invention in the S.A.I.L. model is not in the bottom right quadrant by coincidence. Though we are used to reading from left to right in the English language, the I is positioned in a way that we need to read in a circular fashion. The bottom right quadrant of the model is the point at which we take the forward plunge into action. It is where the wave breaks.

The shift that takes place is a shift from thinking into doing, and is thus linked to the act of creating. The inventing phase incorporates the ingenuity for the creation of new solutions, the ability to synthesize the analysis and take it one step further into its possible manifestations, the playfulness to shift from problem-finding to possibility-seeking and the application of imagination and inventiveness to see more than one solution.

Principles for Inventing

1 Think like a designer (a.k.a. design thinking)

Probably the most characteristic aspect of thinking like a designer is driving towards an outcome. Design thinking entails providing clarity in the journey towards a defined purpose. There are of course many books devoted entirely to the methodologies, tools, and techniques of design thinking. Thinking and focusing on what needs to be created is fundamental to the act of making or inventing.

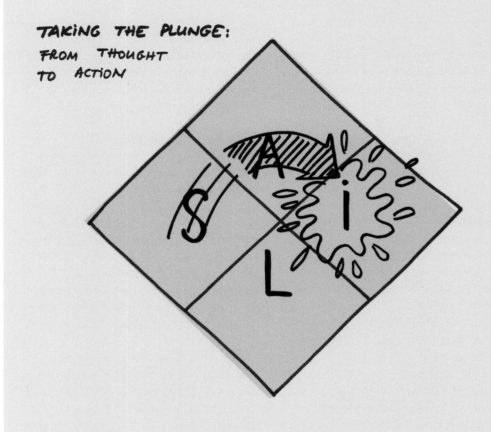

TAKING THE PLUNGE: FROM THOUGHT TO ACTION

It involves gathering perspectives, making choices and trying solutions. What allows you to get into the design frame of mind and think like a designer involves the following:
• Build a project space to make your progress visual: creative acceleration is achieved by letting go of what you are making, always seeing it as a draft to be evolved to the next level. As you let go you keep stepping up.

By having an actual studio space in which you use surfaces like walls and whiteboards to organize your project spatially, you make it easier to share the information but also to reflect back on what you've learnt and what that means for what you need to do next. Make sure there are lots of supplies for prototyping and making at hand as you apply the insights.

- Don't be precious: ideas and prototypes are part of a fluid process of creation and creativity. Invention and creativity are not linear approaches for which only one answer is possible. Keep asking yourself and others, What works? Why does it work? What else could work? Why would that matter? Dare to keep breaking the problem into bits and putting it together again in different ways, this will help you see what is simply nice to have, and what is essential to your solution.

- Ideate and try: in other words, iterate. When prototypes are created, design shifts from the realm of thinking into the realm of doing. That is when unidentified white spaces emerge, challenges become tangible, and the real opportunity to learn what might and might not work ultimately appears. By doing this as early as possible, the waves of thinking and doing or reflection and action become intertwined and intermingled, maximizing the chances of polishing out errors, assumptions, and mistakes before implementing solutions. The magic of this is that by doing, you actually integrate the whole system of interactions into your learning. As the late Professor Ranulph Glanville[6], a leader in the field of system design stated, "The big difference is between those who want to theorize and use design as a convenient vehicle, and those who want to design, and look for ways of exploring the act." The synthesis necessary to move into invention is achieved by conceiving ideas and by trying them out in order to make them happen.

2 Action not words

Leonardo da Vinci famously said: "I have been impressed with the urgency of doing. Knowing is not enough; we must apply. Being willing is not enough; we must do.."In order to keep taking the strategic process forward, action is a must. This includes

- A prototype as ongoing hypothesis: in his book *The Lean Startup*[7], Eric Ries famously introduced the idea of a minimum viable product. I would take it a step further here, and speak of a minimum viable prototype. As the saying goes: done is better than perfect. Action therefore does not exclude thinking. Rather, it includes quick prototyping as a way to convey the essence of the idea and to have a piece that will serve as a basis for discussion within the team and with the different stakeholders. Prototyping materializes the idea, making it accessible to others, allowing the discussion to centre around what is being done rather than theorizing about alternatives.

- Sketching as ideation tool: as you will see later in the chapters that feature the interviews with both pioneers and experts, I am a passionate drawing-activist. An image truly speaks more than a thousand words because drawing is synthesizing an idea so that others can elaborate on it. When we use words to communicate, we actually chop the idea into words. This is a left-brained activity that rationalizes and conceptualizes what we want to convey. When we draw, we integrate ideas, we connect, we arrange the idea so that it actually 'fits' the space where we want to draw and by definition we bring together what we want to convey. It is a right-brained activity in which fluidity and relations between elements are more important than perfection of drawing skills. It is amazing how many things we see and understand when we can look at other people's drawings. This essential ability is great for ideation. Give your team five minutes to draw twenty ideas. You'll be amazed with the results. I can tell you by experience that my clients love this because it reconnects them with themselves and it shows them how much is possible without words!

- Think physically: meaning becomes manifest through form. It is easier for us as humans to interact with things: including props, drawings, 3-D prototypes, wireframes, constructions made from carton boxes, etc than it is to interact with conceptual descriptions. It is just more 'real'. Make sure you have all kinds of materials to play with: carton, clay, paper, markers, straws, string, glue, and so on. Availability of materials is crucial to get going. You don't need fancy stuff: empty food containers like cereal boxes and yogurt cups make for excellent raw materials for quick prototyping.

3 Mix & Match

The Merriam-Webster definition for bisociation[8] reads, "the simultaneous mental association of an idea or object with two fields ordinarily not regarded as related". This lies at the core of any creative effort. Mixing and matching serves the creation of new combinatorial possibilities. It is a means of discovering and uncovering new territories and it can lead to an exponential growth of ideas, because it allows you to learn from what works but also from what doesn't work. You can try out new connections by

• Combining variables in unexpected ways: this is a simple way to steer your thoughts in order to create novel solutions. It involves making a table of variables, which you will then connect in new ways. First, list the main variables of your challenge. Make each variable the title of a column in your table. Within the column list all the variations you can think of. Then, take a step back and select one random item per column. Connect the randomly selected variations and create a solution based on those parameters. This exercise can be done for particular product or service challenges or for your business in order to look at new alternatives.

• Find what you are not looking for: working with analogies often helps us understand what solutions might already exist; by looking at dissimilarities we can see what we are not looking for, which is of course the opposite of what we are trying to solve. You can playfully introduce prompts to guide your thinking like: asking, What would happen if we deported this problem to Mars? How would it be solved there? Or what if my problem were... (an animal, plant, object, etc.)? Or flip through images and make yourself generate an idea that has to do with that image. (It can be helpful to make

a set of simple cards for this, I certainly have). The same can be achieved with random words. (Just browse the internet for lists of random words and you're set to start). By making forced connections you engage the group's creativity to both use their imagination and apply it.

• Look for new ways of applying creativity to form an alternative solution: SCAMPER is an acronym that was developed by Bob F. Eberle and published as a book[9] on creative problem solving, based on previous work by the father of brainstorming Alex Osborn. It is a set of questions to help you create ideas based on seven principles: substitute, combine, adapt, modify, put to another use, eliminate, and rearrange. Each of these takes what you know and matches it with an instruction so that you can generate a solution in that space. They are quite abstract, but they serve as guiding principles of how to unlock your thinking away from what you already know or have tried and into new combinations. Here is SCAMPER in more detail:
Substitute: remove an element of the possible solution, substitute the user, or replace the solution with anything else you can think of.
Combine: make new combinations of the elements of the solution, or the interaction of the solution and the context, to iterate your solution.
Adapt: change whatever is not working in your current solution to make it work by borrowing or inventing whatever you need.
Modify: increase or reduce in scale, change shape, modify attributes (texture, colour, position, attitude).

Put to another use: modify the solution to serve another purpose.
Eliminate: remove something in your solution in order to simplify it further. Make it smaller, lighter, faster, more flexible, or more fun.
Rearrange: turn upside-down, inside-out, change the sequence or hierarchy, or make it go in a different direction.

• Time boxing: during the invention phase there sometimes is a tendency to go on endlessly perfecting ideas. Make sure you iterate quickly and build on ideas rather than put too much time in working out the details of ideas that can be raised to a next level through inventive thinking. Put time constraints on your creative and generative efforts: you want to keep raising the bar rather than losing momentum in ironing out details. It is a matter of subjective appreciation of when to push through and when to deepen out ideas. If you put time boxes on your efforts it will allow you to manage the energy and reflect on the progress you are making during the process itself so that you can keep steering your energy and that of the team to where it is most useful.

4 Contextualize

The importance and relevance of context cannot be overemphasized. It is the difference between a successful implementation and a failed attempt. Mastery is achieved through experience. After all, as Franklin Roosevelt is quoted to have said, "A smooth sea never made a skillful sailor". The sooner we try things out,

"The importance and relevance of context cannot be overemphasized."

the sooner we will be able to distinguish what might or might not be a good solution. Contextualizing the inventions is a non-linear way of approaching the discovery of the most effective way forward. It does not mean diving head first without preparation. On the contrary, it is part of the preparatory process. But there is no check-list to be followed. Linear models actually create redundancy in this sense: they answer their own questions. Contextualizing prototypes pertains to uncovering new questions and challenges that further inform the design process with regards to what is relevant and appropriate in the context. This informs the process in order to further evolve the proposition by testing it in the real situation. Here are some principles to take into account:

• Co-design involves the co-production of solutions between the designer and the end user. Its basic premise is that users are experts of their own experience and that they can best assess what works or doesn't work in a solution and then give guidance towards its

improvement. The actual problem-solving and solution making is done by designers alongside the users. From their perspective co-design allows them to experiment and evolve. This is a generative process: at the beginning of the process you cannot foresee which new questions will arise in the process. It is important to give it sufficient room to freely form, as you learn from and with the end user. Having sufficient materials at hand to allow for communication and representation of ideas is one of the main advantages of co-design. In this process new ideas are co-invented.

• Zoom into the interface: go for the contact moments with the different stakeholders in order to understand the real and perceived effect of your strategy when implemented. In this way you will see which ripples you produce. And you will also identify the gaps and challenges you had overlooked because you will be directly confronted with them. By zooming in you can act upon these issues and take adaptive, corrective actions. As Franklin

Lloyd Wright is thought to have said: "You can use an eraser on the drafting table or a sledge hammer on the construction site." The invention stage is the perfect moment for live-drafting and immersive learning.

• Role-playing: acting things out is the most engaging way of experiencing a situation without actually being in it for real. There are countless techniques that can be borrowed from improvisational theatre to help spark creative thinking and imagination. This kind of rehearsal allows teams to play out different scenarios and invent solutions on the fly that arise from the interaction. This is particularly helpful for services, but also very tangible for products. It is the perfect try-out for prototypes, and there is no harm in failing because the environment of trial and error makes it safe to improvise solutions and interactions as you go.

From Inventing to Learning

Learning takes place as the receding wave reveals what is left on the beach: sand, rocks, beautiful shells and treasures, lost messages in a bottle, or wreckages of capsized initiatives. Within the S.A.I.L. model, learning is a moment of appraisal and reflection. It is a crucial step because we live in a changing, non-linear world in which we cannot always foresee or plan towards pre-defined goals. The vision or direction set through strategic intent is an aim, and learning allows us to evaluate what happened during and after strategy implementation and whether we achieved what we aimed for.

Learning is a step back because it requires zooming out of what we were doing and appraising what was created with a particular future in mind, considering the impact once the inventions are embedded in the new 'now'. Learning is appreciative, evaluative, and ultimately also inquisitive.

Principles for Learning

1 Learning by doing

All problems have several possible solutions. Finding the sweet spot in which inventiveness, costs, constraints, and user happiness are in an adequate balance is more art than science. The lessons learned along the way help guide the total process but are unlikely to yield precise answers. Implementing strategy through the invention stage of the

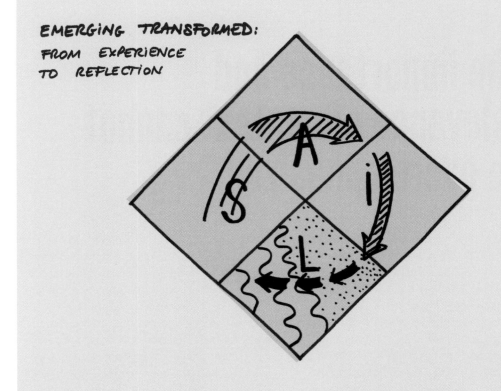

EMERGING TRANSFORMED: FROM EXPERIENCE TO REFLECTION

S.A.I.L. model means taking a position in the context. In order to learn about its effect within the context it is necessary to understand it in practice:
- Experiential testing: this is no more and no less than using your product or service and experiencing it. Most businesses leave this to consultants and external researchers. Learning by experiencing the results for yourself is a fantastic source of insight. Just dive in, ideally in different situations, days of the week, etc.

This works well when different team members go into the context, gather experience and then contrast what they've learned. It is important to focus on feelings and emotions too, not just the mechanical, transactional aspects of the experience.
- Reverse role-playing: in the invention phase one might have used role-playing in order to act out the experience and gain empathy with the user. In this phase, we aim to learn. By doing reverse role-playing we can represent

our roles back to ourselves: what do we look like while delivering the strategic intent through the eyes of others? It allows us to make small changes and adaptations to our roles and our delivery of user experience so that we might improve it even further based on practice-based learnings. By adding a role-playing element we can think ahead of the situations and solve issues in advance of them happening in reality by applying what we learn.

• 20/20 hindsight: create a narrative, storyboard, or customer journey map of what actually happens in practice. Practice, as we have already discussed, proves itself in practice. Theory and practice are seldom the same. Once you have the narrative or journey of what is really happening, it becomes easier to assess the gaps, understand the logic from a user perspective, and discuss new courses of action with your team. Take the time to reflect before running to fix separate aspects of the strategy implementation.

2 Re-analyze: compare and contrast

In the Analysis phase we framed or reframed the problem. Now that the solution created in the invention phase is embedded, we can look back and contrast it with what we set out to do. Reflection is a necessary next step to Action. Here are some ways to learn from our efforts:

• Make a list: every project is different so the list will be different per project. Consider questions that help assess the project, e.g.: Does it solve the problem or resolve the challenge effectively? Is it a reliable solution that users see as an improvement to their situation? Does it meet the constraints in a practical and relevant manner? Does it drive business forward through value creation? You can also add extra questions for bonus points, like, Was it fun to do? Would we want to do this again? Is it original and surprising? Was it fast and effective? etc.

Score this list as a team, knowing that you originally were aiming for high scores. Look for the gap: where did you score as you hoped you would? Where did you score above or below that? What did you learn from it?

• Consider different points of view: use a radar-like chart with several arms -the business, the user, the competitors, the team, the main stakeholders, etc. Score the project on each of the lines. Connect the scores of each of the team members to see how well you did versus your intent and from the point of view of each team member. Have a discussion to extract learnings.

• Reconstruct your insights: throughout the process you have been making new connections of cause and effect. Go back to your project space and re-construct the story with the use of a Ishikawa[10] or Fishbone diagram. (How appropriate for our sailors that the diagram has a fishbone shape!) This diagram will help you make visual what you've learnt from your actions. It helps you literally 'see' what the assumptions were that led you to do what you did at each step of the invention process, and why that mattered. Its value is in mapping out relations and interconnections in the thinking that triggered the actions and identifying what worked and which things may have been overlooked.

• Ask others: user testing gains a new dimension when something is part of the existing possibilities. Until the point at which new business ideas become implemented and embedded, the learning is valid but limited to the lucky few that interact during the invention phase. As business propositions go into market, they start their journey on Roger's curve which is a wonderful opportunity to learn first-hand by comparing and contrasting what was intended and what is actually being experienced. User testing can take many forms, from engaging in a dialogue to hear first-hand about the experience, to contextual interviewing to see the product or service in its contextual reality, through to big data analysis to understand behavioural patterns of large groups and footprints of usage.

3 Feedback to learn as a team

Zooming out of the project (be it a business strategy, innovation strategy, product or service development or any kind of project) will expose the good, the bad, and the ugly of the project. Be candid and respectful: the aim is to learn. Here are some ways of framing feedback so that it is useful for learning what can be improved or what could go better next time:

• Post-mortem: for failed projects, set time aside to analyze what happened. Be objective in your assessment by giving specific examples and objectifying it versus an expectation or a benchmark. Being specific allows for everyone to benefit from the lesson, without finger-pointing or blaming team members. Allow everyone in the team to make a post-mortem analysis providing specific feedback and then compare notes. This allows for group learning, and in such a way it will make it easier to remind one another in future projects. Make sure you are objective enough to include what worked as well as what didn't work.

• Evidence gathering: set some time aside as a team to collect evidence and re-construct what happened. By opening the discussion together, lessons will emerge. Make sure to capture those on sticky notes and cluster the learnings to see the skills or areas that need the team's attention for improvement. Make a plan and a commitment on how you'll work on these. Once the team is more experienced or has worked on similar projects before, you can anticipate on the evidence-gathering during the project by creating a 'treasure box' which you can fill with learnings as you go. So whenever there is an issue or an insight team members can jot it down on a piece of paper and put it in the treasure box for reflection during the learning phase.

• Paired listening: as a group create twosomes or threesomes of team members, ideally as cross functionally as possible. Share the lessons within those sub teams. This is important because it ensures everyone can air his or her views, and everyone is listened to. Feedback to the total group by summarizing each other's views.

• Intuitive scoring: this is a great way of providing feedback in smaller teams. Ask team participants to rate the total project with a school mark. Once everyone has done this individually, draw an imaginary line on the floor and ask team members to position themselves along that line based on the score they gave the project. From those positions, have a quick group discussion focusing on the plusses and minuses from each perspective.

4 New questions

Different people learn in different ways. Individual learning styles have a lot to do with how we engage our senses. Learning therefore also has a generative role, not just an evaluative one. This generative role is linked to what we can learn from our conclusions and which new questions arise. Consider the following approaches to generating new questions:

• Tune in: have conversations with users and non-users of your proposition. What leads them to think or do what they do? Remind yourself that 'silent' and 'listen' have the same letters and that they can both unlock the same kind of knowledge: knowledge that you wouldn't have had if you hadn't tuned in. Let the user talk and let the user come up with new questions, the questions we could not have come up with in theory but which are imminently logical in practice. Use connective phrases to help the others express themselves and allow you to listen. Say things like 'so you say that...', 'I'm quite intrigued by...' so that the other person can build the story as you ask clarifying, open questions.

• Engage your senses: people's learning styles can be visual, auditory, reading/writing or kinaesthetic. Consider what people are seeing and experiencing by walking alongside them using non-participatory research techniques. Look, listen, observe and document what is really happening from these perspectives. It is amazing how much more you can see when you look through other people's eyes and walk in their shoes.

• Context mapping: as the name suggests, context mapping involves making a map of the context of use. This context has now changed by the mere fact that we have (inter)acted in it with a new proposition. This means it is time to take inventory by mapping the context and asking new questions. The aim is to chart things in order to learn from what is happening in the context. Any and all participatory research and design tools are valid as long as you keep the focus on mapping:. Asking for directions (involving users and having them explain) and visualizing the territory with visual tools (reflecting back and asking whether this represents what they are experiencing) will help you map things. Be playful and use what you need in order to generate interactive learning with those in the context itself.

From Learning to Sensing

The moment at the harbour in which we make sure everything is in good condition and ready to embark on new sailing journeys is the interface between learning and sensing. This is where the cycle renews itself. The development and implementation of strategy in a context of ongoing change, with ever more complex problems requires continuous dedication and above all, a mindset. This mindset requires openness to learn and to engage and to sense the world yet again as we interact with it and intervene in it. We need the predisposition to help improve our understanding of it, and get inspired by the possibilities within it and for our positive actions to co-create it: using our abilities for thinking and for doing.

When we start sensing again, it is mandatory to adopt a beginner's mindset. This is a concept from Zen Buddhism, and involves being objective and seeking the actual truth which Buddhists call *Shoshin*. It does not mean we

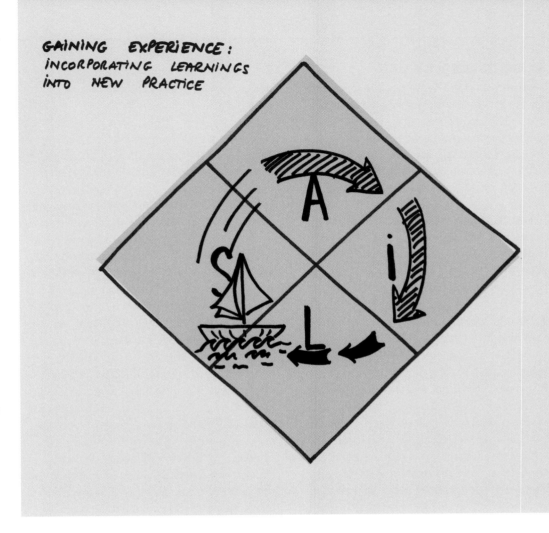

GAINING EXPERIENCE: INCORPORATING LEARNINGS INTO NEW PRACTICE

need to be naïve or forget the lessons obtained by learning. But we must see each wave in the S.A.I.L. model as a new way, with a new set of conditions and opportunities, letting go of our assumptions and filters gained by expertise and daring to look at the context as if for the first time. As Shunryu Suzuki[11] reflects, "In the beginner's mind there are many possibilities, in the expert's mind there are few." Go out into the sea of context and appreciate it in all its vastness to rediscover it again and again with each wave.

Iterating the sailing cycle

Tools and principles don't make the sailor, they are simply a means to achieving the strategic intent. The above principles therefore do not aim to be a compilation of what you should do. They are simply a source of inspiration for what you could do as you adjust your sails during your interaction with the weather and wind of context.

In a time in which ethnographic research, design thinking, and service design are being hyped into step-by-step models I believe it is important to signal that the process does not guarantee the outcome.

The S.A.I.L. model is more than a set of guidelines or principles: it is applied, alive, and real. Therefore as an organic model it is not defined by the procedures and methods but by
• the evolving clarity it gives the team, as they sense the context and generate understanding, the interaction between the team members that helps open up perspectives giving a fuller view,
• the accumulated knowledge of tools of the whole team, which increases the adaptive and improvisational capacity to act on opportunities because what is available to one is available to all,
• the joint capacity of the team to analyse, draw conclusions, and create different possible answers,
• the mixed skills of the sailing team to translate insights into concrete idea, quick prototypes, tangible solutions, and experiences that allow for hands-on experimentation, and

• the distinct and different learning abilities of the team members to help reflect on the sailing journey.

Tools evolve continuously, which is why they are not the focus of the S.A.I.L. model. The mindset of exploration, discovery, interaction and experimentation is more important than listing the tools. The tools for researching come from different places and converge in the sailor toolbox. Some come from design, some from research, some from the social sciences. For reference and to increase awareness of the variety of tools I have made an intuitive list of some of the tools available when you venture out into the sea of context. This list is not thorough; its purpose is to illustrate that there are a variety of alternatives to choose from depending on the aim of a project. It is most important to sense, analyse, invent, and learn along the way. The tools are merely a way to frame your thinking and prepare you for the adventure, but there are no secret formulas. Working multi-functionally will deliver more tools, more approaches, and more alternatives than a list of tools ever could. What counts is the mindset and readiness to experience and explore, in order to make the sailing memorable and useful.

AS YOU SET SAIL REMEMBER THAT A CURIOUS MINDSET, OPENNESS TO DISCOVERY & TRIANGULATING FINDINGS ARE KEY!

CO-DESIGN WORKSHOPS, CO-DESIGN LABS, LEAD USER RESEARCH, CONCEPT TESTING, USABILITY TESTING, VALIDATION ...

PHOTO JOURNALS, CULTURAL PROBE KITS, ETHNOGRAPHIC MONITORING, CONTEXTUAL MAPPING, CO-CREATION, ...

ROLE PLAYING & SCENARIOS, FOCUS GROUPS, ONLINE COMMUNITIES, IN-DEPTH INTERVIEWS, USER DIARIES, ...

BEING YOUR USER: EXPERIENTIAL IMMERSION, OBSERVATION & SHADOWING, VIDEO/PHOTO INVESTIGATION, ...

QUESTIONNAIRES & SURVEYS, DATA VISUALIZATION, STAKEHOLDER RESEARCH, ...

DEMOGRAPHIC DATA, ATTITUDINAL DATA, BIG DATA & DIGITAL FOOTPRINTS, ...

DESK RESEARCH, LITERATURE REVIEWS, WEB ANALYTICS, ...

SAIL

AWAY

Companies setting S.A.I.L.

To further illustrate the application of S.A.I.L. in practice, let's look at what companies are doing in their strategy and innovation initiatives. There are no rules to follow or tools to guarantee outcomes. Sailing is a matter of expertise, intuition, decision-making, and stewardship. Companies aim for a destination and discover along the way what opportunities and lessons the journey holds. This requires collaboration, commitment and flexibility, as we will see in the following projects conducted by pioneering agencies (all of which are featured in more detail later in this book). Each project highlights one of the phases of the S.A.I.L. navigation as a key point of insight within the total S.A.I.L. process.

Sensing in Practice: Dispelling clouds in patient's eyes

Crew: Vision inPractice (ViP) and China Bridge (CBi)

Vision in Practice strives to eliminate avoidable blindness in China by assisting both eye care institutions and eye care professionals to offer ethical, high quality, and financially sustainable eye care in any community—regardless of patients' ability to pay. Vision in Practice is growing an international training network where doctors can obtain these essential capabilities, and provides several forms of transformative consulting services to private and public eye-care institutions that wish to improve their services and social impact

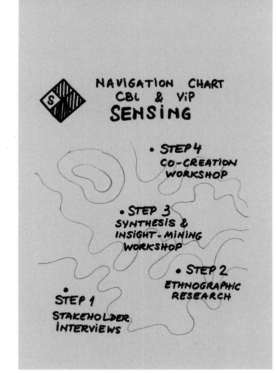

China Bridge is an insight-based innovation and strategy firm, that works with leading organizations when there is an need to innovate and design 'next' brands, products, and services.

Location: Shanghai, China
Destination: to improve surgery conversion rates of cataract patients by evolving and enhancing the patient service strategy.

Approach: through the use of ethnographic research and co-creation, engage locals and collaborate with medical experts in order to sense where the real issues lie and help create a programme to address them.

Steps of the journey:
Step 1- Stakeholder interviews: learning the knowns and unknowns to help identify and reach alignment on where to start
Step 2 - Ethnographic Research: participatory observation and in-depth interviews
Step 3 - Synthesis and insight-mining workshop: compile research findings into coherent mapping, highlighting key pain points across critical steps of the medical outreach service.
Step 4 - Co-creation workshop: ideating and selecting new processes and engagement concepts to address issues in the medical outreach process and to gain trust by better addressing patient's right to care.

Logbook of the journey: Cataract is an age-related visual impairment disease. It is caused by clouding of the lens inside the eye, which leads to a gradual decrease in vision.
In a small village in Shandong Province, China, doctors describe the symptom of cataract as "Clouds in your eyes" to help villagers, especially elders understand what cataract is.

Despite being a curable disease through simple surgery, many Chinese cataract patients are left out from receiving treatment. In order to learn directly from practice, CBi and ViP collaborated with the Xin YiMin Hospital.

A lot of insights were generated during the Sensing phase due to the immersive nature of the research conducted by the team.

"Sailing is a matter of expertise, intuition, decision making, and stewardship."

Travelling with the outreach teams from village to village to promote, conduct screening, and pick-up patients provided a great opportunity to understand the outreach teams needs as well as interacting with the potential patients that needed screening. Because the low-income patient group is difficult to reach mediatically, the teams use a vehicle with a public address (PA) system that loudly broadcasts messages about their services, attracting attention from the villagers.

The research team learnt that although the work itself can be quite tough, the passion for serving local communities and making positive impact keeps the team members moving. The medical outreach teams had to be very flexible, as there are plenty of unexpected situations in the field and from ethnographic observations, it became clear that the team was very skillful at handling changes and quick to find new solutions. Work took place under difficult conditions – from setting up clinics in barn houses or outdoor areas, to handling large amount of patients, keeping them in order, to patiently explain the cause and treatment procedures to undereducated patients etc.

The insights gathered became the basis for a Synthesis and insight-mining workshop. The sensing phase had uncovered a total of eight barriers that drove patients to decide not to accept surgeries, and most of these issues were hinting at deficits in the promotion and communication process. Quite simply, the audience could not understand nor value the promotion and communication tools.

CBi helped ViP evolve The Patient Service Strategy and localize The Business Model:
• Advising XinYiMin Hospital on "WHAT needs to be improved", "WHO could be involved to make improvements happen" in the short and long term
• Defining principles for service strategy implementation- Based on research insights as well as service concepts generated and evaluated by Xin YiMin's staff

The value of sensing as a first step in the cycle is demonstrated in this case by the ability to uncover what truly needs addressing. Should the team not have taken this step the essential issue would probably have remained unaddressed. In this manner they combined design principles and the deep study of local conditions only then to develop a solution according to the insights uncovered. The team thus saw that what might seem small aspects can make big difference on the impact with a little change or improvement. For example: improving the layout of the poster that will be used on telegraph poles and suggesting to adjust the colour tone to be more easily readable by old people.

The sensing phase delivered measureable, real results as the outcomes of the initial work became the foundation for successfully prototyping, capturing and refining a new business model. A model that provides a better route to health care in China, moving Vision In Practice one big step closer to their purpose of eradicating needless blindness.

Outcome of the journey: The success of this project is best expressed by the surgery conversion rate. Within half a year since adopting the new service strategy recommendations, surgery conversion rate almost doubled – from 35% to 63%!

Crew: Lo/Jack Argentina and +Castro

Lo/Jack is a global provider of technology products and services for the tracking and recovery of stolen mobile assets. The company is headquartered in Boston and is operational in more than thirty countries throughout North America, South America, Europe and Africa. This case refers to work done for Lo/Jack Argentina within the Argentinian market.

+Castro is a leading creative agency where all kinds of new, experimental and exciting projects are continuously brewing. They are the first "Innovation House" in Latin America, combining advertising creativity, cutting edge technologies and production capacity with the objective of offering big ideas that create a turning point in the life of a brand.

Location: Buenos Aires, Argentina

Destination: The challenge was to enlarge and renew the image of Lo/Jack Argentina by connecting to end users in new ways.

Approach: Lo/Jack created the stolen vehicle recovery market more than twenty-five years ago and has since earned a ninety-plus percent recovery success rate on cars, trucks and SUVs. Historically, Lo/Jack Argentina's growth was linked to insurance companies

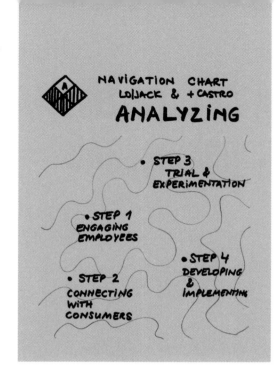

and mainly a business-to-business model. As such, the brand was almost invisible to the end user who contracted Lo/Jack Argentina's services in the hope of not having to use them and as part of a contractual clause in their insurance policies. Any brand awareness that end users might have had was linked to sponsoring activities in professional soccer or racing. They had a well-recognized logo for some, but with little or no brand association.

Creating a step-change in the model, shifting from business-to-business (b-to-b) to business-to-consumer (b-to-c) was understood by +Castro as a cultural change rather than just a change in communicational style.

Lo/Jack Argentina knew a lot about their market and the insurance companies, even the competing offers that were specific and diverse given the complexities of the Argentinian security landscape. What +Castro challenged was the ability to define the offering from the inside out in order to become a preferred solution for the end user. +Castro set out on a quest to find the differential aspects, unique to Lo/Jack Argentina's DNA which would make them stand out and be preferred by the end user, from the heart of the company.

Steps of the journey:
Step 1- Engaging employees to get to the heart of the matter and redefine the challenge
Step 2- Connecting with consumers to chart the context of use holistically
Step 3 - Trial and experimentation: creating Lo/Lab as a space for innovation
Step 4 - Developing and implementing Lo/App

Logbook of the journey: The first interviews included Lo/Jack Argentina's employees. The team at +Castro spoke to different departments within the company and finished their process of scoping out what Lo/Jack was by testing each of the Lo/Jack Argentina products, experiencing them personally. This process led to the first and most fundamental conclusion: Lo/Jack Argentina is not simply a security company, but essentially a technology company specialized in security matters.

"In order to innovate, one must be innovative."

This key finding defined the project on three levels.
1. As a brand, the intent for Lo/Jack Argentina became: positioning themselves as the leaders in technology and modernity. Bringing out to the surface what was an integral part of the heart of their operation, and making that distinctive.
2. From the product itself: defining a need to design an innovative software application that would manifest this brand positioning and provide an interface for interaction with the user. The importance of the interaction led to a quantifiable goal of four hundred to five hundred monthly downloads of the application.
3. From a business/industry perspective: to become the most innovative player, applying state-of-the-art technology to the security domain.

These three aspects were integrated into a design briefing: to invent an iconic product, which in and of itself becomes the carrier of the transformation of Lo/Jack Argentina towards the end user. Conveying that Lo/Jack Argentina is not just another security company, but a leading technology company with intrinsic understanding and years of experience in the security market.

Second, connecting with consumers via qualitative user research led the team to understand things from their perspective. People see security as a whole, including their own personal security, their material goods, their loved ones, etc. However, the security industry provides product-driven solutions which are disintegrated: home alarming systems, surveillance cameras, car security, personal security, pet security, and so on, all are offered separately from one another.

This added a next level to the design briefing: how could Lo/Jack Argentina connect their own technologies in order to offer a single, integrated security system to the end users? In order to think this way, it was imperative to let go of everything Lo/Jack Argentina had come to consider obvious in the industry.

+Castro suggested to think like a start-up: launching a new product in an existing market.

The design of solutions was done from a newly created department, in which the team was able let go of the boundaries between agency and client. Lo/Lab was opened, integrating people from different backgrounds who opened and officially the first space for technology experimentation within the company. Probably the most important lesson for the team was that in order to innovate, one must be innovative. This sounds redundant, but was actually crucial to the way the team spun-off a new way of working that helped changed the culture at Lo/Jack Argentina. They embraced the fact that they were in entirely new terrain, doing entirely new things, while at the same time relying on Lo/Jack Argentina's strength: technology.

The team felt convinced of the need to interconnect their solutions, so they created Lo/App the first interconnected security system to be navigated through digital platforms (mobile and web). It was an ongoing process of prototyping where they not only learnt from their own mistakes but also from the valuable feedback from users who were connected to the project throughout. One of the users in the beta phases said: 'it is like having a dialogue with the full breadth of my security system'. This referred to the possibility of programming different interactions between the solutions.

For example, when a customer arrives home late at night by car, the home recognizes the car by geo-proximity and turns on the lights in the home to welcome its owner.

The design phase also included research as a way of obtaining quick and valuable feedback. Because the main purpose was design, the type of research was highly experimental. During one month they provided two different families with access to the prototype version of the Lo/App and tested out its working in 'real life'. The lessons from this phase in the design process were massive: by seeing the real interaction they gained insights that no survey, questionnaire or lab-like situation could provide. They were able to experience how the users looked for ways to tailor their usage of the app, customize the functionalities, and personalize the services, which pointed them in the direction of untapped product benefits they hadn't even foreseen themselves.

Another important thing is that this phase of design research gave them a lot of story-material in audio-visual formats which they then, innovatively again, shared on social media. Sharing the stories of the two families who helped them shape Lo/App into its final form made it tangible to potential users and gave it meaning in the 'real world'.

Later, they took this even a step further by creating Lo/JackTV a digital platform with web-based episodes in which users could share the interaction with the app and the security system, based on their experiences and everyday behaviours.

Outcome of the journey: Lo/Jack Argentina made a tangible, concrete and effective step towards manifesting its positioning as a technology leader in the security market. Quantitative tracking on brand perception, currently signals Lo/Jack to be perceived as the undisputed technology leader in the Argentinian security market.
LO/APP was the first integrated security app in the world, spearheading the technology transformation of the security business not only in Argentina but elsewhere. The objective of monthly downloads was exceeded and stands at a seven hundred monthly average, increasing month after month. During its launch, Carlos Mackinlay (CEO of Lo/Jack Argentina) said, 'We are not just presenting a new product, we are presenting a new company'.

And finally, thanks to this new, recognized position in the market, new parties are approaching Lo/Jack Argentina for its expertise to partner on new projects. Most recently, the French car manufacturer Peugeot, with the request to develop CAR SAFE a new security service for their clients, developed with Lo/Jack leading technology.

Inventing in practice: Differentiating the value proposition through 'Why'

Crew: KYOCERA Document Solutions Europe and Point Blank International (PBI)

Kyocera Document Solutions Europe was established on the first of April 2012, and was previously known under the name Kyocera Mita Europe. Kyocera Mita Europe had been established in January 2000 following the merger of Kyocera and Mita, two of the most innovative companies in document management.
The change to Kyocera Document Solutions Europe reflects the company's growth as a global supplier of solutions to consistently develop and deliver customer benefits, technological innovation, and environmental sustainability.

Point Blank International (PBI) is a Berlin based consultancy which acts as a strategic partners to business. They help their clients to craft compelling marketing strategies through research, innovation, design, and training.

Location: Germany, Spain and the United Kingdom

Destination: To set up and deliver a qualitative research and consulting project to help Kyocera Document Solutions Europe position their MDS (managed document services). Helping Kyocera chart a path towards future brand success –in Germany, Spain and the UK (as pilot markets).

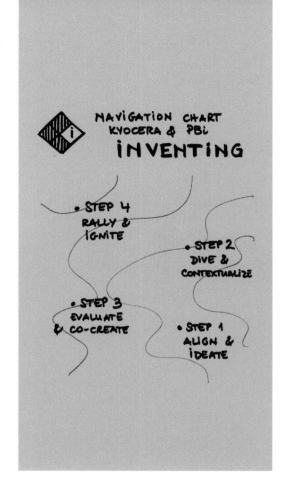

Approach: When KYOCERA Document Solutions Europe approached PBI with their request, the team felt excited:

Here was a client intent on a strategic partnership – a collaborative learning journey that PBI as an agency would co-design and that they'd be part of throughout the process.

From the get go, Kyocera was very open to going beyond mainstream qualitative research processes towards incorporating an ethnographic lens, co-creation and stakeholder workshops.

The insight and marketing teams' intention to build an MVP as a result of the project –a 'minimum viable product'. Reading Eric Ries' book[12] one might easily conclude that qualitative research is hardly an appropriate tool for the creation of what he calls the minimum viable product, but the team set out to prove otherwise.

PBI's task was to help Kyocera chart a path towards future brand success – in Germany, Spain and the UK (as pilot markets). In today's environment, a printer and copier manufacturer needs to look beyond hardware and printing – the future of managing documents and information is digital, and such a future promises huge business service potential.

PBI proposed a 'tandem' team of one lead researcher and one designer to build and run the project across all stages. In turn, the Kyocera team was happy to invite PBI to be part of the project beyond the narrow confines of research fieldwork and reporting.

Steps of the journey:
Step 1- Align and Ideate: kick off and ideation workshop

Step 2- Dive and Contextualise:
get the Real Life Story
Step 3 - Evaluate and Co-Create:
to discuss, challenge and rebuild
Step 4 - Rally and ignite:
go from what to why to how

Logbook of the journey: In a kick off and idea-tion workshop, PBI brought together Kyocera stakeholders and Kyocera's creative and digital agencies. Everyone exchanged their personal motivations and project objectives and PBI pooled the existing knowledge. On the basis of this, they collaborated to spark ideas for Kyocera MDS positioning territories.

Up until the beginning of the fieldwork, PBI continued to support Kyocera in developing and sharpening the territories. In doing so, they left the classical space of the 'neutral' qualitative researcher, and instead putting on their business design hats. PBI's goal was not to check retroactively whether their client stood a good chance for success with their ideas, but to do their very best to help them craft successful ideas in the first place.

PBI then visited IT managers in small to medium sized businesses and spent time in their work environment over the course of a day. Here, PBI set out to get the real-world story of how decisions on document manage-ment solutions are made and how real people use them.

In the evaluation and co-creation stages, PBI invited CIOs as well as IT and procurement managers to discuss, challenge and rebuild the positioning territories that had been developed earlier. PBI made sure to have enough scissors, glue and images on board to let participants cut, paste, and create at will to come up with the kind of ideas and bene-fits they could relate to.

This project was only going to be a success if key stakeholders at Kyocera including local marketing managers and other key stakeholders were fully on board. So, after presenting the results (a slide show presenta-tion, and five personas in cardboard poster format plus an A0-sized interaction poster showing how decisions on MDS in companies are formed), PBI came back one month later to host an activation workshop with Kyocera managers and project leads from the crea-tive and the digital agency. Their goal was to enable them to own the results and create a common thrust for action.

PBI knew that Kyocera managers had been deep in discussion about the right product mix that would pave the way to success, but they had also learned in the field that the functional elements of the offer were already quite familiar to IT decision makers and there was little to no potential to differentiate the Kyocera brand by just bundling these.

'What' is the somewhat generic term 'MDS', meaning managed document services. It transpired that the question of 'How' these solutions were offered and 'Why' people feel motivated to change established work patterns offered far more branding and thus business potential.

It was at this point that PBI's team recalled Simon Sinek's *Golden Circle* approach to build-ing a differentiating value proposition – and decided to design the activation workshop around the Golden Circle, with personas employed as 'human-centricity lenses': Outside in, they tried to define MDS by its 'Whats' and realized there were no elements for creating a differentiating proposition at that level. Then they team-worked their way through 'How' Kyocera might do things differently than com-petitors and, finally, they went on a quest for the 'Why' – for the big mission that Kyocera might be serving with building up a document sharing world beyond printing.

PBI kept it playful, for example by encouraging the participants to imagine how they would use a huge pirate treasure buried in deep beneath the headquarters. But then, after a while, PBI put a curse on the pirate treasure so the participants couldn't use the money to de-velop product features, but had to think bigger.

PBI certainly didn't expect to come out with the uniting cause for a global tech company in just one day spent together, but they managed to create a space in which the Kyocera managers could look beyond their company lens by adopting Personas and role play with them, and where they could look beyond the product level by thinking about the deeper purpose of Kyocera and about how the brand could do things differently.

Outcome of the journey: Together, PBI paved the way for Kyocera to further develop and prototype their MVP –and they rallied together country managers in the understanding that this is the beginning of a journey rather than a set of solutions.

Learning in practice: Evolving and refining the business model for growth
Crew: Food Bazaar and Idiom

Food Bazaar is a food market within a hypermarket. With more than two hundred stores spread across India. They cater to the changing needs of both the traditional and the modern consumer and transform the traditional Indian kitchen into a modern one, ensuring that cooking stops being a mundane chore and becomes a creative and stress-busting activity.

Idiom is a Bangalore-based design firm with varied design skills under one roof. Idiom incubates business ideas, ideas for societal transformation and ideas on life and living. Delivered, as strategy, as design output, as

transformational tools and processes and as robust, ready-to-run businesses.

Location: across India

Destination: Roughly fourteen years ago, Idiom started from a blank slate, to create version 1.0 of this format. Since then, they have worked in tandem with Future Group –the company behind Food Bazaar-, to evolve Food Bazaar in terms of its the design and the spirit of its business, brand and experience across local geographies and locations, working together with the Future Group team, designing and researching their way into success.

Approach: Food Bazaar was born out of its founder's ideal to create a modern retail food format / proposition for the Indian consumer, within Big Bazaar, India's first original hypermarket.

The collaborative approach between Idiom and Food Bazaar, spanning a period of fourteen years, has ensured that the FoodBazaar model has evolved and refined over time, responding to local communities and the changing consumer and environment. While the soul of the idea – of creating modern food retail, and embracing change while keeping continuity of culture, has remained intact, the model has seen constant design and innovation, based on continuous research.

For the creation of version 1.0, the business and design teams gathered together at a long table, in a garage design office. The founder of Food Bazaar acted as the mediator, doing the synthesis of the discussion and agreeing that to have a successful model they would need familiarity for the Indian shopper as well as newness and discovery. A model was created and put into the market.

When the time came for version 2.0 the question was raised: what do we add new? How do we integrate what we now have learnt and understand about our target audience?

This time the approach was characterized by observation, there was not much formal research necessary since these were Indian women who were visiting their stores daily. The observations showed that these women wanted to keep the positive labour when it came to food preparation and shopping. In Indian cooking there is a lot of negative labour: like breaking coconuts, or chopping difficult vegetables. Food Bazaar let the women keep the positive labour and focused on solving the negative labour, making a differentiated offer across the country.

Research and design blended seamlessly in this process. Through community research by the Future Group team, together they added layer upon layer upon layer of understanding as the model and the business kept evolving to cater to the needs of the local communities. Understanding each particular community around the store and creating specific value as different versions of the business model kept emerging and evolving. The experience design thinking in the store referenced the local bazaars. The traders' shop provides depth with an endless variety within a product type, the corner store provides width with variety in merchandise, the seasonal vendor brought in dynamism and freshness. All the time, integrating with local communities, by providing specialty food interventions.

Steps of the journey:

Step 1: Going back to the target audience: outlining user groups
Step 2: Co-creative artworks: as a map for thinking and cultural codes
Step 3 - Deep insight: through holistic, cultural interpretation
Step 4 - Applying the lessons: design of communication, format and version 3.0 of the retail formula

Logbook of the journey:

The opportunity arose to take one full-year to open a store. Again the integrated team went back to the target audience. They segmented the users into two groups: the migrant woman and the traditional woman. The migrant woman has moved within the country into another region or city and wants modern convenience while seeking traditions that are familiar to her. The traditional woman has a stable infrastructure at home, with family, in-laws, etc. She wants to keep tradition while she also wants to try new things.

To remind the FoodBazaar team constantly of who they were serving, of these user groups they created an artwork. This artwork was an integral part of the work space design of the FoodBazaar team. The variety, the festivals, the many communities and cultures also were represented within the workspace. The research essentially created thinking and cultural codes, and as teams were exposed to this, innovations and ideas that could add value holistically, naturally flowed.

From a design perspective, Idiom looked holistically at the cultural aspects that could create greater customer loyalty and retention, as a sweet layer on top of all the design and innovation that was being detailed into the experience.

A very deep insight emerged – the idea of selfless service or Seva is a key aspect of the Indian tradition and mindset, it involves performing a service for another person without expecting anything in return. This provides the giver with a sense of fulfillment while contributing to the wellbeing of others.

Seva became a huge inspiration to the design team. They decided to incorporate the idea of selfless service and the spirit of service into the store. By turning philosophy into a design system.

Which begins with Communication –about the fact that FoodBazaar is here to serve you and various ways in which FoodBazaar is serving you ... differently:
A. Meals Ready: Ready to eat fresh and healthy meals for working couples and strapped-for-time families, that can take the customer from breakfast to dinner
B. Taste Maadi: A taste and try service and counter space where new things can be sampled before they are bought
C. Aapka Swaad: Fine specialty food that is true to the communities and localities surrounding a particular FoodBazaar

The format developed and refined over time, surprising services, at no additional cost, like
- Cleaning, peeling, cutting, grating vegetables in different styles for different communities and their dishes
- Going from grain, to customized grain mix, to flour, to dough, to finished breads for optimum health and incomparable convenience in the most transparent manner, with no wastage.

"Business navigation is a cyclical and transformative process."

By designing a few properties that would be the carriers of this value. They designed the services by converging all the research findings into an added service layer on top of the modern retail that was part of version 2.0, giving the new version 3.0 values of a corner shop.

The result is an unusual modern retail format where there is complete familiarity and a deep relationship, which goes beyond just engagement, between the customer and the store management.

Future Group and its founder, its customer and business teams, all resonated with the idea of Seva. Seva, although developed as a culture for FoodBazaar has become the cornerstone for Future Group's culture and a belief system. Articulated as 'At Future Retail, we believe that Seva that is practiced unconditionally towards all stakeholders will result in disproportionate joy, happiness and empowerment.' In order to make Seva integral to internal culture, each store of Future Group now has a Seva

charter, with clear action points to make Seva the culture of the store.

Based on this idea the characteristics of Seva were defined: self motivated, empathetic, positive and humble. Those who demonstrate these characteristics are celebrated and their stories shared with everyone in the organization.

Design thinking, informed by culture which is essentially research on changing behaviours of people can lead to powerful insights. These insights, when converted into ideas and implemented by those who have been conditioned to believe in a certain way of thinking, can be an extremely powerful force. Leading once again, to new learning, new opportunities for design.

Outcome of the journey: Food Bazaar is a dynamic retail formula that is loved by the Indian public because of its attention for the local community, modern retail qualities that

include convenience, hygiene and choice and for its attention to the traditional Indian values of openness and sensory stimulation in the shopping environment. Ongoing research and the ability to learn and integrate customer views at every stage of the format's evolution have been instrumental to achieving this position. Design has played a key role in guiding the further development of new layers of the offering, bringing business closer to the community's needs at every step of the way.

Design's openness to learn from what the customers need has paid off in the growth of the company but also in the discovery of new and unexpected areas of business. So, for example, Food Bazaar today is very successful in the sale of women's fashion, which is a direct result of knowing the Indian women well and delivering to their delight. FoodBazaar is always in step with the consumer and several steps ahead of the competition due to the fact that it has integrated design and research seamlessly.

The S.A.I.L. journey is transformative

As these four cases show, teams that complete the sailing cycle are transformed. You don't arrive at the shore as the exact same person that ventured out into sea. Team members can be transformed by the new understanding and empathy obtained in the initial phases of sensing, or by the understanding they gain though analysis that leads to re-define the project, or by the effect and impact of their inventions and experiments or by the realizations that come from assessing and learning from their journeys. And maybe, even by all of these.

Pull of adventure, Swirl of Discovery, and Inspiration of new shores

Static planning has become a thing of the past. The times when we could plan ahead, develop and implement according to plan, and then accomplish as planned belong to another era. These days, business navigation is a dynamic process in which everything becomes cyclical, and at every turn of the journey there lies an opportunity to re-visit the course and re-adjust the sails.

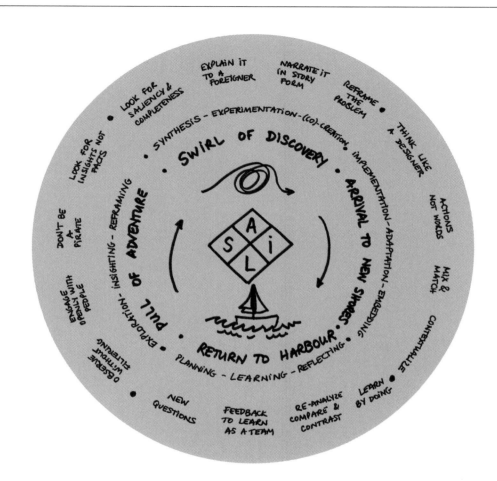

The S.A.I.L. model is an approach based on daring, doing and learning. It is not a process or a method but a way of doing things together. It is dynamic, organic and alive. It recognizes that business teams are teams of real people dealing with real issues in real time. It acknowledges that complex problems benefit from team work and flexibility and that they find a sense of accomplishment in a joint journey in which the combination of insight, understanding, (re) invention and growth allow teams to be successful in all kinds of conditions and to transit even turbulent waters with a sense of purpose, an increased resilience and an eagerness to exceed their own initial expectations of what is possible.

Like sailing, what drives the process of innovative business strategy is the pull of adventure, the swirl of discovery, and the inspiration of new shores.

5 EMERGING PRACTICES

'Twenty years from now you will be more dis-appointed by the things that you didn't do than by the ones you did do. So throw off the bowlines. Sail away from the safe harbor. Catch the trade winds in your sails. Explore. Dream. Discover.'

- Mark Twain

Dialogues in the real world

Change is an ongoing process, so business design practice is constantly evolving through those practitioners who in their work are already integrating research, design and business strategy.

These dialogues constitute an immersive exploration into the emerging practices, by diverse pioneers across the world, to help us get insight into the roles and interactions between strategy, research, and design. These conversations are aimed at bundling strengths, enabling a dialogue, and capturing emerging practices. I invite you to tune into the conversation, by reading through the different views, perspectives, and insights on this emerging area of business practice included in this chapter.

The format of these dialogues is the same for all, because these are the topics that frame the conversations. There were only four questions, which served as a guideline.
- What is research?
- What is design?
- How are they different?
- How are they similar?

My aim is to understand what pioneers are actually doing and how they define research and design within their business practices. These findings add a more practical dimension, allowing us to understand the application and adoption areas of these practices for strategic planning, insight, innovation and brand and business renewal.

The dialogues

A total of twenty-one pioneers took part in the dialogues. Each of them provided a unique perspective that can help us better understand how practice is evolving. All of the conversations were live because that makes the process richer and more personal. Had I sent out questionnaires, I am certain I would have received very 'logical' answers. But this format has allowed for a more personable sharing, which I am sure you will recognize in the tone of the interviews.

The interviews are organized in a continuum from more research-based practices, to those more design-based, and to more innovative hybrids. The pull of this process is innovation and business renewal. The flow of the interviews follows the dynamics of the S.A.I.L. model: progressing from thinking to doing and from understanding to creating.

Words and images

Next to the verbal communication and the metaphors, analogies and other forms of expressions through words all pioneers have provided a drawing[1]. The reason for th is is that while language is a cognitive mechanism that allows us to deconstruct and reconstruct meaning, drawing is a more intuitive, integrative means of communication. To draw something that another person can understand and relate to, you must make choices and you must achieve a synthesis. These drawings are therefore an important part of the conversation, not in the least because they are a representation of how the pioneers see the future of strategy, research and design. A brief explanation of the meaning of the drawing has been captured too. After finalizing their drawing each of the interviewees was asked to explain their drawing by answering, How do you envision the future of research and design within the business context?

Yin-Yang Research and Design

Hans Lingeman
CEO
Winkle
Amsterdam, The Netherlands

Who is Hans?

Hans Lingeman is one of Winkle's co-founders and leads the Winkle team. With over eighteen years experience in global market research, he is a true pioneer in the market research industry – being amongst the first to implement online data collection on a global scale ('96-'98) and experimenting with customer dialogue marketing (2001), co-creation techniques (2006), Lead User concept (2007), Facial Coding (2010) and real time interaction (2012).

What is market research?

We engage in research, because companies wish to make informed business decisions in order to stay around and thrive. Thinking of it that way, market research is an excessively strong human belief in our ability to make sense of the immeasurable world of consumer behaviour.

The real world is immensely complicated with many unknowns (that we do not or cannot measure) which can have an impact to human knowledge, attitudes, and behaviour towards categories or brands. As such, I would rather go back to the origins of what may be the fundamental definition of science: market research is the scrupulous process to satisfy curiosity about the working of our (consumer) world, in order to making sense of the past, the present, and possible future scenarios.

This requires a unique skill set for those who want to excel in research. One needs to be naively curious about everything, and combine this with the capabilities to decompose business questions and designing a methodical research framework. It's not surprising only few make it to perfection.

I think market research as it is being practiced nowadays goes through a deep crisis. There are four clear signs it's at the tail end of its own S-curve: (1) The industry latches on the use of empty terms, with an almost maniacal empha-sis on new tools, even before the "old ones" are being validated or proven faulty (Read industry magazines and visit events regularly, and you see it's all about tools and methods). (2) We try very hard to ignore the fact that research access panels are skewed and over-used, that some target groups completely stopped filling out research surveys or particip-ating in 'fun, engaging, gamified' communi-ties. (3) There is a relentless effort of industry bodies to enforce regulations and ISO-imple-mentations to practitioners of research. (4) Last, prices are eroding to a point that you may seriously start doubting the quality of our work. Where the profession needs to liberate itself, it's digging its grave in the rigid, smelly soil of research fantasy-land.

Market research does not require a question-naire. It requires the ability to think beyond the obvious and to generate hypotheses for the different directions in which businesses can change and evolve. Like I said previously, mar-ket researchers serve an important purpose in helping businesses to stay relevant and to grow and we should do this by providing a simplified framework of the real world.

What is design?

Design is meaningful; it gives purpose to someone's life. Humans have an urge to create and build. This can be executed by the arts, like paintings, architecture, and literature. But I think growing a family, or building a company should fall under the same definition. The connecting element is that we transform something that wasn't there to something that is eminently present. That way, design can get us to places we wouldn't have gone without it. Design provides direction, not limited to its physical manifestation.

How are they different?

Design is far ahead of research. Take the utopic idea of a 'one button machine'. It seems so intuitive for consumers to want a one-button coffee machine that always prepares the perfect coffee in an instant! Or, think of the one-button washing machine which washes, dries, irons, and puts your clothes in your closet in one-go! Wouldn't that be great?

Actually it is great. But, ironically, people want to suffer or engage in activities they do not like to an extent. Because it makes them feel they lived a life, they have been on Earth for a purpose, they created something themselves. A shirt that you ironed yourself feels very different emotionally to a shirt that is perfectly ironed by a one-button machine. The first arouses rich emotions during the process of drying the shirt [frustration and anger], ironing the shirt [fear to spoil it] and wearing it [proud]; while the latter delivers just flat emotions. And people would rather have ups and downs than a 'steady and mundane' life.

Design understands the balance between supporting us and eliciting feelings, it is multi-layered.

How are they similar?

What both have in common, is the aspiration to simplify the cosmos around us. Both research and design are exploratory. Genuine curiosity is probably key to create design or engage in research. Both add to the understanding of how things work, and have a built-in, default innocence -an ability to see things as if for the first time. Also, when done well, both should be actionable, triggering new ideas or decisions.

How do you envision the future of research and design within the business context?

As I grow older, the obvious and ancient wisdom becomes clearer to me: We do undeniably have one world only -one globe, which we share with eight billion friends. I wish for a world in which research is like a satellite orbiting our planet that looks after us, identifying opportunities and threats for humanity and organizations in particular. Design helps manifest change in the world (cause), or our response to change (effect). Both, in pure harmony, support society to survive, evolve and grow. Very yin-yang indeed.

Connection, curiosity and exploration

Jochum Stienstra
Owner and director
Ferro Explore!
Amsterdam, The Netherlands

Who is Jochum?

Jochum Stienstra is a qualitative market researcher specialized in narrative research. He is the director of Ferro Explore!, a company he has worked at since 1989 His ambitious goal: pushing the limits of qualitative research. Jochum is active in producing new methods of research and uses Cognitive Edge methods, focused on developing new methods and tools to assist organisations with truly complex problems and opportunities.

What is research?

Research is the exploration of uncertain fields with the aim of finding a logic within them. Research acts as an interactive hypothesis-probing mechanism that allows us to make sense of what might really be happening in the field we investigate.

Traditionally, there are two definitions for research:
• Scientific research: which is the systematic and objectivising way of searching for the building blocks and explanations around a given phenomenon. It requires the researcher to start with a hypothesis, the mapping out of the consequences and manifestation of that hypothesis and the deepening into some parts of the hypothesis that are relevant for that particular study. Once conclusions have been reached, they are applicable to the area of study only. To apply abstract findings into other areas would be the equivalent of fantasizing. For you cannot know for sure whether it would apply, too. Within this paradigm, measuring is an instrument for knowing.
• What I call natural research: this is an inbuilt capacity in all human beings. We all do this, continuously. As it is natural, there is a flexible, explorative, more intuitive and systematic search for meaningfulness, for applicability and for insight. Here, the hypothesis is a creative leap, which manifests beyond your cognition and which is a consequence of being open to learning and allowing

serendipitous impressions to create a broader picture and new connections.

I believe every research is a combination of these two forms of research. You could see them as two forces that operate together: the first is a stopping force that freezes things so that they can be interpreted systematically. The second is a disruptive force that challenges models because an explanation is not a full representation of reality. It cannot be. This disruptive force is more intuitive and pops-up in the moments in which we are 'not thinking'.

However, in this fast-paced time we live in the interaction between these two modes of research needs to happen faster than ever if we are to keep pace with the reality around us. It is no longer possible to try to make things manageable through the use of static models. We need to be able to challenge and revise the models all the time. This is difficult because even the complex reality appears simple at times. Just when businesses and people think they've got it sorted out, things change again.

Research is well positioned to help us understand the order of things around us. However, we need to understand that things cannot be forced into control. We need to recover our sense of wonder and we need to let go of our preconception if as researchers we are going to help make sense of the world around us. More often than not, things around us are complex which means that there is more to it than meets the eye: we have to dare to acknowledge that.

What is design?

Design is a form of expression, from an attitude of playfulness with the reality that surrounds us. It is about making something and achieving an effect. It looks into the fundament of things, it's not just a sauce you pour over things. Design goes all the way from defining the problem to solving the problem.

How are they different?

In my view, market research has traditionally been guilty of linear thinking. This reflects badly on the market research practice.

Typically, market research has dedicated itself to the search for explanations based on a premise. This premise would then be broken into the different manifestations that were found in the world to either support that premise or challenge it with new information. However, questioning the premise or any of the assumptions that go with it was not part of the research. And this is where I think research and design are different. Research needs to recognize that the premises and assumptions are the core of the problem. And explaining them will not widen the scope of the discussion.

"When the terrain is complex, doing is probing and probing is doing."

Design embraces reality with all its subjectivity. Research is traditionally objectivising and separating. This is the domain of consciousness. There is nothing unconscious or intuitive in objectivising, because the whole point is to work within existing systems. Design's role is to change existing systems.

Design researchers aim to put themselves in the shoes of those they research. They dive into the world, which makes it impossible to separate the research from the designer. The designer is the explorer who works towards the formulation of a powerful vision they can then use to guide their design. When the terrain is complex, doing is probing and probing is doing. These skills are narrowly interconnected, making the labour of design research much richer.

By contrast, research uses tools that involve a higher degree of intervention, almost interrupting real life, like interviews for example, which demand answers from interviewees. This will only deliver very poor answers, produced under stress. That produces the language of the comfort zone, of the most trodden neural pathways and of what we know already. We don't need more of that, because that is not making anyone any wiser nor making business more relevant.

How are they similar?

As the market research paradigm shifts into a less analytic and more interdisciplinary form, it gets more similar to design. The similarity lies in the sensemaking.

The value of research is not in the conclusions. Rather, it is in the ability to look at things together and to develop joint conclusions about the matters at hand.

Some scholars talk about 'the science of the hunch' or abductive thinking. This to me, is the space in which design and research meet.

The very fundament of the way these disciplines think is about the generation of new systems -not from the language, codes or explanations of the old systems, but through a quantum leap of knowledge, giving new meaning by giving things a new perspective, a new twist, a new angle of understanding.

How do you envision the future of research and design within the business context?

I think the future will be characterized by a collaboration that will come naturally to all of those involved. Like in nature, there are exchanges going on all the time. And everyone benefits. If you take a picture, it may look static. But a tree is growing, taking minerals from the ground, water from the rain, giving shelter to birds and other animals, etc. And things grow and unfold in their natural course.

This exchange takes increasingly the form of dialogues, co-creations, joint initiatives that lead to joint narratives, without a reductionist or interventionist approach, but from our natural human needs to connect, to be curious and to explore together.

Collaboration and complementarity

Luis Woldenberg
CEO and founder
NODO research and strategy
Mexico City Mexico

Who is Luis?

Luis Woldenberg has been in the research industry for thirty-five years
and has been strategic advisory to
multiple projects throughout his
career. Luis is currently president of
the AMAI in Mexico, the Mexican
Association of Market Research
Agencies. He also heads NODO one
of the top five research agencies in
Mexico, where he has pioneered
several initiatives including the
social sentiment monitor.

What is research?

I think a distinction should be made between
market research and market intelligence.
There will always be a need for market intelligence and basic data collection. But that is
not enough. Market research is the ability to
compose and decompose information about
the market and people, and to conduct analysis on that process that leads to new insights.
Research is about understanding not just
about information.

Everybody has access to information. How
can we as researchers pretend to help our
clients if all we have is information? They
don't need us for the information. They need
our support, as we say in Mexico, to provide
'the medicine and the treatment'. Our talent,
our contribution in a collaborative setting
with the client is about providing analysis,
conclusions, possible strategies, and proposed ways forward in which business can
add value. Just prescribing 'the medicine' in
the form of a report on research findings
will not help the client in understanding the
relevant 'treatment'.

Research is about discovering opportunities
and solutions. It is about mapping the way
forward based on learnings from studies of
different kinds: qualitative, quantitative,
trends and databases, internet research and
surveys. Research has all these tools to create and deepen understanding.

There is no added value in being a messenger
of the questions from our clients towards the
audience, the value is in helping them understand what the questions might be based on,
what is happening out there and deepening
their understanding so that they can have
more relevance in market through their
business activities.

What is design?

For me, design is something that relates to
form. Design is about shaping solutions. Based
on a defined problem, design develops conceptual directions and answers to that problem.

Design works hand-in-hand with research.
Our research teams are constantly scanning
the market and evolving our understanding of
people, society, and culture. This allows us to rise
above the obvious, above the level of information
that everybody else has access to. We digest,
provide insight and foresight, and build the
emerging stories. We create meaning from the
findings. Then we work in tandem with design to
iterate potential ways of addressing this meaning
in the form of business solutions.

We see design as the key to ensuring that the
solutions we propose to our clients reach the
market in relevant ways. Particularly, design
means a/ that products and services will be
purchased from our clients and b/ that they
will be used and consumed in ways that add
value to the consumers.

How are they different?

I consider research and design to be quite different. Research allows us to focus on what really matters, not just what is convenient, on-strategy or on-brand. It shows us where things are going and what we could do about that to maximize business effectiveness, impact, and ultimately sustainable profits.

Design on the other hand, consists of tools that allow us to ensure we achieve the desired effect with our actions.

Designers often want a defined problem to work on, so that they can think of many solutions. Mostly, they are not in the 'war room' with the strategists. Researchers work alongside strategists because we help gain understanding and insight which feeds the strategy.

How are they similar?

It used to be so, that both for design and for research, the work would start when the client provided a brief. That has changed. Both researchers and designers now have to participate in the process of briefing, to get to the heart of the matter. This means that the skills in the future of design and research will not only be defined by the educational background (from mathematicians and statisticians, through social scientists and designers, to anthropologists and management professionals) but that we will see hybrid teams of people who

are joined by their eagerness to question, their curiosity to understand, and their ability to integrate insights into relevant strategic direction.

How do you envision the future of research and design within the business context?

I am hopeful that we will see a future in business much more characterized by collaboration and complementarity. There will no longer be 'stars'. We will have experts, yes. But we will finally understand that analyzing any topic from just one vantage point is not enough. We need a variety of talent if we want to make a meaningful difference.

We need people at the table who understand finances, brands, people's behaviour, emotions, design. They sit around one table, addressing issues together. The table's legs that make it solid are: people understanding (insight into human dynamics and culture), and the ability to engage emotionally. Shaping business and creating meaning can never be an isolated and clinical job. It is about people, for people and with people. It is a job we need to do together re-valuing what each of us contributes and opening up to what we can learn from each other.

Shared Purpose

Gustavo Lohfeldt
Founder and CEO
Provokers
Buenos Aires, Argentina

Who is Gustavo?

Gustavo Lohfeldt is an industrial engineer with a career in business and market research. He is currently Provoker's founder and CEO and has held different roles along the way to his current role: Today he works with clients on projects around consumer understanding, challenging strategies and innovative actions.

What is research?

I would define market research as a tool to understand situations and people in order to generate actionable insights.

Research can be descriptive, for example by mapping out a certain situation of usage or interaction. And research can be explicative, for example by explaining the drivers, points of view, and barriers for a given person or group of people.

In the complexity that surrounds us, I think market research is generating two streams. On the one hand you have the ultra specialized, technique-driven research agencies. They are excellent whenever you need to track and validate. They inform with accuracy on narrowly defined subjects.

On the other hand there are market researchers who integrate strategy and design into their practice, becoming like a kind of General Practitioner in medicine. They have the sensitivity and the knowledge to really understand and interpret the information and data they collect. And because of that, they dare to go a bit beyond, integrating the consequences of that information or data into their role.

Researchers today are no longer 'specialists'; rather, they have become 'partners'. We help clients generate solutions. Nowadays we are seeing clients pressured for results in short time, with a lot more information to process and with teams that are more fluid. The organizations have less hierarchical structures, people change jobs more rapidly, and the average process has six months to thrive or die. If you take longer to understand and act on your research, then your competitors will have made a move or society will have changed again. This means that researchers, as suppliers to business, need to be quicker, more integrated, more holistic, and more agile.

What is design?

Design is about adding value in a concrete way. It is much more than aesthetics or form. It is about taking an idea, capturing its essence, and translating it into something that is of value and relevance to the consumer.

Designers use research as a source to inform their design making. Clients in the business world today are asking for a clear and integrated thread of thinking. Learnings need to be integrated as you go. Design has an integrative role as it creates a solution. You cannot create a relevant solution if you do not integrate what research shows to be meaningful.

How are they different?

At the very specific level of expertise, they are different. Creativity and production within design are unique to the domain of design. Data gathering is part of the domain of research.

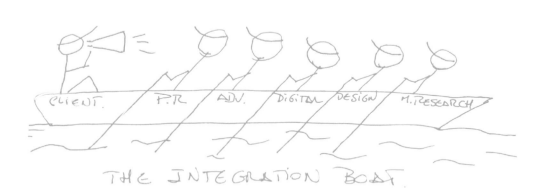

THE INTEGRATION BOAT

The skills are all necessary: strategy, numbers, creativity, promotions, advertising and communications. But the client is not asking for the skills: the client is on the lookout for the result of these skills applied to strategy.

This brings research and design into a space in which they converge in their ability to create solutions that are integral, integrated, and profitable for business. Clients are no longer willing to do the integrating themselves. They reward agencies that do the integration for them.

How do you envision the future of research and design within the business context?

I think we are moving towards a model in which all parties share the same purpose: to deliver relevant and useful business solutions. This brings us together from different disciplines as partners to business. While our clients can concentrate on managing existing business, all the different suppliers can congregate and share skills around their joint purpose of adding value to business. This is a considerable shift from the traditional thinking that if we all did 'our' job well, we were providing business with what they needed. Now it is the reverse, by providing business with what they needs we will apply our skills as necessary and understand where we need to collaborate and where it is our role to help others think, as their sounding board and inspiration.

These differences actually generate a problem for the client. Businesses used to have time to do a lot of project management, and they were so-called in control. So first they would go ask a researcher for help, once they had that they would re-evaluate their strategy in the light of the findings. Once they had that they would think of a marketing plan or a brand plan. Once they had that they would think of the design aspects of communication, packaging, brand values, etc.

The problem with pigeon-holing the disciplines is that it is more work for the client. They have to integrate everything .Plus, it takes forever.

I think the differences will remain for the specialists. Designers are not likely to go into big data or statistical analysis. Researchers are not likely to go into interaction design or graphic design. For the rest of us, the direction of growth is of a generalist approach with a bit of salt and pepper, to make it unique, to make it surprising, and to make it interesting for business.

How are they similar?

There is an incipient change. We are seeing it at the level of medium-sized companies. They combine and integrate the disciplines. There is a convergence towards collaboration.

Interrelated and interconnected

Malex Salamanques
Project Director
Space Doctors
Brighton, United Kingdom

Who is Malex?

Malex Salamanques is a Project Director at Space Doctors in Brighton, UK. Malex specializes in applying semiotic thinking and hands-on design expertise to the optimization of brands' visual language. A pioneer in this field, she leads the Design Semiotics offer, which brings strategic vision and executional guidance to the process of design research and development.

What is research?

As I work in the area of commercial or applied semiotics for brands, I will define research based on my practice. Semiotic research is all about going beyond the surface, to reveal layers of meaning.

The semiotics mindset, for me, is like being a foreigner in a new land, reading things with new eyes, looking for the unfamiliar with an open mind, finding patterns. Ideally, this 'look from the outside' is combined with the local cultural 'software'. This combination allows you to understand what is relevant for a given context and importantly it also allows you to know how to break paradigms, where to innovate.

It is not about asking people, but about reading the context they live in, in order to better understand their aspirations and needs. Very often consumers can't articulate what they want or need. They are capable of playing back from what they know. It is very difficult to understand a future landscape for innovation or product planning based only on consumers responses.

Why would anyone try to understand a complex world by only asking people? Science and culture evolve and, thus, what something means and what things signify changes through time. Within the semiotics toolbox we look at residual, dominant, and emerging codes. If you ask consumers, you will get the codes that they are immersed in, which

is never the whole picture. Or if you look at trends you will see emerging expressions but not in the context of the code trajectory of that expression: where it came from, where it's heading. All of these things have value. Semiotics helps you by giving you a map: what is emerging today will be dominant tomorrow, what is dominant and mainstream will turn into residual, and even residual codes may turn 'vintage' and make a comeback.

What is design?

As a designer myself, I like the definition by Milton Glaser. He posits that design is an intervention in the flow of events to produce a desired effect.

Designers are constantly scanning their environment, because everything is a possibility. They look for ways of mixing two different things to produce a third. Design acts as an eye-opener, offering a vision of the things we could not have discovered otherwise.

How are they different?

Semioticians are interested in the granularity; I think most designers designers are not interested in interrogating more than they need. Yet curiosity comes from the same place. There is a considerable difference in terms of their purpose.

I've seen so many sterile research exercises, which are very shallow, self-referential, and ultimately useless.

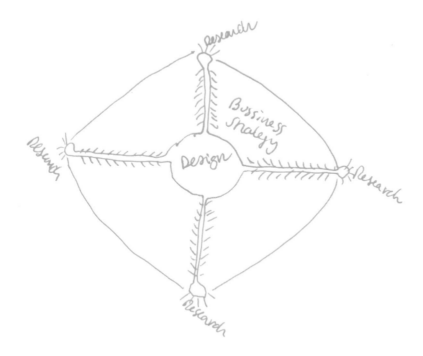

How are they similar?

All designers are intuitive semioticians. All semioticians look at design to gain understanding. I believe there are a lot of similarities, and also a lot of complementarity, or maybe synergy.

Designers can see so many possibilities; sometimes that can be overwhelming for a brand team. Semiotics can help to focus, to ground the options, and also incorporates richness into early stages of a project.

When design and research work together, the result is a more profound, deeper understanding, and they are more nuanced and better tuned to what is truly relevant, what is potentially achievable, and what is most useful.

How do you envision the future of research and design within the business context?

I have drawn design in the centre, at the core of business development. Research is the antennae, which reaches through and beyond business strategy, which is the matter that surrounds the core of design. Research comes from design and goes through strategy out into the world. This is how I envision the future, where things are interrelated and interconnected, where business is listening and tuning into its environment and where design is shaping things with a purpose.

Semiotics is more profound. It does not set a limit or expectation on what is to be found. Because of this, what's discovered usually constitutes inspiring, flexible, replicable platforms for creative execution. It can spark an almost symmetrical thought on what the solution could be, which is where design comes in. If you take design language and look at the research from a design point of view you start linking what you are discovering with what you can create with it. These two different disciplines generate a new hybrid when they work together: Design Semiotics.

Another example where we capitalize on the different strengths from semiotic research and design is the less purist application of semiotics in co-creation: Semiotics is utilized to get insight from how users say things rather than what they say. We would ask things like 'what are your significant objects' and why. In this case, the framing comes from design, which is mainly about finding the right questions, and the depth, the substantiation, comes from semiotics.

Serendipitous Journeys

Christoph Welter Strategy Director
and **Virginie Gailing** Strategic
Designer and founder of The Cookery
Point-Blank International
Berlin, Germany

Who are Christoph and Virginie?

As the resident Strategy Director at
Point-Blank International, Christoph
Welter is responsible for pushing the
envelope in new thinking and practice
with the team. He stands for actionable and people-centric research and
consulting approaches.

Virginie Gailing is a true hybrid thinker
and design activist, devoting her design
skills to meaningful and visionary
innovation. Mixing, distilling, and connecting information, she is a creative
researcher with a holistic vision.

What is research?

At the very heart of research is connecting
people. We see it as a social activity that
connects people in order to uncover
emerging truths.

In a sense, we compare research with magic.
It takes knowledge and expertise, yet also
charisma and intuition, to conduct great
research. Like a professional magician, you
take a lot of care preparing, setting up. You
coordinate a time, a place, the appropriate
conditions, and also a spell or a potion. And
then, within that setting, emerges a serendipitous moment. As Louis Pasteur said,
chance favours the prepared mind.

Researchers are uniquely positioned to help
understand, to catch and find patterns, and to
help others see how they can take those patterns further, without pretending to be right or
wrong. Research allows you to understand the
context. It provides a point of view, which is
sharp and helps build a vision. It gives you the
curated details in a world where we have too
much information.

There will always be a risk of missing bits of
the information. To eliminate the risk of just
being conceptual or just be providers of information, which is, at best, neutral, researchers
need to impact decision-making. Research actually has to lead somewhere, as you research
you see where the energy is, what to focus
on, what to deepen out. Inspiration is not
enough; it is a basic condition. Beyond that,
what matters is whether something new
or beneficial is created out of the research
findings.

What is design?

Ettore Sottass' definition feels the most
appropriate. He describes design as the
transformative process that helps to create
objects, love, eroticism and politics. "Design
does not mean to give a shape to a more
or less stupid product, for a more or less
sophisticated industry. It is a way to devise
life, politics, eroticism, food and even
design." It is a great quote that looks at
design by including the concepts of systems, processes and the act of designing
design itself.

Ultimately, design is a mindset. Of course, it
is focused towards action, towards doing. But
it is so much more than the tools alone. It is
learning through doing.

What sets design apart is that it is synthetic,
systemic, and project-driven. By synthetic
we mean that designers embrace complexity
and look for ways to simplify it. The systemic approach of designers is linked to their
ability to see all the parameters and all the
things that interact. And the project culture
of designers is about dedicating oneself to
something and to grow with it.

How are they different?

We'd like to contrast rapid-action with deep-thinking. Research overstresses deep-thinking. In research we look at the full laddering, from the level of people's lives and conversations that emerge in research all the way into the meta level to build explanations into a thought palace. Research allows us to see the connections. Rapid-action comes from design. Designers make things very concrete.

Where research is immersive, design is action oriented. The point is that neither is enough by itself. The potential for synergy is huge. Design needs research if it really wants to under-stand things, to contextualize and to elaborate propositions rooted into people's behaviour. Researchers have an in-built ability to see things further and more deeply than the obvi-ous. But research also needs design to get real, put thoughts into action, iterate and prototype around ideas from the get-go rather than going ever deeper into analytical metalevels with-out having a proof of concept. Designers look for possibilities and embrace the fact that the creative process is uncertain. This is essential in the current context: we cannot know ahead of the research what the outcome will be. And we have to accept that. Because it is not as simple as: here's a business issue, here's an answer. Both research and design contribute their competences to this process of unlocking business issues within a complex world.

How are they similar?

Most companies have difficulty in formulating a vision. Research and design can join to bring inspiration, offer new perspectives and create a new, emerging truth for companies and brands. This is not a merging of the disciplines, it is rather a common journey,

We see both research and design as key players in the process of innovation and vision making. Both researchers and designers are people's people in their own ways. The lead is a pivoting lead: sometimes research leads in un-derstanding, sometimes design leads in action. In our practice we have seen research grow into this role through the incorporation of de-sign thinking processes into our projects: these have allowed us to come closer to design and to truly see the project as magical, serendipitous, and creative. What design and research share is that magic.

DESIGNER
CLIENT
RESEARCHER

A serendipitous journey to impact
Christoph W.

How do you envision the future of research and design within the business context?

We have drawn two pictures: one to show the future, the other to depict the journey we hope design and research will embark on together.

The future we hope for is one in which research and design each bring their own tools and thought processes to create a common vision for business. In the picture there is one eye, but there are two brains. They both share, compare, and integrate their observations while they both contribute towards the thinking process from their own competences.

The picture that shows the journey shows an integrated process, on a joint road where the researcher and the designer do hyperbolic movements by going further out into their fields of expertise and then going back and sharing with each other and with the client. This shared road is also a bit like a maze, with serendipitous detours in which the journey itself is the goal. It changes those in it.

Growing integration

Kevin Mccullagh, Founder
and **Debbie Nathan,**
senior consultant
PLAN
London, United Kingdom

Who are Kevin and Debbie?

Kevin McCullagh: Design strategist and thought-leader with a twenty-year track record for breaking new ground. Kevin founded Plan in 2004. With a background spanning design, engineering, marketing and social forecasting, he also writes, speaks, and curates and chairs conferences on design, business, and society.

Debbie Nathan is a senior consultant at Plan and heads up Plan's consumer research offer with a particular focus on moving from insight to strategy. Her background combines a first-class degree in industrial design, a Philips-sponsored Masters in Design Practice and professional experience in design research, product-service innovation, and pure qualitative research.

What is research?

Research is about understanding, sensemaking and inspiration. It is a process by which we understand attitudes and behaviour –be it observed, heard, or reported.

Research is one component of insight development. We use consumer research together with other sources of information to triangulate information that will allow us to deepen our understanding. Consumer research involves direct and planned interactions with consumers. We integrate what we learn from these interactions together with other sources of insight, such as trend research, desk research, and expert and stakeholder interviews. Additionally, new sources of insight are emerging such as big data or digital tools that provide a wider palette of data sources.

The current context requires our research practice to be forever changing, so we turn to mixed methodologies. However, we would say that at the heart of research lies the understanding of user behaviours and attitudes. With our clients and partners we find that we are working more collaboratively: researchers are being seen as the voice of the customer and invited to bring that voice into the conversation rather than solely preparing a document that is about the voice of the customer.

What is design?

Design is about problem solving in a cultural context for developing new products and services, and involves making decisions about functionality, usability, and meaning.

How are they different?

Research and design are different things that interface with each other. They are not mutually exclusive. Research can assist design. Perhaps that is the main difference. Research is one component to the design process, whereas design is not necessarily a component of the research process, but rather a potential input.

Where design research differs to a pure design process is the rigour of the data collection and the analysis of the data, not always immediately weaving it into a design process. Research allows us to structure information in a tangible way that is then easy to embed in design processes. Yet research does not necessarily need to respond to one specific design. The big value of design is that it's immersive and contextual. This means that the designer becomes an experiential expert through the process of design and gets to truly understand what is going on.

How are they similar?

Clients are coming from a situation maybe until five or ten years ago where they could manage projects sequentially, in a waterfall fashion: first do the research, then think of its implications for strategy, then start designing. Now the time pressure, the degree of competition, and the demands of the market mean they have to run things in parallel. Big companies have to form more agile processes.

This need for agility has caused research to change, to be more beneficial to design and also has caused a shift in the design practice, transitioning from product design to the design of product services. The need for more agility has led to a greater need for empathy, so the way research is conducted has changed into more collaborative forms. There is a need for client teams to be immersed in the consumer context, because experiencing the interaction

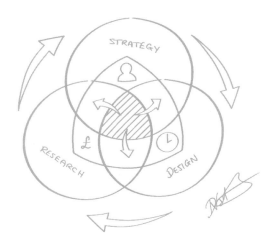

first hand allows them to tell their own stories and to stand behind the insight. We are seeing clients wanting to learn the research skills to go out and research themselves in order to truly understand what is happening and to gain ownership of the insights. This is very different from getting a report from a researcher who is telling you what someone else said.

Design has also adapted to research and has taken on a role to help widen and sharpen the research questions and the research objectives. Designers don't just appear after the analysis of the research has been done. When designers get involved early on in the research we also see that they look at things differently because they understand what can and cannot be manifested into reality,

what the possibilities are. This leads them to ask different kinds of questions to get the necessary understanding in order to create.

Another thing they do have in common is that both are about openness to possibility and awareness of change, but in quite different ways. Sometimes it is very appropriate to go really open into the research and learn. But at other times, it can be useful to have designed something in order to research. That might sound like it's the wrong order of things but in actual fact, you have to begin somewhere and design can be equally instrumental to opening new possibilities in a dialogue with consumers. It is beneficial for research that the design is already underway. Research and design are ultimately not separate processes but part of a continuous process where things happen concurrently or in parallel.

How do you envision the future of research and design within the business context?

We have drawn a Venn diagram of the intersection of research, design and strategy. We envision this intersection growing: more people, more time, more money will be channelled through that intersection. Around the Venn diagram, the world keeps spinning at high speed, meaning more agility will be key.

What we wanted to portray is that these disciplines will become increasingly integrated and that their relevance to companies will grow.

Collective thinking and rich ideas

Laura Williams, consultant
and **Brian Millar**, director
of strategy
Sense Worldwide
London, United Kingdom

Who are Laura and Brian?

Laura Williams is a designer, strategist and project manager specialising in insight, innovation and business strategy. In her early twenties Laura co-founded and ran a service design consultancy. Then she co-founded a tech-start up and is currently developing a learning programme called AcadeME.

Brian Millar is head of strategy at Sense Worldwide, where he works on innovation projects with leading clients. He started his career in advertising at Saatchi and Saatchi and Ogilvy, became a speechwriter for CEOs, and then decided that strategy was more creative than either. He writes regularly on design and innovation in Fast Company and Wired.

What is research?

Research is the act of gathering information that will lead to insight. Insight is a step beyond the information itself: insight provides you with a new understanding about a subject and can point you in a different direction.

Research brings the consumer voice into the commercial decision-making process. It's essential to innovation and strategy because you can't know what your different customers need without involving them.

Research needs insight because while existing data and other information might tell you 'what' is happening, insight is obtained by unpacking 'why' things are happening.

Whilst most standard research methodology tells you about the 'now' and the 'then' of any given situation or subject, it does not go beyond that into the 'next'. It is still a key part of the context for innovation and strategy: by understanding and learning from what has worked previously, you can verify your hunches on what might come next.

What is design?

Design is the application of creativity to solve human problems. This can be anything from a more user-friendly kitchen appliance to an integrated digital financial management system or a physical retail experience.

Design involves creating products, services, and businesses beyond the constraints or boundaries of the current context in ways that serve people's needs. One thing that designers often have is empathy and imagination, the ability to put themselves in someone else's shoes and design around their needs. In this way, design is much more than a skill set. It requires a particular mindset. This creative thinking that helps designers design solutions to a problem or challenge is the way they go about generating solutions. Central to this is the idea of playfulness: it is about exploring with a big smile or even a cheeky grin.

There is a danger these days that people think that design is a chin-stroking exercise, yet the gap between ideation and making something that resonates with people deeply is what defines design: it's a balance between design thinking and design doing.

How are they different?

Research allows us to understand the boundaries of a topic. Design allows us to break those boundaries in order to redefine a topic in a new way. You can take a creative approach to getting the insights you need, but encouraging people to come together and generate ideas based on the insights is naturally more embedded in creativity.

If design is used well it helps people become more open to learning from mistakes and more likely to help things be repurposed around emerging customer needs.

Design has a broader scope than research. We would even say that it is possible to design without research. Like the Hubble Space Telescope for instance, you can be sure they did not do focus groups for that, although they may have asked astronauts for input on the interior design and other practical design attributes. There is such a thing as design without an end user in mind, and there are also lone geniuses. And in some circumstances that works.

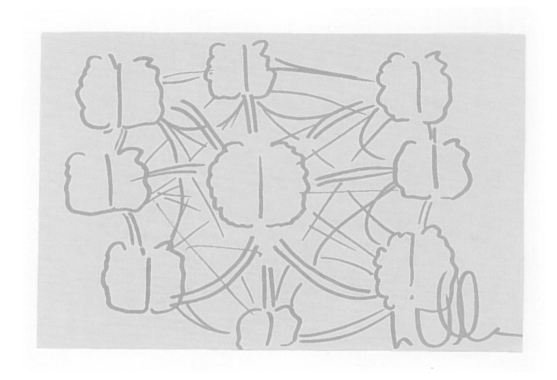

How are they similar?

Both research and design are about creating learning organizations and people. Research can learn from data and feedback and generate continuously evolving hypotheses and help explore personal and cultural boundaries that already exist, or are starting to shift. Great design is about pushing these boundaries, and emerging beyond or building upon what is fashionable or normal. It's an exploration into the unknown.

Research and design have to fulfil their potential within a business context. A lot of commercial research is used to understand what's happened previously. If a company wants to innovate they need to understand why new things are happening, but from a research perspective that's a much harder internal sell. Within large companies, research is too often used to kill ideas, which can cause tension between the research team and the design team.

"Both research and design are about creating learning organizations and people."

Designers have to introduce new ideas, while people evolutionarily do not like new things. No wonder designers find it difficult to gain acceptance for their ideas.

Working towards insight is the main area in which design and research work symbiotically. To get to deeper meaning, both integrate feedback into their learning process and pivot the lessons learned into new opportunities and new questions.

How do you envision the future of research and design within the business context?

Brian has drawn a big light bulb with many little light bulbs within it, inspired by the principle that the big idea is always the rich idea, that is, an idea interesting on many levels: products become a medium and consumers can influence the future shape they take.

This symbolizes what we see happening at the intersection of research and design: co-creation. No design department can keep up with the speed with which consumers' demands change. The most creative consumers start acting as valuable muses to design, and research has a role to play in getting that inspiration. Together with the consumer, the ability to see new perspectives and to integrate those perspectives is where great ideas take shape.

Laura drew brains in a network, to symbolize collective thinking and the ability for all people to learn. All the brains are equally big, yet there is one central brain that helps connect. This image speaks to the capacity for collective thinking and to the way in which collaboration brings people together to create more effective learning hubs.

DISCOVER.
EXPLORE.
TRANSFORM.

Architecting and Constructing

Will Leach
Founder
TriggerPoint
Dallas, Texas, USA

Who is Will?

After seventeen years of consumer insights experience in the CPG, Biotechnology and Energy Industries, Will Leach saw an opportunity to blend his passion for consumer insights with his expertise in behavioural science based design. TriggerPoint is the result of that passion. TriggerPoint is a behavioural research and design firm specializing in identifying and influencing the subconscious factors guiding consumer decision making.

What is research?

Research in its essence is the act of bringing understanding into an organization. There are many methods to do so, ranging from data analytics to qualitative studies. This 'understanding' can help organizations understand 'what is happening' and 'why its happening' which is pretty important to know. However, I'd suggest that there's an even more important mission for research; behavioural change. Research's sole goal should be to provide the insight needed to change consumer behaviours. Not preferences...behaviours. Therefore I evaluate all research and insights through a behavioural lens and its ability to change consumer behaviours. This to me is the most important thing that research provides companies and the future of our discipline.

The idea that insight's purpose is to understand the drivers of consumer preference is outdated. Measuring consumer preferences are often meaningless because they change so often based upon (1) context and (2) psychology and how we're feeling at the moment of decision. These factors very often trump our preferences in-the-moment and we act 'irrationally'.

To truly understand where people are going to spend their money, you'd better not waste time on understanding and messaging to their preferences. It's much better to focus on understanding how psychology and context come together to drive behaviours -and more importantly how to design for it.

So how do we take on the challenge to move from only providing consumer insights to also driving topline growth? I believe it comes from the intersection of insights and design -Behavioural Design.

What is design?

Within Behavioural Design we define our role as creatively merging behavioural sciences with design to transform existing behaviours into preferred behaviours. Simply put, behavioural design helps you understand and change people's behaviours.

How are they different?

In essence there is a missing bridge between behavioural research and behavioural design.

Research focuses on the understanding of people. It's a whole industry that focuses on better measurement and better techniques for better human understanding, but unfortunately, not driving behavioural change.

Behavioural Design is focused on changing behaviours and doing so by understanding and influencing context. Designers create the new experiences that drive the way people behave. But they often lack the scientific understanding behind why people do what they do and

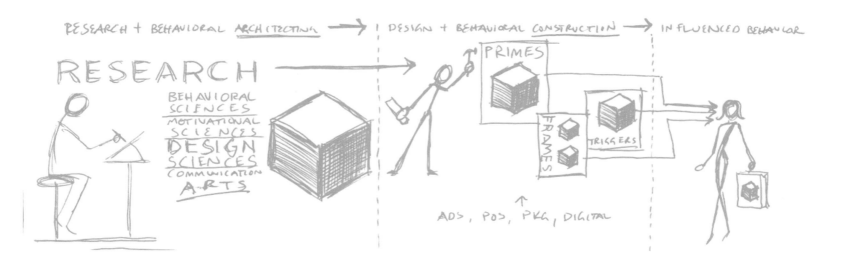

aren't skilled in the behavioural methodologies needed to guide their design.

How are they similar?

It seems almost incredible that these disciplines currently work in isolation. They are both about driving better consumer experiences.

I relate the ideal relationship of research and design to building your dream home. When building your dream home you need a great architect to listen to your dreams and build the blueprints for construction. These blueprints are then given to a master builder to make these dreams a functional reality. The connection point between these two jobs is the blueprints that bring ideas to execution.

Similar to an architect, a good behavioural researcher intimately understands their consumer and uses motivational theory and behavioural economics to build their ideal experience 'blueprints', if you will. But it's only when these blueprints are given to creative behavioural designers who can turn theory into beautifully designed products,

marketing or experiences will true behavioural change occur.

How do you envision the future of research and design within the business context?

The future of research and design will come from the intersection of the researcher (the architect) who will use motivational science, behavioural science to create the blueprints that behavioural designers will actually translate and build these into aesthetically beautifully activations that ultimately influence behaviours.

Circular integration

Rikke Ulk
Director
Antropologerne
Copenhagen, Denmark

Who is Rikke?

Rikke Ulk, Antropologerne, is the CEO, Chief Anthropologist, and founder of a project-based consultancy firm in Copenhagen. Pioneering the approach of combining anthropology and design methods with co-creation, Rikke continuously strives to ensure that insight and change lead to innovation that is valuable for people, society, and the planet.

What is research?

Research is exploring and creating knowledge by gathering different kinds of material. This includes any and every form of research from desk research to field research.

For good research it is crucial to understand at the outset what the underlying assumptions are that are driving the urge of knowledge. This is important because the questions you put out always define the answers. A clear outset also leads to the 'how', that is, how to gather the empiric material, which methods to use, how to conduct the research.

Knowledge is not lying out there waiting to be gathered, it is something you build in the process of doing research. Research is an active act, a way of interfering in the context of investigation. Since knowledge, at one level, is a product of the lenses through which we see and discover the world, it is also subjective. As researchers, we need to be clear about the subjectivity of our research and make it transparent. This is crucial to the quality of our findings.

We should not, per se, be looking for answers, but for the right questions to put. And look for different ways of asking questions, ideally also involving several people so that everyone can ask questions from their perspectives. There is no single truth out there and therefore we should uncover as many positions, rationalities and voices as possible. Research is

an exploration; otherwise we would just be confirming what we already knew.

What is design?

Design is a discipline and a set of skills based on making solutions to problems. To design is to do and to create, not just to understand. Design is about authoring a new solution through a well orchestrated and structured work process.

As such, design takes things a step further and has the ambition of obliging people's unmet needs and everyday challenges. It contributes with a solution, making things tangible, visual, and directional. This is why design is so instrumental to making change happen.

Ultimately, design makes something new that changes a situation for the better, whether that is a new product or service, or a new way of organizing local communities.

How are they different?

What makes research and design different is their end goal. Creating knowledge is to be able to say something with some kind of qualified documentation. The end result of research is an insight, which is intangible. It includes assumptions, knowledge, and praxis that help understand certain people in a given context.

Design, on the other hand, aims for a solution or change, by bringing something new to a situation. Good design is based on deep insights because it is so much easier to develop brilliant concepts from understanding the conceptions and everyday practices involved.

Yet the product of design is always tangible. Even for service design or interaction design, it is always something that you can use, you want, you can understand or interact with.

How are they similar?

When research and design work together they strengthen and enrich one another and blend their skills in a very synergetic collaboration. Research is instrumental to opening the hearts and the minds of people who are creating things for or with other people by uncovering what is needed, what are the difficulties to be obliged, and what motivates people. This makes the design effort much more focused and successful.

In turn, design has tools that can be shortcuts to uncovering latent, implicit knowledge. Via tangible exercises, probes, and interventions you can really dive deep into more latent levels of knowledge, (ie. what people dream and wish for), understanding people as full beings with a sense of the context, achieving results that otherwise take a much longer time.

Wanting to understand and solve the needs of either a society, a group of people or an organization is what brings research and

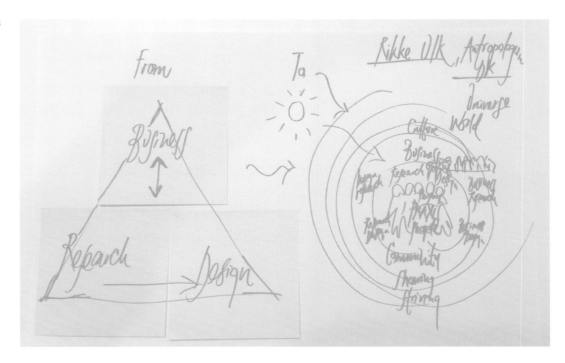

design together. Both disciplines contribute to understand how people interact with each other, the places they visit, and the world they live in and has the aim of making people's lives better, create value, improve systems and create relevant things. Research and design help to make meaningful innovation and a meaningful world.

How do you envision the future of research and design within the business context?

In my view, we will move from a hierarchical model in which there is an established order from research to design in order to make business and strategy (at the left) to a more circular way of work (at the right) where research, design, and business merge and integrate in new and different ways having people and praxis at the centre.

Hopefully research, design, and business will work in a people centred way, serving a greater goal than just business, striving to create a better living conditions for people, a better environment, better societies, and ultimately a better world. At least, that is what I hope.

Continuous learning and applying

Marc Rettig
Principal,
Fit Associates LLC
Pittsburgh, Pennsylvania, USA

Who is Marc?

Marc Rettig is founding principal of Fit Associates LLC, where he helps companies, teams, and institutions create in complex social situations. He has worked with corporations in many sectors, as well as numerous startup companies and nonprofit organizations. In addition to his consulting practice, Marc is on the faculty of two universities: Carnegie Mellon University's School of Design and the Masters in Design for Social Innovation program at the School of Visual Arts in New York.

What is research?

My view of organizations is that they are living processes, which sense the world, then make sense of that input in order to conceive an appropriate response. This is a creative process, which is essential to the life of an organization.

There are many ways of sensing. Quantitative research is a way of sensing. And so is qualitative research and all sorts of other methods, ranging as wide as cool-hunting, socio-cultural trends, and data analytics.

Research is a tool that helps organizations sense the world, and be transformed by that act of sensing. Its main role is to help designers, developers, managers, etc. become connected as people, so that they can create something true, something that is good for the world.

What is design?

My working definition of design is a process definition: design is a way to create in uncertainty, through a repeated cycle of understanding and making.

The design process entails two activities: understand and try. The first, 'understand', begins with the basic assumption that you do not understand. The world is too complex. Other people see the world differently than you, and you cannot see what is ahead: a hole, a snake, a tree, or whatever else might be there.

The light reveals just enough for you to move safely forward. By moving, you also move the light and so see something different, sufficient for the step that follows. The second activity, "try," is about daring to take those small steps that will bring you new perspectives, a different understanding.

The heart of design is intention. By following your intention into the world, you improve your understanding. And as you understand better, you are likely to revise your intention.

The engine of design is iteration. In complex domains it is key to be able to listen for just enough information to be able to develop a sense that something may be worth trying, and then do an experiment. As you do several safe experiments in parallel, you start finding patterns of what is beneficial and what works.

How are they different?

An organization is a vehicle to connect senses to the world. Research is a label for the way our understanding grows through the process of sensing the world. Design is a context in which research is carried out. There might be other contexts, of course. You might do research to measure something you need to know, for example. There are countless ways of doing research, but what you aim to do is to get understanding. Ultimately, you want ideas for things to try that are different from what you would have had without the research.

Design is about opening your creative system and process to the world. Design involves a way of seeing, a way of working, and a way of being: a stance of openness and a willingness to keep creating despite uncertainty.

I'd like to note that what I call 'understanding' is different than having an "explanation." Researchers often create diagrams or a list of 'key insights' that attempt to explain what they've learned. Managers look at those diagrams and think they understand, but really they only have a story about what's out there in the world. The kind of understanding I find to be essential to the creative life of an organization is much more personal. It's the difference between reading the recipe and tasting the food, the difference between reading the rules and playing the game, or between reading about colour and looking through a prism. Quality attention -the kind that yields personal and organizational understanding- comes from direct experience with the world.

How are they similar?

For both research and design, what is standing in the way is not process or ideas but organizational culture. Organizations are complex systems, driven more by habit, belief, and story as by intellect. We see all sorts of symptoms, some stand in the way of real sensing -the cultural equivalent of hands over your ears- and others stand in the way of aligning actions with research results. For example, departments that don't talk to each other. We see organizations consistently oversimplifying the world, seeing customers, partners, markets and processes through the lens of mechanistic models handed down from the industrial age. However it is mainly humans that make the system, each with a will of their own in a social dance. Cause and effect are no longer something you can count on. An experimental approach is called for.

Both research and design are evolving in this model of complexity. Research is not only short term in its understanding. Resilient enterprises will recognize a grand shift as it unfolds. Design is being called upon to act with purpose, integrity, and coherence as a way of seeing and of being through iterations and helping embody different new possibilities.

How do you envision the future of research and design within the business context?

I envision an ecosystem with many creatures of all different sizes. They are all interrelated: their roots may intertwine at soil level, but also above the ground there is a natural exchange. They all thrive through this exchange.

Each of these creatures senses through its living processes the presence of the others in the environment and understands that the best way to have a healthy self is to have a healthy whole.

There is a continuous dynamic of learning and applying the learning. For example, a tree might sense that the soil is dry and grow its roots deeper. All responses become true, based on who each creature is and where it stands. It is a cycle of things coming and going, each in its own right, with resilience based on the ability to contribute and participate in the grand cycle.

Harmony on scale

Lekshmy Parameswaran
Director of Insights and Strategy
fuelfor healthcare innovation,
design, and consulting
Singapore

Who is Lekshmy?

Lekshmy Parameswaran is a founding partner at fuelfor, an experience design consultancy specialised in healthcare and co-located in Barcelona and Singapore. fuelfor develop award-winning products and services using a design thinking approach that they have specifically tailored for healthcare challenges.

What is research?

Research is the stage of any project that involves framing the right questions to address the particular issues involved in the project and the plotting out of how we are going to get to the answers.

Research gives inspiration, confidence, and credibility. Without research at the front end of a creative process we cannot create meaning and value for people.

The research process involves the setup of how we are going to get to the understanding of the issues within a project. We look at different research tools and compile a bespoke toolkit that can help us unpack the issues to get to the essence: not as a Q-and-A but in a multi-layered approach that allows us to get through the different levels of complexity.

What is design?

Design is the translation of an insight into some tangible and meaningful form. It can lead to different outcomes, e.g. a book, a clinic, a communications campaign The magic of design is in the translation: to embody meaning and communicate it.

Sometimes clients wonder why research is necessary as part of the design process. We find that the quality of the outcomes is precisely in the subtleties of the choices we make as we research and then design.

This leads to different qualities, features, communications, and messages. This is a joint process of seeking to understand and seeking to embody. In this way we work across and within the multiple layers of meaning and then bring it together in intuitive, design-driven ways. The result is that the people who are confronted with the outcome 'get it'. It makes sense to them, in their context yet via new interpretations and manifestations.

How are they different?

Researchers are driven by the need to report, capture, and convey what they truly saw, heard, and learnt through their research.

Designers, on the other hand, tend to be driven by inspiration. They empathize so much sometimes, that they tend to make huge leaps of synthesis.

Research wants to stay out of the solutions, whereas designers pull towards solutions. When research is done with the end in mind, driving towards design outcomes, it feels like this pulling in different directions enriches the process. The team is then like a big creature, with lots of eyes and the capacity to see at very different levels getting a much fuller picture.

The skills are different. Researchers are much better at the actual interaction, helping people to open up and share and get the conversation going. Designers that are involved in the research phase tend to be excellent at picking visual and atmospheric cues. Working together gives us extended abilities.

How are they similar?

Both research and design share the qualities of being creative, collaborative, and intuitive. Both of them have process and rigour.

Much like our thinking, which involves left-brain and right-brain abilities, research and design both require a dynamic and flexible approach to make sure we connect with the full scope of opportunity in any given project.

We take our clients into the research and involve them: so they get to immerse in the setting of the project while using their right-brain capacities as they go through a process that is systematic and analytical.

For design, we see that a lot of our clients are into 'design thinking': they like the idea that it is a nice, clean, linear process. When it gets down to 'design doing' and prototyping, things get messy and we shift out of the 'linear' comfort zone. For us, the total process is iterative, seamless and fluid.

The similarity between research and design as I see it, is in their generative capacity. Unlike market research where information is an end in itself, design research is a means to a design outcome. This means we are focused on where the research could lead as we move towards design.

Our clients tend to be very familiar with market research. We feel that market research reports need to be complemented. Those reports give data and evidence, in a way that can be distanced from reality and context. There is an underlying need in any business to connect with people in the context of their lives. This is where research and design have a role to play in order to help companies make the connection between so-called insights and business plans.

How do you envision the future of research and design within the business context?

I have drawn research, design and business in an integrated way. In my view, this is the only way forward: the idea of multiple disciplines working together. You could see my drawing as the generic description of a team working together to come up with more strategic solutions by combining right- and left-brain abilities.

Today we see that designers are educated to develop research and design skills in combination, this was not the case ten, fifteen years ago, and it is a positive development in design education. Today's designers can also conduct research and vice versa. This affects my drawing, since in the future there may not be three *separate* people working together, but these same three skills embodied in several people.

My ideal future is one of harmony on a larger scale, as opposed to just harmony in moments. This drawing represents that. We notice through our work that in order to get projects going we need to break through disharmony, building resilience to carry on. The resilience is built in those magical moments of harmony. Yet a lot of time is spent in helping people embrace change, to feel less threatened, to step into the unknown, to align views with the reality of the users. But a lot of our work is still about managing the energy within teams in order to move projects forward. My hope is for a future in which we can put the bulk of our energy where it is most meaningful and where the creative process can flow again.

Broad, connected networks

Abby Margolis, Director of Research And **Rich Radka,** Founding Partner
Claro Partners
Barcelona, Spain

Who are Abby and Rich?

Rich Radka has led technology, creative, and research teams for fifteen-plus years to creatively solve business problems in both developed and emerging markets. He is a founding partner at Claro Partners in Barcelona, Spain. Claro's mission is to transform understanding into value for people and for business.

Abby Margolis has an Anthropology PhD In her role as Director of Research at Claro Partners, she helps clients navigate disruptive shifts in business and society. Through her work Abby combines perspectives from social science, design and business to create frameworks that transform disruption into real opportunities for business innovation and service design.

What is research?

For us, research is part of a broader set of activities we simultaneously engage in to solve problems. Through research we uncover both what is important and what is unknown about a particular context or situation.

We are not really keen on terminology, though. The term research suggests a validating approach. We prefer to look at research through the social sciences without pigeonholing those skills. They are enablers to help us solve problems. The way to solve problems is to understand people and to apply tools in order to create solutions, but this needs to happen in an integrated way. Research is not 'phase one', which you have to clear before you do the rest of the phases.

Research is a continuous effort to make sense of the world by understanding what is important to people, where we think that things are going.

What is design?

Design, like research, is a verb. We don't see it simply as a skillset or a domain. We like to think of design with a big D: the Design of Solutions. Design is ultimately scheduling a problem for solutions.

Its not just people who went to design schools that do design. Actually, that can sometimes be limiting. If you do design at the simplest level, for example because you are hired to design some graphics, you will not have strategic impact and it would be wrong to expect so. The struggle here is how to integrate thinking and doing at a higher level.

How are they different?

Research and design are converging. In a world in which change is accelerating and business models can be copied very quickly, there is not only a need to make things more quickly.

We need to all bring in tools and processes from design thinking, theories from social sciences and start layering those in ways to help solve problems.

Research and design are like two different hats you can put on. They involve different skills, not different attitudes. Sometimes you need the big picture, the sweeping overview and models; other times you need to dive into the details and communicate that back within a particular context.

How are they similar?

It is no longer a matter of pointing in one direction and then building a bridge to get there. Conventional Strategy 101 processes have fallen apart. Improving what you already have doesn't work for most businesses anymore, their markets have been disrupted. You need a purpose. You need something that doesn't answer all the questions but that helps you answer the questions as you go along. If you know who you are and you know what people expect from you, then as things change you can continue to be relevant based on that purpose.

In this fast moving world, we need new approaches linked to creative skills and synthetic skills. We need nimble thinkers who think by doing and learn about what's going to work. People who are smart, who can make connections, and who can empathize with others. The underlying philosophy is that you need to create a bond with people.

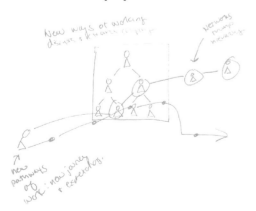

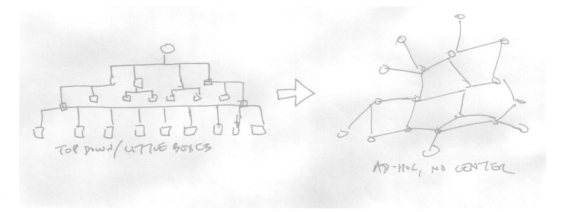

The real learning happens in the project as we learn together and create a synthesis together. This gives clients deep understanding and exposure to a new set of skills, which they seek not only as organizations but also as individuals.

How do you envision the future of research and design within the business context?

Rich has made a drawing to show our changing world. We can no longer deploy teams like an army in a hierarchical manner. We are moving towards a world in which people work together. To the left is the traditional hierarchy: a typical organizational chart with a big boss at the top and a structure in which everybody has their little role, in a little box that fits in a certain place. To the right is the new state: it is an organic and chaotic-looking network of ad-hoc connections between different people, with different experiences, points of view, skills, and passions.

Abby has made a drawing of what a new company might look like when we recognize that we are all nodes in a broader network. She is inspired by Anti-fragile: hierarchies are intrinsically fragile because being siloed makes them inherently more fragile than when they are connected. Networks that take on new forms can improve and learn and get better. The company of the future might look like her drawing: with porous boundaries, people coming in and out, networking within it and beyond it, coming together in different projects and fluid structures.

Both point to a future in which we all embrace and accept change as ongoing and in which business has understood that to get value out of the network you cannot control it but have to let strategies emerge from it.

Dynamic engagement

Sonia Machanda
Cofounder and Creative Chief
Idiom + Dream:in + Spread
Bangalore, India

Who is Sonia?

Sonia Manchanda is Cofounder and Design Chief at Idiom Design and Consulting, a vibrant trans-disciplinary design firm, and a design evangelist, leading projects with business leaders and corporations, making design thinking integral to their businesses, culture, brands, and experiences. Sonia is the initiator of the Dream:in project, recognized in 2013 as a global gamechanger and as a global platform for stirring up an entrepreneurial culture and empowering people.

What is research?

Research gives us a feel for how issues are forming and, instead of being a long and linear process, it is an integrated conversation in which we integrate research and synthesis as we keep bringing in all the information alongside with design development. At the beginning of any project, there is a stage in which you go deep to gather insights, talk to the customers, study benchmarks, involve a network of sounding boards to gather knowledge on different levels. We call this 'stage zero'.

Whenever we have an idea, a thought, a problem, an opportunity, or a challenge, we first look at this from 360 degrees. This is crucial and it is necessary because often we know we want to get from point A to point B, though we have no idea what or where point B is.

Once within the projects we have an ongoing approach, where everything merges into new solutions, taking into account qualitative research, quantitative research, ideas, and final execution and blending it together much like entrepreneurs do. A highly qualitative process of staying open and responsive to inputs, with a constant churn or synthesis, so that knowledge remains dynamic, informs decisions and actions. If research is an independent, one-time effort, knowledge runs the risk of becoming static.

What is design?

I see design as a way of approaching challenges opportunistically, with the conviction that in every problem lies an opportunity. Designers are able to see things positively -through a curious mindset that doesn't give up until it can create something that didn't exist before. Design knows that there are new spaces to be explored, new solutions to be developed with great elegance and beauty. Design seeks solutions that are unified, simpler, and better.

In the context of business, design can be a vehicle to take ideas to market with skill, speed, and imagination. Design gives ideas form and shape, fast and holistically so that people can respond to it. The refinement process then, is continuous.

Currently design is present in business in two ways:
a/ design interventions: where design participates in a limited capacity, as an intervention for a particular element in a business idea, like the design of a website, a product, or an experience.
b/ design as creation: where design is engaged in shaping and spreading an idea to help it grow and proliferate. Design becomes the process itself and fuses seamlessly with business. Here businesses are no longer driven by plans; rather, businesses are designed. They are shaped through a yin and a yang of business and design that collaborate to incubate ideas and make them grow,

I believe in the latter. That is the work we do. Design is an integral part of business: it nourishes it and helps it to grow by seizing opportunities.

How are they different?

Design and research both work together to get to the fundamental truth, something that will lead to a game-changing idea. They are not the same, but I find that they are not entirely different either.

I would say that research is divergent, generating lots of data, quantitative and qualitative. It is astute and looks for new answers. Design is convergent, bringing the answers together while remaining open and curious to get to the essence of the idea. Synthesis is the bridge between the two, where the search for truth takes place.

How are they similar?

Time is moving fast. Nothing is as obvious as it seems and there is a need to be innovative in the approach to projects of any kind. The similarity between design and research is in their openness, their ability to think outside of the box instead of with linearity. At the core, design and research have the same mindset: they are just different expressions of that mindset.

I think also that design is a research process as you learn through your design and that designing research is mandatory in order to

make the most of it, just like a design project. Research and design interact dynamically as the process of developing businesses evolves, while continuously focusing on the user and adapting to the changing context.

We are seeing that using the same proven and tested approach doesn't always work anymore. Particularly in a country with the diversity that India has. For example, you may want to design something for a given user group, but you are not them and it is not possible to generalize what they may need because you are looking at people's needs through your eyes. The similarity between research and design is that they go out there and look at the world through other people's eyes.

How do you envision the future of research and design within the business context?

I see design and business merging seamlessly as research flows through them.

Research is not a stage but a mindset, which flows through the various stages and versions of a business. As the business keeps evolving, research needs to engage dynamically. Design becomes the main driver of business growth.

There is a certain churn to this model: it is not circular and it is not linear. It is like a spinning wheel, where users are also the creators who help refine the ideas and develop business further.

Manifesting the future

Cathy Huang
Founder
CBi China Bridge
Shanghai, China

Who is Cathy?

Cathy Huang founded CBi China Bridge in 2003, the first insight-based innovation consulting firm in China. Years of successful design practice have allowed her to become an influential leader in the field of design today. Her 'Five Elements' theory and 'Observe, Learn, Ask and Interact' methods have been acknowledged and appreciated by professional and academic societies.

What is research?

Research informs businesses' decision-making. It is the foundation. Research provides information from many angles: through market studies, competitive analysis, company identity, client profiles, etcetera.

You could compare a company with a person. Research is like food, it is something you ingest and you incorporate into the body. It is essential; without it a company has no foundation. Research is like the nutrients that you take into the body; however, whether it is transferred into energy is up to the body. That is not something that research, as food, can force upon business.

Continuing with this analogy, I would say, research is at the source, and the purer and more organic the source, the better. Like food, when you know where it comes from it is honest, it is unpolluted and it is useful. Otherwise it will hurt the body, as bad research ultimately hurts business.

What is design?

Design is the act of making things real. Design turns research into ideas and ideas into implementation. Design is the process of abstracting the research and then applying it to create something useful your organization needs.

Again, if we compare a company with a person's body we will see that the five vital organs are interrelated. In Chinese medicine, the system of vital organs is referred to as *zang-fu*. Everything is interconnected. This is also true for design because design is the creative process of transferring research input into ideas, products, services, and any solution that will help organizations be more competitive.

How are they different?

Well, you can research a lot and never really get to ideas. Traditional market research and academic research both do research that is never put into practice to create things. They seek better wordings, papers and publications, reports and presentations but never really go beyond the conclusions and findings. And government is actually funding this. As are big corporations because there are still many business people who like numbers as the easy way to account for their decisions and back themselves up by 'research', even if there is no obvious connection. Research for the sake of research is meaningless,

Design is a process that turns input into output. However, without research design is like a magic wand. People think you just wave the magic wand and come up with something pretty.

More often that not they work separately, though designers increasingly understand that they have to embrace research as a method to communicate to higher levels in the organization.

Designers have a greater chance of their ideas gaining buy-in when they adopt research. Not just qualitative but also data-oriented research at that.

How are they similar?

I would state four areas of similarity: curiosity, an open-mind, explanation and the ability to make the unknowns visible.

There is a difference in approach. Both research and design are part of a process. This process is all over the place nowadays; anywhere you look you will see people going through the phases of Discover, Define, Develop, and Deliver. All these processes are the same, with slightly different names.

Research is to help clients to look at what they could do next: what is their next product, their next service, their next competitive advantage, their next market, and so on. And it only really works when the process and tools are not fixed. It is the people that execute the processes that make the difference. Mainly through collaboration: amongst themselves as a team, with the client, with the users.

The same is true for design. Design is about shaping the next product, service, competitive advantage, or new solution. But it only works when there is an environment that nurtures the innovative culture: open-mindedness, collaboration, open discussions of the chal-

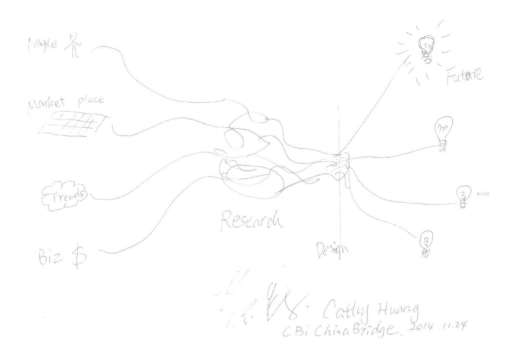

lenges, joint definition, and redefinition of the scope.-not as individuals behind desks but as a collaborative team effort.

How do you envision the future of research and design within the business context?

To the left I have drawn research: for it is needed to research different things: people, the market place, trends, business needs, etc.

Research then mixes this information into considerations for design. Design, in turn: filters, refines, extracts this information into something useful, tuning in to opportunity and turning ideas into what manifests as the future.

Shorter iterative cycles

Ashlee Riordan
Research Lead
Thick
Melbourne, Australia

Who is Ashlee?

Ashlee Riordan works for Thick. They help organizations to have a positive, sustainable impact on the world, whether it be social, environmental, or economic. Thick's clients generally belong to the Australian government, healthcare, education, and not-for-profit sectors, but they work with select commercial clients too. At Thick, Ashlee leads design research and straddles service design and strategy. Her passion is for helping organizations to learn what they need to know, so they can decide what they need to create, and get where they need to go.

What is research?

Primarily, research is a learning process. We all do research all of the time, its how we inform decisions and it's what enables our agency. In the business world it is more formal and structured because we need to show how we came to certain conclusions, but essentially it happens all the time.

Research can be about exploration or it can be about confirming and testing our understanding. As an explorative process, research allows us to learn deeply about the world and understand how it works. In such cases, the point is to describe the state of something so that we may understand it and then make decisions about what we want to do. Confirmatory or experimental research is about establishing feedback loops as we interact with reality with the goal of changing it. It is about testing the impact of our actions on a given slice of reality or system -measuring changes, testing cause and effect, or assessing the effectiveness of efficiency of the changes we are making to the products, services, websites, apps, etc. we are looking to improve.

Both types of research are necessary and it is important to select methods and techniques that are fit for purpose. Qualitative, social research techniques are valuable because they are people-centric; they are geared to learning about people's different experiences of reality. Qualitative research traditions come from a point of view that you can learn from the differences in people's subjective realities. Quantitative research in the business world is usually more product- or service-centric and helps us to know if things actually work and how we might help our products and services deliver the value to people, in the most efficient and effective way possible.

What is design?

Design is a creative problem-solving process. The outcome of design involves the transformation of an idea into something novel, purposeful, useful. At the conceptual level, design is something you can apply to anything, tangible or intangible.

Because the process of design can be tailored for many different goals, the design discipline appears to the outside world to be a very fragmented discipline. However, the unifying aspect of design as a discipline is that it is a creative pursuit. Designers apply creativity to deliver an outcome. There is an art to it; there is a point at which there are no hard and fast rules you can follow or sets of criteria you can apply.

This means that good design entails the use of intuitive criteria that help the designer know when something is meets the mark. To an extent, this may seem like it is just a matter of opinion, but designers develop intuitive sets of criteria over time and with experience. Expert judgment is like a muscle that needs training and practice to develop, and importantly, it is not something you can learn to master academically.

How are they different?

Research's goal is learning. Design's goal is creation. They are different points in a larger process and they each fulfil different needs.

The bigger, meta process is a strategic one, with the aim to learn about the world and interact with it to achieve a goal. Within it, research and design are complementary activities. You could think of 'strategy' as the operating principles which define why research or design might be useful and instrumental to get from point A to point B. Implementing strategy fundamentally requires a combination of both research and design activities.

At an abstract level research relies on critical thinking whereas design is arguably slightly more skewed towards creative thinking. Research uses the critical thinking to analyze, synthesize, and put things into frameworks by teasing out the relationships between things. For design, the differences are the creative cycles. While designers also use the critical skills for the evaluative part of those cycles, the goals of design are principally creative. When you think about them as components of a larger process, design and research balance out creative and critical thinking almost like the flipped image of one another.

"Research's goal is learning. Design's goal is creation. They are different points in a larger process."

When you consider them both as part of a larger process, really one cannot exist without the other.

How are they similar?

Both research and design are strategic processes. They are about figuring out how to move from point A to point B. Research is about figuring out what is known versus what is not known. It's about reducing a knowledge gap.

Design bridges a different gap; the gap between what doesn't exist and something that will exist.

Neither research nor design is a hard and fast science; they both have an 'art' component. They both require human interpretation and judgment at different points in the process. Researchers frequently make choices about what information gets transformed into insight.

When researching complex social systems, these choices are often guided by your gut and rationalized later. As I mentioned earlier, the same is true of designers and how they figure out when perfection is reached. Both research and design require a certain maturity and experience of practitioners before work can be meaningful and useful.

How do you envision the future of research and design within the business context?

In my drawing, I have divided reality in two. On one side is the reality as experienced from within organizations. On the other side is the larger reality of what is going on holistically in the world. The outside reality is changing and dynamic, which is why the ability to keep up with the pace of change is so difficult and important for organizations. The border between the two is a dotted line that I have dubbed 'seam of compatibility'.

When researchers and designers sit at the strategy table, two things happen. Researchers bring an appreciation of how complex and dynamic reality actually is by making the dynamics of that reality visible to the organization. Designers bring an appreciation for rapid iteration and shorter design cycles.

The result of these two things is that organizational research and design cycles become shorter, iterations occur more and more rapidly, allowing organizations to remain informed

as reality changes and therefore able to adjust their efforts appropriately. Currently, in many organizations, those cycles are too long and it is critical that business leaders understand that it is a giant waste of effort to develop strategies in long cycles because any new product or service will be out of date by the time it reaches the market. We are seeing this shortening of research and design cycles already

across the more innovative and sophisticated organizations of the world. In the future, as more companies invite research and design to support strategy, we will see an increasingly fine-tuned ability to stay connected with the dynamics of complex adaptive systems, which, at the end of the day, translates into more effective and efficient use of precious natural and human resources.

Reconnecting with our humanity

Miguel Melgarejo Fuentes
Senior Innovation Consultant
Cirklo
Mexico City, Mexico

Who is Miguel?

Miguel Melgarejo is a Mexican designer focused on social innovation, strategy development, and the promotion of the design discipline. His work focuses on qualitative research, generation of business models, and systems for products and services across multiple industries.

What is research?

Research is an excuse to understand what is really going on. I think we all go about our lives without really questioning anything. We just assume we know or accept things as they are.

Research allows us to pull the world apart into tinier explanations and helps us make sense of how it all builds up to form a system, with its own parts and purposes. Even if we are not researching something really big, research is the starting point of breaking the whole into smaller parts so that we can understand how those sub-parts interconnect or don't connect and why. Sometimes things seem connected but they are not. Sometimes they seem disconnected and there are in reality a lot of connections and ongoing processes that were overlooked at first sight.

For research to be effective it needs to meet a couple of conditions. First, it requires an open mind and the ability to see things as if for the first time. Letting go of pre-definitions requires a certain degree of freedom that can vary depending on the context in which the research is conducted. Some constraints are of course okay, but within the defined search area the research needs to be an exploration, without biases or preconceptions if we are going to learn anything new. The second condition is that there needs to be an interpretation based on the information gathered, a new deductive conclusion that stems from the observations and unifies the findings in a new understanding. This new understanding is what makes research actually valuable and not just an exercise of observation and fact finding.

What is design?

Design is a discipline which allows you to see the world in a new way. With design you can imagine a different future, define courses of action to achieve it, and then create solutions that challenge the current reality and impact it towards shaping the new reality you envision.

Design requires the abilities to
• understand what is going on and what could be changed,
• imagine a different situation or outcome by making links/connections and creating a proto-type in your mind by making new combinations
• and finally as a last step making the solutions tangible in the form of a product or a service.

I think that the ability to deductively link understanding to different possible outcomes and creating a new projected reality is the core of what design does. In my career as a design-er I initially felt very limited by the idea that all I had to do is create an artefact. From the moment that I came to realize that design is a mindset, I understood my role as a designer of solutions. This significantly changed the way I approached the creative process, it is no longer just outcome driven. It is an open process in which one progressively learns.

There simply is no design unless there is a process. Without process, it is an expressive form which you could call art. The process is the instrument of design because you form and shape your practices as you design. As a design practitioner you also design yourself: you gain understanding of what you can contribute, how you can contribute, where you need others, where and how you evolve in your practice and understanding.

How are they different?

The end result of research is the understanding of a reality. The end result of design is the projection of a reality. This is where they differ because, in this sense, design has a stronger pull and a greater responsibility towards building a new reality.

Design triggers an effect that goes beyond just understanding or explaining. I think in a sense design is more subtle. What design wants to achieve is an effect, not just communicate information.

I have this image of design, in which designers 'object' reality. Just like in the movies where lawyers looking for the truth interfere with the presentation of facts by saying loudly: 'I object, your Honour'. What designers do is they 'object' reality. It sounds like a play of words because we make objects, traditionally. But it's like we introduce a new object into the reality around us and thus change the reality,

impacting it through our interventions and creations. In this sense it is different from research. It feels like researchers look for a different kind of 'truth': they don't look for ways to change things; they look for ways to explain. They don't look to 'object' or say what is wrong, surprising or could be different. They look for object-ivity. Plain and simple, yet so important as a starting point for understanding.

How are they similar?

The similarity is that they both contribute towards creating meaning. Research puts explanations into words, creating the possibility to develop a common language and communicate about what goes on around us.

Research and design go together. The purpose of designing may be more or less linked to the purpose of research, depending on the challenge at hand.

In the business world where things have gotten complicated and there is a whole system that requires designing or redesigning, research is essential. You cannot see the whole system; it is crucial to understand it systemically, through its dynamics and sub-parts.

While the explanations research provides go through the rational route of presentations, graphs, and other models, design focuses on tailoring solutions that will work.

And both are necessary. Our clients are humans too. A lot of what design does feels right to them, although the term 'design' is still foreign. Design is a medium for realizing change by making things work for people in business because people can see things working for them.

Yet design alone could not do the whole job because we would try to drive change too quickly versus the understanding that the system has of itself and that could be counterproductive. The added value of research is creating a common understanding and a common language so that the issues that need attention or need changing can be addressed while creating a basis for adoption by the system (the business) itself.

Addressing the identified issues through joint programmes and initiatives is important because it increases ownability by the user, something that design knows how to make happen. We see it in our work at Cirklo: a lot of what we do is labelled 'pilot' or 'experiment so that the clients can experience the result and the impact of design without scaring off everyone with solutions that are ready to implement without them understanding their meaning, their purpose, or how it even fits the broader scheme of things. We can then scale from there, having proven that it will work for them. And once people believe, magic happens and things take flight.

"Designers 'object' reality."

How do you envision the future of research and design within the business context?

I have drawn a person. My feeling is that in business today the human aspect has been lost. Once we engage together by learning to understand and learning to design, we will reconnect with our own humanity. It is like a returning to being, a possibility to open up again. Without openness there is no connection and without connection we cannot build meaningful businesses that are sustainable across time.

One dynamic evolving system

Ari Popper
Founder and CEO
SciFutures
Los Angeles, California, USA

Who is Ari?

Ari Popper is the Founder and CEO of SciFutures, a foresight and innovation agency that uses sci-fi prototyping to help their clients create meaningful change that is relevant for the Exponential Age. He is a passionate sci-fi fan and amateur sci-fi writer.

What is research?

Research is the process of understanding the world in certain given conditions. The aim of research is to get clarity and insight on whatever subject we're exploring. This is done via inquiry in a structured way.

I think research can be done for two reasons, the yin-yang of the research practice:
• Research to satisfy intellectual hunger and curiosity. This is research in its purest form and it is used to understand the conditions and conditionings around us. I think all people and business ultimately, in one way or other want to move forward. Moving forward necessitates an understanding of where we are here and now. Research is then aimed at gaining that understanding and it is a natural human need to make sense of the world around us.
• Research as insurance. This is research in its controlling form. It is used to dot the i's and cross the t's as due diligence without any other goal than to justify actions. It's an easy way out because people are used to seeing research as part of a process. It is research by inertia which may or may not be used; it probably won't. Stakeholders will want to judge and evaluate any endeavour based on facts. So this second kind of research is based on that: providing some kind of argumentation or back up for something you want to do.

The research practice is having a hard time within the business context. For a long time the dominant paradigm has been one of left-brained, analytical, factory-like, and empirical-scientific skills. This has served its purpose, but it is now breaking down. I call the current paradigm 'the exponential age'. The conditions around us are changing so fast that any tool used to looking at the existing conditions is per se obsolete. This is why most research is ineffective: because it goes out of date so fast.

A well-known and frequently cited example is McKinsey's 1980 prediction that mobile phones in the United States would reach a grand total of 900,000 mobile phones by 2000. The actual number by the year 2000 was of 109 Million. This prediction guided the decision-making at some telecom giants, who only entered the mobile market too late once the writing was on the wall and the signs that this was a huge, booming segment were here to stay.

The assumptions that underpin research have to change. Some businesses that buy research and many of those who produce it have an outdated view. They have this idea that if you research a topic, your findings are valid and predictive for an extended period of time. But the usefulness of research fades because the conditions change. If you are looking and reporting on existing conditions, once you report this information it is already obsolete. Conditions change continuously and they change fast.

"Both research and design can be creative, dynamic, intuitive, flexible, and robust."

What is design?

Good design is taking an existing condition and making it useful. Great design can change the world and literally transform society and cultures.

An eloquent and beautiful design is an articulation of how the world could be, typically in the form of products. Design is a form of inspiration: it is beautiful, intelligent, useful, and human. Design makes the unreal real. It helps to conceptualize and bring to life what did not exist in the real world.

We work with thought design and narrative design to come up with new futures. The power of stories is just incredible. Stories are a way of articulating new realities taking into account our fundamental humanity. Human beings are social creatures with basic needs and basic truths. Humans like storytelling because they can relate and connect to the stories. It is a language that we all understand, that appeals to our emotion, to our imagination, and to our ability to collaborate and build on each other's stories through our own interpretation.

People's belief systems shift through stories, sometimes more so than through facts. This is scientifically proven. There have been experiments to see how far stories would go. And guess what? People believe stories more than facts even when they have been informed in advance that the story is not true. That is huge power, and it has to be dealt with appropriately. So, if together we can build stories that connect, that inspire, that motivate,we can make positive changes, that include everyone. Design has the capacity to narrate new, meaningful stories. And this can be world changing.

How are they different?

Research is about inquiry. But unlike design, it is limited to the here and now. And that can be constraining. Because research ultimately over-emphasizes linear- and conditional thinking, which is not conducive to building the future. You don't want to put time and space constraints into the future, simply because when you create something in the here and now, its valid in the context of the here and now. And you can be certain that tomorrow's context will be different.

I think in the best of circumstances research can be supportive and constructive. Yet design goes beyond that, adding dimensions of human-centricity, imagination, and creativity. Design has a goal, it wants to get to a new articulation of something. It needs inquiry, too, but also goes beyond that in order to learn and apply the learnings. Any good designer knows that research can inform and guide the design process.

How are they similar?

At its best, research should feel like good design. I think research has lost touch with that. Both research and design can be creative, dynamic, intuitive, flexible and robust.

In the end, technology is just technology. It's just gadgets if it doesn't have utility. It is meaningless if it is empty of human connection. For this reason a good designer will always need to do research, to guide and inform the design process.

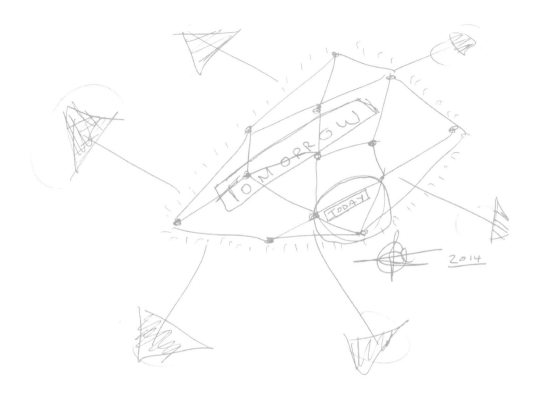

How do you envision the future of research and design within the business context?

I envision a future in which we are truly, humanly connected. We are joined by our ever-increasing understanding of what it means to be human. The dots represent people, businesses, customers, and human beings in all kinds of interconnected relationships, which are represented by the lines.

In the future, we will have acknowledged through our behaviours that we are one big dynamic and evolving system. Right now, our understanding and thus our behaviour in accordance with that idea is about 'this' small.

Smarter together

Slava Kozlov
Co-founder
Summ()n
Eindhoven/Astana/Moscow
Netherlands/Kazakhstan/Russia

Who is Slava?

Slava Kozlov is a co-founder and director of Summ( )n, the Netherlands-based collective that supports companies and organizations in their strategic innovation initiatives. Summ( )n provides in-depth understanding of people's behaviour and values today and explores the societies and cultures of tomorrow, helping to change personal and collective mindsets using 'serious games' and other transformative techniques.

What is research?

Research has a role of informing what is happening today and inspiring to imagine what could be possible tomorrow.

Informing and inspiring is not only about going into the field, gathering insights and reporting those back, expecting the results to speak on their own. Research has evolved as an activity: now it is more participatory, more active, more pragmatic, and more opportunistic. The goal of research is not to produce stand-alone 'data' or even 'insights' since it does not really allow people to experience for themselves the implications of what is being shown.

I think research has the role to help us understand people better, to understand their activities in contextually-based situations and in a more systemic way. We need to move from reductionist frameworks of treating people as 'users', 'consumers', or 'patients' toward more holistic view, of seeing people as, well, 'people', complex beings acting in different social and cultural contexts.

Understanding people is as much about today's practices as about the possible practices of tomorrow. We do it by exploring, probing these possible futures, and by using new methods that will help us understand the ever-changing nature of the relationship between people and products/services/propositions.

What is design?

Design is about inspiration and 'showing' what could be potentially possible. It is a way of thinking differently and continuously challenging oneself to stretch the boundaries.

The aim of design is to create these possibilities, not through getting more certainty, but by increasing uncertainty. This opens up new, unpredictable scenarios, which you cannot predefine nor foresee from the start.

The approach of design is iterative, through prototyping, creating and feedback loops. It also helps to obtain better understanding by playing with alternatives, by suspending beliefs of the existing paradigms, and by developing the alternatives. It is an iterative process of playing, reflecting, and playing again. Not being afraid to make the wrong things is very crucial, because there is simply not such a thing as a wrong draft.

How are they different?

The difference is in the tension between their roles of informing and inspiring. Researchers seek to inform, which per definition means that they will look to collect accurate, grounded information. Increasingly this is being done in new, broader, more contextual, ways, which helps to widen the ideas but also verify them more.

"Research and design require the ability to suspend one's own assumptions."

Design goes beyond that. From its role of inspiring it helps construct, show, visualize, experience. Design is not just about the outer layer, the exterior or look and feel.

Design is way more than merely 'look and feel', it can really redefine the role that certain products play in our life, or even create entirely new roles. But to do so is a very hard work. Thus there are a lot of sketches, iterations, trials and errors as well as dead-ends before a relevant design can be created.

How are they similar?

Both for design and for research, open-endedness is a key aspect. These are both disciplines in which you simply do not know what will happen until you get going. They require a mindset of openness and the ability to suspend one's owns assumptions for the purposes of discovery.

There are a lot of similarities: they are both about exploring the new, about future probing and multiple encounters. I think there is a lot to be won by the integration of the skills in an iterative exchange because while they are similar, they are not the same. We need a multiple encounter approach interweaving research and design, where we iterate understanding and experiencing. As these develop and intertwine, we can co-develop an aligned vision of the future.

It is still very infrequent though, to join the similarities into a blended pool of skills. I think there is a lot to be gained here, by enhancing the collaboration in a process of co-discovery, where designers are brought into the field to gather insights and experience what is happening, where researchers participate in the acting out of scenarios and playing with possibility, where in the process we better

understand both what is happening and how we could contribute. These are transformative processes where we all learn to think differently and embrace duality, or even multiplicity.

How do you envision the future of research and design within the business context?

I envision it in the form of a neuronet with different hubs connected to each other. This network is similar to our brains, but out in the open with no skull around it. Businesses are not one hub. There is no such thing as one brand or one company. It is all a connected and collaborative system.

Design and research could be seen as neuro-transmitters within the network. Their role is to facilitate extra connections. Research is busy with the flow of making connections by understanding whether they are possible and what is needed to make them possible.

- companies, organizations, agencies

- existing connections

- exploration of new possibilities (Research)

- making new connections (Design)

Design's role is to make those connections real, to forge them and make bridges so that the connection becomes alive, pulsating and conductive. Design facilitates the process of stretching the neurons so that synapses can grow and reconnect.

In the future, what we see, therefore, is that the whole brain gets smarter and the whole network gets wiser. One neuron can not be smart. We all get smarter together.

Intertwining flow

Martta Oliveira
Service Designer
Engine Service Design
London, United Kingdom

Who is Martta?

Martta Oliveira is a Finnish-Portuguese Service Designer based in London. Her background is in management, and she has training in design thinking and innovation. She has worked and studied across Europe and Asia, and is passionate about designing meaningful services. In the past she has worked in a range of consulting firms specializing in service innovation, digital strategy, and operational excellence, now she works at Engine Service Design.

What is research?

Research encompasses the process of answering questions, discovering possible solutions and finding your way in a particular context.

Within the design process of discover, define, develop and deliver, research is the first step, but it also happens at other stages of a project. Research is fluid; it happens in various different moments and feeds into the generation of solutions. It is an integral part of an iterative cycle.

In my view, any time that you are understanding the context and the needs, synthesizing those learnings and refining what you've done with those learnings by asking new questions: you are researching.

What is design?

Design is about bettering things. You design things to improve them, in any way. Whether it is aesthetics, functionality, or any potential way of improving things for society, for the users, for service providers.

The most defining characteristics of design are a process, which you follow, that allows you to infuse empathy into what you are designing, whether it is a service or a product or anything else.

Business problems do not happen in a vacuum, and design brings in the contextual aspects into the generation of solutions. It does not assume that the world is stable; it actually assumes that it changes all the time and it integrates this into the process of making things better.

How are they different?

Research is a part of the design process. It is design. You could see them as concentric circles, with research in the middle of design. By nature, research is an essential part of design. However, design goes a step further. Research informs the design process, and then design creates an output.

In order to make things better through design, you need to know how things could get better. That is the role of research in the design process. Beyond that, there are moments in the process where you are not researching, at those moments you are designing the solution by fine-tuning it further based on what you've learnt, visualizing and explaining, or creating solutions. For example when you produce a service blueprint. At other moments you are learning more intuitively by interpreting behaviour that has been revealed through research or understanding what has not been said; these activities are design activities that go beyond research.

So there is a slight difference, in that design is broader than research and needs to be informed by it. But they are not separate; they need one another in order to arrive at solutions. For design to be successful, every aspect of the outcome must make sense to the people you are designing for, which is what you get from research. Whether you are creating a journey map, a persona, a service blueprint or the end solution you generate, it all needs to be in line with the research.

Perhaps the key difference is in what they put value in. If we pull research and design apart to its more extreme forms in order to better understand them there are differences in how they contribute to the total process. Research focuses on the process of research and the outcomes thereof, because its aim is to produce learnings that will enhance the design process going forward. Whereas the designer is focused on the end product of the design, on finding the solution that will solve the problems.

How are they similar?

There is an important similarity in that they both bring empathy into the process. It is thanks to research that design adds value to business because it really boils down to creating empathy with the customer or with the user. It's about understanding how things work, and this it where research and design add value: not as a separate activities but as part of a whole creative process.

I find that the moment you start sharing the process within the team, research and design

morph into one. Whether it is during work-shops to further deepen what you've learnt and what you are doing with those lessons. or while testing things out to better understand the constraints that affect your prototype and interpret the type of need for the solution you are creating, they both start flowing together and merge into one. I would say that research never leaves the design process; it is always there ready to jump in and support as needed by keeping a link with the context.

Finally, I would say that research and design both work well in chaotic environments. They can cope with chaos because they follow structured processes that make them work by applying a structured approach to dealing with complexity and chaos. They help us under-stand how things are evolving and moving and how to move forward from there.

How do you envision the future of research and design within the business context?

I have drawn a braid-like flow in which you see business and design intertwining. They each come from different places, and they are tangling with each other to become one. In the process of integrating design into business I envision a future in which busi-ness and design collide in a positive way, crossing over a chasm and merging into a new way of doing things.

There are some arrows coming out of the braid to symbolize what is lost in the process. These are the things that don't really matter: old preconceptions, old ways of doing things, and anything that does not add value. In that process we will be distilling the essence of design and business, generating a better future together.

Continuous Beta-mode

Nicolas Pimentel, Co-founder and **May Groppo,** cultural transformation consultant
+Castro Innovation House
Buenos Aires, Argentina

Who are Nico and May?

Nicolas Pimentel has been working in brand experiences for more than seventeen years. Before opening +Castro he was BBDO Argentina's Director of Integrated Communications. Under his lead +Castro was selected a creative standout in 2012 by Creativity Magazine. Nico has been identified as one of LatinAmerica's top creative talents.

May Groppo has a hyper-eclectic background. As a cultural curator, May Groppo has been a pioneer in Latin America for the past decade. She initiated the PechaKucha Night in Buenos Aires and launched the first crowdfunding platform in Latin America called Ideame. She likes empowering people and leads a multi-disciplinary team at +Castro that helps bring about cultural changes within organizations.

What is research?

Research is the necessary process you go through when trying to understand a problem or an issue.

Great research contains an element of curiosity, of taking the matter you want to investigate seriously, and the daring of finding things you didn't even know you were looking for.

Insights keep evolving and changing throughout the process. It is not about predictions or even macro and micro trends. Research allows us to test and retest our hypotheses as these take shape in the creative process. First in a more abstract way, and then becoming increasingly tangible in the type of research we do, getting closer to the user and to the context where those ideas will manifest and act.

What is design?

We see design as a focal lens that allows us to prioritize. From the totality of possibilities available to solve any given challenge, design allows us to discard and underline, guiding our creative process as we separate wheat from chaff. Design provides us with a blueprint which evolves and iterates as we take something to its best possible version.

Probably one of the main skills when designing is knowing what is good enough and what needs more work. Everything can be perfected. All of the information and insights you gather could potentially be useful. This part of the process alone could go on forever. However, design as a skill allows us to know what to let go of during the process and therefore also what to keep.

How are they different?

The difference lies in that research not necessarily leads into action. In design there is action, it is intrinsic to the act of designing. Design internalizes the knowledge, experiences the possibilities. It is not just about knowledge as a cognitive discipline; it is about applied knowledge.

The traditional separation of research and design as is often seen within business, has led to an over-emphasis of abstraction and synthesis, and while these can be relevant to gain understanding they do not exist as such in the real world. So statistics, hard facts, etc are nothing on their own.

In large corporations, research and design have been divided, they are separate activities.

"To get to the heart of the matter you need to experience it, get close to it, to live it."

This leads to a lot of inefficiencies across the system: in budget spend, in the time lost in meetings, in the dissonance in the communication. These inefficiencies have been covered up or hidden for long.

But in a world in which absolute certainties and defined 'truths' are crumbling, on all orders of life -religious, political, you name it- there is no place for inefficiencies caused by disconnection in organizations. We are in an era in which we are allowed and even empowered to question anything and everything: the tools and the method, the how and the what.

This may cause the differences between research and design to narrow down in the coming years. In fact, they are already blending into each other, taking new forms. We are seeing in our clients the need to give shape to their ambitions and dreams and to give resolutions to their problems. These organizations are looking for tangible results and for messages that they can own. Not to be state-of-the-art or bigger/faster/cheaper than their competitors as they traditionally aimed, but in order to shape their companies and brands through a connection with the user that is lasting and relevant.

How are they similar?

Both research and design are continuous processes. In this day and age one needs to keep scanning the possibilities, the changing landscape. We see it as our responsibility to stay in touch with the world, to feel what is going on, to experience the emerging culture around us.

In our practice we combine research and design by what we call 'chronic curiosity', an attitude which defines us because we take nothing for granted. If we are not continuously asking questions, it is highly unlikely that we will be in any position to help our clients find answers.

In our pre-idea phase we do a lot of research. But as the idea keeps taking shape we don't stop researching because research helps us contrast and compare with what is out there and keep shaping our ideas.

Research and design are linked to human behaviour. Both in the perspective of the user as within business teams. For all people, whether user, manager, designer, researcher, what works best is to use your common sense. We need to regain touch with our common sense. Otherwise things get pretty weird. Why would anyone look for solutions if they haven't even understood the problem? Is there even a problem? And does it even matter? Research and design are curious: they dare to question the question and then to defy the answers. To get to the heart of any matter you need to experience it, get close to it, to live it. If those of us who design solutions get distanced from those who use our solutions, all we will have been doing is an exercise of our imagination.

How do you envision the future of research and design within the business context?

We envision lots of happy people: people who feel listened to, people who can reach their potential by co-creating solutions based on true talent and not blah-blah or imposed roles, people who are connected and interconnected. We imagine a world where companies are in continued Beta-mode: they are based on algorithms that keep mutating, keep taking new

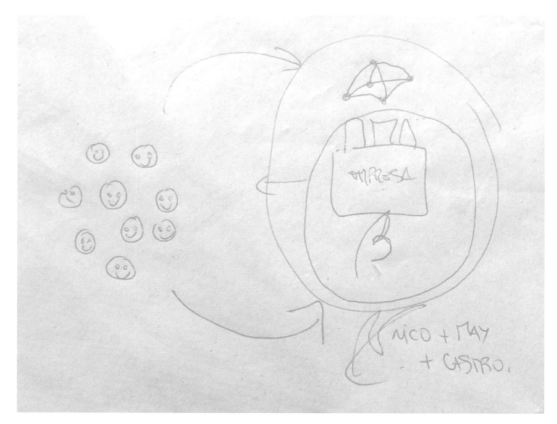

forms, and keep providing better solutions. There will still be a lot of uncertainty, but we will finally have understood that the angst that goes with uncertainty is linked to the daring of those who change the world for the better. And we will also see that it can be done, by working collaboratively and by humanizing the interaction between companies, brands and people.

Emerging practices

Every single one of these conversations has been valuable in trying to understand how research and design are changing in practice to support business. The inspiration that they all provide is that you must do. If there is one common element amongst the pioneers it is the fearlessness with which they embark on their own adventure as agencies, relying on their skills and their ability to make sense of the world by interpreting, by doing and by learning.

In this age of creative empowerment that is perhaps the most important lesson for business: strategy is better when we dare to embark on it as a journey, when we dare to acknowledge all that we don't know in order to open up what can be known and what can be discovered and rediscovered -the ability to learn openly, to build strength out of diversity in teams, and to integrate it all in meaningful ways.

These conversations constitute a point in time. Both in the evolution and growth of those interviewed as in our collective levels of consciousness and awareness. They show us what is happening: we are opening up as human systems, in order to integrate new learnings and new skills that make us more adaptive to the complexities of our changing context.

The pioneers show us the value of anticipation, not merely as a tool to pre-empt competition or gain advantage above others, but as a way to stay in tune with the world around us. They show us the value of collaboration, not as a way gain access to specialized views, but as a way to open our perspectives and create fertile ground for new combinations and connections. And they show us the value of adventure in a path that is not linear, where there is value in daring to take the plunge and a thrill in venturing into the unknown to emerge more connected, more involved and more aware of our effect within the context.

6 CONVERGING TOWARDS COLLABORATION

'A traveller who has
lost his way, should
not ask: Where am I?
What he really wants
to know is, Where
are other places?'

–Alfred North Whitehead

Purposeful convergence

The experts interviewed in this chapter are academics, recognized leaders of professional associations, and most are also published authors on these topics. They have been chosen by their ability to contribute their views, their eloquence, and their clarity of vision. Interviewing experts gives a view into the state-of the art and emerging explanations for how practice is changing, and the consequences of these changes on how the disciplines are understood and taught.

The dialogues

All interviews were conducted in the form of a live dialogue, a conversation on the topics of research, strategy, and design. The structure of these conversations is the same as with the pioneers: we addressed the same four questions, then the experts each made a drawing and reflected on their drawing by answering one final question.

The questions of What is research? What is design? How are they different? and How are they similar? and How do you envision the future of research and design within the business context? are very difficult to answer because we are in a period of change. There are no right or wrong answers and there are no ready-made definitions of these subjects. My aim was not to get to definitions but to provoke a conversation in order to understand how the thinking is taking shape at the expert level. How do those who actively research these subjects look at how they are emerging, transforming, and merging? Each conversation is unique because, like with the pioneers, the dialogues took the form that the interviewees gave them. My role was to offer a structure and a space in which these dialogues could take shape.

Like the pioneers, the experts were also asked to make illustrations[1] at the end of each dialogue. The reason for this request is that putting things into words necessitates left-brained skills: we artificially break up concepts into words in order to transmit our thinking. Also here I wanted the interviewees also to engage their right brains in order to distill the essence of what they were saying. Drawing is a holistic, integrative activity and especially important to help us see where things are going in the views of the different experts all over the world. The result is a wonderful gallery of illustrations that depict the future of research, strategy, and design as well as detailed, revealing explanations of what is happening and how research and design are transforming business strategy.

Interconnecting disciplines

Naturally, many of the experts have to label their work depending on the disciplinary area in which they are active. These labels are not strict; they just help define the place they take within the academic or professional arena. Their disciplines and the ways in which they themselves view them are changing too. In this changing world, none of the labels are static.

We are moving towards a networked and interconnected future in which collaboration is the central theme to bringing skills together and joining our transformative power to generate better strategies, create better business, and ultimately contribute to a better world.

In the interconnected space of research, strategy, and design the interviews span the full scope of backgrounds, including experts from business schools, to research associations, and design schools. A total of twenty-one experts participated in the interviews, which I have organized in clockwise direction around the convergence of these three disciplines: from strategy to research to design.

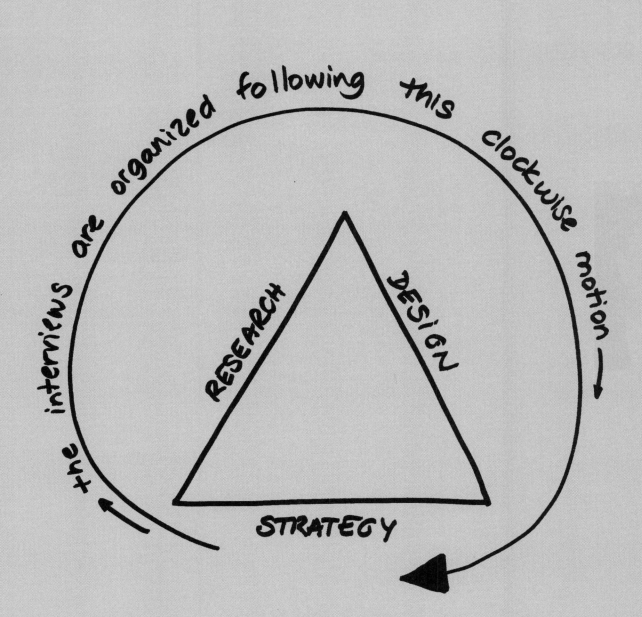

A learning ecosystem

Prof. Henry Robben
Professor of Marketing
Nyenrode Business University
Breukelen, The Netherlands

Who is Henry?

Henry Robben is Professor of Marketing at Nyenrode. His research interests include strategic marketing, innovation management, and new product development. He has regularly published on these and other topics in academic journals. Henry has co-authored several books, is a regular speaker at academic and managerial conferences, and acts as an independent consultant to companies.

What is research?

Research is the systematic and replicable search for answers. In my view, it is composed of a question or hypothesis, a method or instruments, respondents and the analysis of observations, and the formulation of conclusions.

In big lines, research always follows these steps. You start with something you want to understand. Whether your research is scientific, or more ad-hoc qualitative/quantitative, when you conduct research your starting point is something you would like to know. Based on your initial question you can formulate new possible questions or define a quantitative method, which you will need to answer that question and validate it in the real world.

You may or may not have a questionnaire. Sometimes a question is more qualitative and you may not know all the questions up front. In such a case research helps to identify patterns and gain understanding on the issues that are at play within a particular theme. Your starting point is the theme or topic of research. It is something you want to explore and clarify.

Quantitative research has the ability to provide robust conclusions. Whether you use surveys, experiments, or data comparisons. There is a clear object of research and a defined questionnaire. You can describe phenomena based on the findings, though you will not always get insight into why. In such cases, alternating qualitative and quantitative methods as you learn is advisable.

Each piece of research provides a defined, finite, number of answers. The great thing is that because research is systematic and replicable, you can repeat it as often as you need to deepen your understanding of any given issue.

What is design?

Design is the creation of a product or service in response to a question. This question can rise out of curiosity or be defined by a client. Designers then look at the real need and the ways in which it can be fulfilled.

The focus of designers is the interaction between a product or service and its user. Designers are taught to look at any given problem from as many possible sides.

How are they different?

Researchers limit their questioning to surveys and qualitative tools, whereas designers have a lot more freedom in how they look at a given problem. I think they see any piece of information as one piece of the puzzle but never the whole picture. So designers are interested in research as one of the many sources of information but they will look for many different perspectives.

The systematic approach required by research removes the possibility of chance encounters. In this sense, the research instrumentarium provides businesses with ideas of the implications of a given, predefined issue on their organization.

The design instrumentarium on the other hand looks for solutions. And solutions do not exist in a vacuum. Solutions are tangible, objectified in a product or service, and are fed by observation. This means that design has access to other kinds of observations which research may overlook.

Researchers look for consistency, robustness, and clarity. Designers look for options and thus have much more freedom in which information they integrate into their solutions. The main difference to me is that for designers the object of research keeps changing, keeps evolving. Designers switch more easily from one method to another, with the ambition to learn. They are driven by the need to understand and open perspectives and are unafraid of adding complexity. This makes them better able to deal with a world around us that is ever more complex.

How are they similar?

In the context of business, organizations need to make a profit. The big question is how. Companies need to be resilient if they want to be strong and sustainable.

Research and design both have a role to play in helping devise strategy and plans as to how to do this by understanding what companies are good at, what matters to users. Research is instrumental in helping to generate insight, identify gaps in what is versus what could be, and showing avenues for progressing business. The flexibility that characterizes designers allows them more freedom in integrating different points of view, formulating a vision and providing possible solutions for turning that vision into reality

How do you envision the future of research and design within the business context?

As an ecosystem. I think, increasingly we will work in teams to learn from each other's expertise and learn together. The ecosystem or network thrives through value creation. There is a continuous dynamic by which those who add value and interact to shape better business, do well and those who are unable to add value and contribute to value creation die off making place for new and better adapted forms of collaboration.

Cyclical and fluid processes

Reineke Reitsma
Vice President, Research
Director – Market Insights
Forrester Research
Amsterdam, The Netherlands

Who is Reineke?

Reineke Reitsma leads a team at Forrester Research that helps their customer insights professionals understand how technology developments influence the market insight industry, and how to adapt in order to stay successful and relevant. In addition, she leads a team responsible for data innovation at Forrester. This team tests and evaluates alternative data sources and research methodologies, and it looks at new ways of visualizing data. Reineke is a speaker at numerous events, market research and marketing conferences.

What is research?

Research is the activity of providing information to different parties within an organization. To do so, research looks at what is happening in the market and what is yet to come. Based on this information from the market and the customer, researcher can help define the next steps that an organization needs to take.

Ideally, research covers four different levels of information. These four levels include: data, insights, knowledge, and foresight. At the most basic level, research is about data collection. That is not enough because data in itself is not actionable for decision-making, which is why researchers translate data into insights. Again, insights won't give you the full picture. So researchers deliver a body of knowledge that is of value for decision makers as it provides a basis for argumentation. Finally, researchers can go beyond what is and into the domain of foresight and help make predictions that steer the direction of a company into the future.

Currently, a lot of the research studies are carried out in order to confirm something that was already known. At least sixty percent of the research studies thus look backward at what already has manifested or check data. This means in practice that research is too late to the game and that the decisions are sometimes made independently of research and left for research to check or validate. The great contribution of research is in exploration and understanding; this is more valuable, creates more relevance and is much more efficient.

What is design?

Design is the activity by which ideas are translated into a working product or service whether it is at a tangible or a conceptual level. Design brings ideas to life in such a way that people can interact with those ideas.

What characterizes great design is thus high usability, when something really works and is engaging to the user.

The aspect of making things tangible is central to design. For this reason it is easier for design to claim ROI -return on investment- on its activities. People can actually see what it is that design has done or accomplished. You can easily measure success based on a design: whether that design is an infographic, a prototype, a service, or a product in market.

How are they different?

As a researcher, one is primarily busy with information. It will always be about an estimation of what is really happening and thus it is more abstract than design. On the other hand, design starts from something abstract and maybe even ambiguous and shapes it into something concrete. Design is on the side of the output whereas data is less tangible.

Designers also have the advantage that they can build on what consumers say, give it a new twist in the form of a solution. For researchers that is problematic. Yet we know that people cannot always tell you what they need.

The skills required for design and research demand different types of personalities. One of the biggest frustrations for researchers is that nothing is done with the conclusions from research or the recommendations they give. At the same time, they do not go out there and involve others to get it done. Designers are more action-oriented and more readily step up to people with their ideas to get them done.

How are they similar?

Both research and design translate data into meaning. A good researcher has an interpretative role: looking into the data and reading between the lines to extract meaning in the form of conclusions. The same is true for design. A good designer looks at the data available, defines new questions and potential answers, and through that process designs a solution that meets the needs of the end user.

Both designers and researchers want the best for the customer. They will both ask questions like: 'Are we doing the right things?', 'Do we really know what matters to the consumer?'. Researchers aim to be the voice of the customer within organizations. Designers want to improve the customer experience. They are

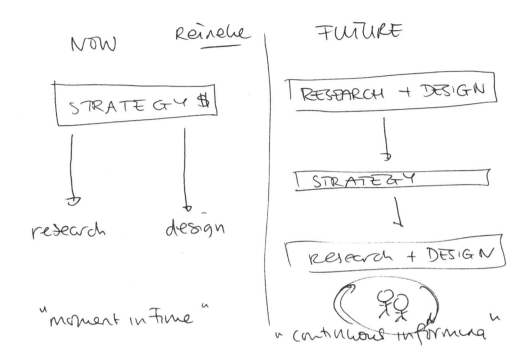

both customer-obsessed and see the economic performance as a result of having the customer at heart.

How do you envision the future of research and design within the business context?

I hope to see processes in large organizations that are more cyclical and fluid instead of top-down. Now, we are seeing a top-down set of mandates: 'research this', 'design that', which is more financially driven. By keeping the lines short and the directions simple there is an assumption of efficiency. But this is actually

inefficient and highly ineffective. There is little or no interaction between research and design.

I see a future ahead of us in which design and research work together and interact with strategy in a continuous loop, there is continuous informing and there is an interactive dialogue. This leads to better alignment instead of hap-snap in-the-moment decision-making which can be short-sighted.

Exploring strange new worlds

Lenny Murphy
Editor-in-Chief
GreenBook
New York, USA

Who is Lenny?

Leonard "Lenny" Murphy has been in the market research industry for over a decade in various senior level roles. Recently, his attention has shifted to working with multiple organizations to help advance innovation and strategic positioning of the market research industry, most prominently as the Editor-in-Chief of the GreenBook Blog and GreenBook Research Industry Trends Report, two of the most widely read and influential publications in the global insights industry.

What is research?

I believe market research to be any process that seeks to understand that which is not understood and to explain it in an impactful way so decisions can be made.

Methodologically speaking, market research is so much more than 'asking questions'. The realm of understanding includes all kinds of new activities from listening and observing through to big data analytics. What defines tools as market research tools is the fact that they support the core purpose of research, which is to understand, to explain and to make an impact.

Ultimately, the aim of understanding is not knowledge gathering. The pursuit of knowledge has no value in and of itself. Research seeks to understand something so that you can change some variable(s) and create a new result.

The ubiquity of 'insight' as a word makes this clear. It has been co-opted by everybody! Importantly, it is used almost as a synonym for creating change.

Market research is traditionally methodological, scientific, structured, and rigorous. All of these are code words for 'unimaginative'. We are seeing the market research spend shift away from traditional methods into new domains which are more observational ways of data collection. They start to include elements that are more emotional, more behavioural, and in many cases more interpretative.

The reason for this shift within market research is that it is no longer enough to check metrics through a dashboard. These sources of data do not help companies to manifest significant changes in direction or make strategic choices.

What is design?

Design is taking the unstructured and providing meaningful and useful structure. It is not only about something aesthetically pleasing. Design is about usefulness: it creates things people enjoy but importantly also, things that are a useful use of people's time.

Design has so many different applications. I think what matters most in the context of business is that there is usefulness as well as usability. Design for the sake of aesthetics has a place, but is not a great contributor to business in itself. You can make a pretty chair to put in a gallery, but that cannot be the purpose of a chair. Chairs are not to things to look at, they are to sit on. Design thus also addresses to practicality and adoption by the user. Design can answer to a need, provide a practical application of something that is missing.

How are they different?

Design goes into user experience, where research stops. From a research standpoint we too often still ask questions without thinking of the experience.

We can learn from this because this shows us that we need to think like designers and act like researchers. When we take elements of design into research, amazing things happen. A greatly designed experience feels seamless to the participant; people get so engaged they forget what they are really doing and value emerges. Take for example the Frito-Lay's crowdsourcing campaign for new flavour development. That is essentially research: it is concept development and concept testing! People participated willingly, they loved the experience, and in the process they created completely new products that added value for everybody.

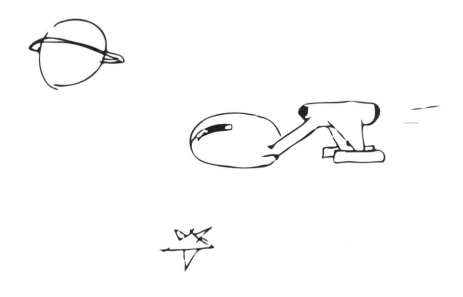

How are they similar?

On a very philosophical level I'd say that the nature of the universe is creating order out of chaos, as humans that is what we want. Design and research are both structures of thought that enable us to create understanding and bring order.

The principles of research can be incorporated into design and vice versa. I am optimistic that the emergence of new technologies will allow us to integrate research and design more quickly

than we may foresee. It is a business issue: the more businesses start understanding the value of creating opportunity for new discoveries, the more we will see value in new tools. We are now able to create prototypes faster, more cheaply, and more easily than ever before. This will create an agility in the innovation processes, in the capacity of businesses to integrate the user and thus will develop arguments for scaling up these kinds of practices.

How do you envision the future of research and design within the business context?

I have drawn the 'StarShip Enterprise' from StarTrek. In the future we will be together exploring strange new worlds. We don't know what we'll find, that is unimaginable from the current paradigm. What I do know is that we will 'boldly go where no man has gone before' and that we will find new ways to create and deliver value through these explorative pursuits.

A joining of hands

Finn Raben
Director General
ESOMAR
Amsterdam, The Netherlands

Who is Finn?

Finn Raben is a 'third culture child' who was born in the Far East and grew up in Europe and the Middle East. He went to university in the Netherlands and Ireland. He has spent most of his working career in Market Research and is currently the Director General of ESOMAR -the association for international market research.

What is research?

Research is the means by which we can discover and test hypotheses in order to refine what business, society, and governments can do. Of course there are many different kinds of research, conducted across a broad number of industry sectors. Yet, regardless of the exact type of research, the best research is a continuum, an ongoing conversation. That is, there should never be a presumption of knowledge. The purpose and the value of research would otherwise dissipate. Research is a constantly evolving conversation wherein we can ask and help answer successive questions through which business or government sharpens its understanding of what it needs to do.

More recently, there has been a growing expectation that research should always provide Einstein-like 'aha!' moments and that if it does not, then it is not good research. But the magic bullet for problem-solving does not exist. Research never tells you precisely what to do, rather, research provides you with options. Research guides and assists management, it does not, and should not, replace management. Good research is an integral part of good management because it is the researchers' role to help define and refine decision-making through that ongoing dialogue.

What is design?

In my humble opinion, design is an interpretation or a manifestation of the link between emotion and purpose. Designers create their manifestations through their own, personal interpretation. Each designer has a different interpretation, so, using the same information or materials, different designers will create different things. Anything that is iconic and original usually has a source linked to the individual interpretation of the challenge and which has been made manifest from the perspective of the designer.

How are they different?

Research and design serve different purposes. Design creates something that will be understood and appreciated by its user. Research usually defines the parameters within which the designer is able to work.

To illustrate with what might be termed an 'anti-example', let's look at the Ford Edsel story from the late 1950's -a classic marketing blunder Ford was looking to create 'the perfect car'. So they interviewed and surveyed large numbers of people for almost three years. Each step of the design and production process was over-researched as they looked for the 'perfect' solution, with 100 percent approval. This took so long to achieve that by the time they went into full production, without continuing the dialogue, market and consumer desires had moved on, had changed significantly, and the car flopped.

The lesson of the Ford Edsel story may be summarized in the 80:20 principle, or the Nike slogan: 'Just Do It!'. Eighty percent right is better than 100 percent wrong!! It is impossible to be 100 percent right, 100 percent of the time. The aim should be to get it 80 percent right, then launch -'Just Do It!'-, and then allow the research continuum to help you continue to refine the proposition.

Whether the first study delivers 50 percent or 60 percent or 70 percent, and whether follow-up research delivers a further another 10 percent, 20 percent or 30 percent, there will come a point eventually where you have to decide and to act. It's better to get it out there and refine it than to wait for it to be perfect. Both research and design can contribute to that process from their own angle.

How are they similar?

The similarity between research and design lies in the interpretation. A bit like qualitative research, design will always be a bit personal. This is the unique quality of design. The same applies to qualitative research. Two different qualitative researchers would produce two different reports. This is the beauty and the wonder of qualitative research, and sometimes also its weakness.

While there are some basic research rules that are design-agnostic, such as not asking leading questions which would bias the answers, both research and design seek out information and in that process make decisions on aspects such

as the order of the questions, the structure of the questions, and the type of setting/interface in which those questions are asked.

Generally speaking, qualitative research is about prompting conversations, not about leading them. Research starts the conversation without pre-defining the parameters. I would suggest this is the same with design because if the design parameters have been pre-defined, then the end result may be more evolutionary than revolutionary. ;

Good research and design are the result of freedom to interpret these parameters through the 'continuum' of the dialogue/project. To ensure this outcome, research and design should both do some ruminating and reflecting on their findings and propositions with the 'buyer' -end client- and shape the process together.

This collaborative engagement is what most enriches decision-making as this approach provides external input to the business process in the form of an evolving conversation that enriches all parties involved.

How do you envision the future of research and design within the business context?

In the future, there will still be a 'storm' building around us, which will continue to be 'fed' by economic pressure, thus lowering standards and dumbing down processes. The red, white, and blue hands are a reference to the fact that we're based in the Netherlands. But there is a universal principle in the joining of hands because if we work together and collaborate effectively, there will be nothing but sunshine, fair weather and a bountiful harvest for everyone.

Creating all kinds of value

Celiane Camargo-Borges
Lecturer and research coordinator,
Imagineering Academy
NHTV Breda University of
Applied Sciences
Breda, The Netherlands

Who is Celiane?

Celiane Camargo-Borges, Ph.D. is a lecturer and research coordinator at the Imagineering Academy, NHTV Breda University of Applied Sciences in the Netherlands. She is also faculty at the TAOS Institute. Celiane has worked in many settings including communities in Brazil, international healthcare in Taiwan and cross-cultural communication at KIT in Amsterdam, the Netherlands.

What is research?

Research, to me, is the capacity of inquiring, to be curious, to be puzzled by something with an aspiration to explore it further. I believe that we are all researchers. Every one of us participates in a continuous process by which we engage in making meaning, producing knowledge about a specific matter, modify and evolve our views and in turn, have an impact on what others do and think. Depending on the format in which you do that, it will be legitimized as research or not.

Historically, science had a privileged position when it comes to knowing, having the power of deliberating what is considered good research or not. The current changes in our society are connecting people from a variety of backgrounds and this phenomenon is changing the landscape. Nowadays you can see alternative practices of research, even within the academic context. That shows that there are so many other ways for researching and for producing knowledge and understanding that we don't need to restrict research as an activity that belongs just to science.

What is design?

Design is related to the urge and/or ability of sensemaking, of producing useful artefacts for people and society. Designers embrace a dynamic process of action and reflection that allows them to continuously feedback their learning loop into what they are doing. This means that learning by doing is at the core of design and the approach is by definition experimental and focused on utility. Designers always aim to achieve a useful result, one that is meaningful and desirable to the community involved.

What I most like about the design field is the openness to new questions to emerge during the process, always based on what will be useful and on what makes sense to people involved in a specific context. To me, this approach increases the success of what is created as there is flexibility and focus on what is needed.

How are they different?

The main difference derives from actionability. Research is about investigating a matter, systematizing understanding, producing new meanings. It allows us to construct and deconstruct old patterns of understanding and revisit our knowledge, meaning and practices in order to make sure they are still fulfilling for the lives we want to lead. The problem with researchers is that we have traditionally not learnt 'by doing' and there is no tradition of including other voices/expertises into our work, basically you have a researcher as the only expert following a method and drawing conclusions from it. Design has in its basis the action-reflection mechanism. It does not place knowledge first, as there is a risk that you will be theorizing about something that is not per se useful for people in a specific context. The design approach connects knowledge development to actionable knowledge, engaging and inviting other people as also experts on a topic, generating more meaningful actions.

How are they similar?

Research and design have complimentary roles. What research and design have in common is the ability to listen and dive into the moment. When research and design are well done, the toolbox of techniques from both research and design are merely seen as resources. These tools enrich the practices by being held lightly, though seriously, allowing the practitioners to embrace the messiness of the process knowing that the tools you need can be brought into the process and used to explore, not just as sequential steps of a predefined plan.

At the Imagineering Academy, we work with a design approach called Imagineering, which has as a central focus on designing for evolution, aiming at the emergence of new stages in business development. The Imagineering design methodology utilizes the collective creativity of all involved in a project in order to cope with the complexity of today's business landscape. To me, Imagineering is a great example of uniting research and design to reach the goal of reframing complex issues in inspiring ways, leading business to more desired directions.

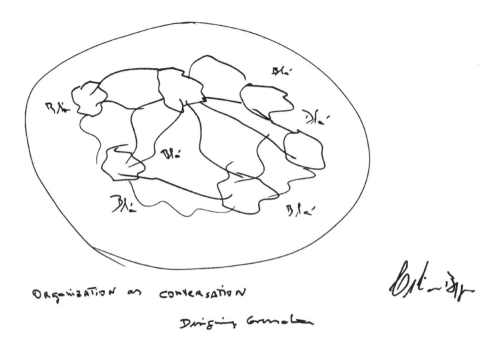

ORGANIZATION as CONVERSATION

How do you envision the future of research and design within the business context?

I envision a future of research and design working hand in hand to help the emergence of a new business logic, where organizations can be seen as a community of people working together. Organizations and businesses should be human-centred and as designing research holds relationships as central it can be very helpful with creating a new enterprise logic. Design can help support and guide the creation of conversations by giving them form, space, and different vehicles. This is crucial to create a sense of urgency, in which is needed

for business to succeed in sustainable ways, creating all kinds of value: monetary, societal, customer.

Research and design together can help with transforming the logic of business, helping entrepreneurs to do business for good instead of just good business.

In this endeavour, the researcher-as-expert can be turned into the researcher-as-offering-expertise, helping to co-create the type of change that is most meaningful and impactful for sustainable business.

A project-based future

Joyce Yee

Co-author, Design Transitions
Programme Leader Interactive Media
Design at Northumbria University
Newcastle upon Tyne, United Kingdom

Who is Joyce?

Joyce Yee, Ph.D. is a senior lecturer at Northumbria University's Design School in the UK, teaching interaction, service and design methodologies across undergraduate and postgraduate levels. She has over ten years working experience in academic and professional environments as a graphic, interaction and service designer. Joyce has published regularly since 2003 and her research interest is bound by a common theme of exploring and identifying how designers develop and improve their own practice.

What is research?

My understanding of research is based on my academic practice. From that role I would define four levels of research. The first is academic research: possibly the purest form of research because it is self-driven and self-motivated. The topic is selected by a researcher who spends time finding an answer that constitutes a new contribution to the knowledge base in a given field. It is governed by an interest in the field and a search for knowledge.

The second level of research would be research projects, which are usually funded by government agencies or by organizations. Research projects involve teams working across boundaries and have a higher complexity due to the motivation of the research: it is no longer 'blue sky' but there is a research need driven by the funders.

The third, layer is consultancy research. Companies come to a research team at university or to their own internal teams such as research and development or market research departments. Research is formal but it is not publishable as it contains strategic information that companies want to keep to themselves to increase their competitive advantage.

Finally, the fourth level is the most empirical and practical: design research. This kind of research is conducted by smaller teams that cannot afford research or need to do this within a project but less thoroughly, e.g. in the form of a contextual review. It is a more informal application of research but it is being increasingly recognized as a research tool within design thinking and service design methods.

In short, research is a whole scope of activities aimed at gathering knowledge that go from the more abstract/scientific studies to the more practical/personal level.

What is design?

I think design is primarily about the orchestration of activities to create engagement with an end user. It involves a whole set of skills: encompassing creative approaches, visualizations and the ability to imagine possible and preferred futures.

Design also requires the ability to be comfortable with uncertainty. It creates a studio-space condition, based on the principle that there is not one single right solution. In this sense design is both the end game and the way through.

Design creates artefacts by distilling and synthesizing information. These artefacts are tangible and 'criticable'. The draft concept becomes available to the whole team: by showing it, you can bounce ideas and use the evolving concept as a clarification point. The way a designer works is by experiencing; a model is just one way of probing and iterating the way towards a solution.

How are they different?

I believe in research through design, that is, to use the design practice to answer research questions. This brings out the complementarity of the disciplines: research historically sits in academia and science while design historically has been vocational, practical.

Scientific research is about understanding a current phenomenon. Design goes further. Design is about projecting a future scenario, a future question, a possibility.

In design, repeatability of a research project is not relevant. Design requires usefulness. The information and insights obtained have to be useful. It is much more engaged, you have to be continuously conscious of what you're doing and why you're doing it. A design researcher is aware that at every point you are making a decision of where you go next. It is less contained than research that seeks to understand a given situation or answer a given question.

How are they similar?

Research and design use similar thought processes and similar skillsets. You have to be interested in the world around you, to be informed, to be curious, and to ask lots of questions. Research is about understanding. This is a crucial aspect of good design because both research and design are about making connections and seeing patterns.

The relationship between research and design is shifting. As research through design is becoming a more valid way of researching, the similarities are increasing. Designers are starting to see that research can be a useful tool. Research is being seen to be an important component to a design process in professional practice, while in a research practice, design methods and tools are being used as a vehicle of research.

Designers are needing to become good at research because just researching is not enough. Design provides a context in the form of an itch. Once you have an overarching itch you want to scratch, you will figure out different

ways to scratch it via research, via prototypes, via new questions, via visualizations, etc. Bringing research and design to an entirely new level.

How do you envision the future of research and design within the business context?

My vision for the future is project based. Teams of people pulled together, with many skills and competencies working, with an aim in a project setting. Projects are extremely powerful because they provide a sense of ownership. There is a beginning and an end, which allows people to have a sense of achievement.

Project teams deliver, projecting, literally, a new future. I think we will start to see more of this, not only at strategic level because projects help unite teams through a sense of purpose, a 'why', as Simon Sinek brilliantly posits. This way of working is not new but it's a way of working that designers are used to. Many designers take for granted that they work in projects. While a lot of people are just carrying on with 'business as usual', which is not sustainable because it is not sufficiently motivating and can be quite disheartening. In the future we will have lots of project teams, guided by people with understanding of skills, people, project management. Not just people in 'management' who are disengaged from reality because they are too far away from it.

Business like music

Aditya Kedia

Research Associate and Lecturer
School of Design, The Hong Kong
Polytechnic University
Hong Kong, China

Who is Aditya?

Aditya Kedia works as a design
researcher and lecturer at the
School of Design of The Hong
Kong Polytechnic University. He
believes that design has a great
potential to enable social, economic
and environmental sustainability
in an era of unpredictability and
chaos. His interests and practice
include using human-centred design methods for driving business
and social innovation.

What is research?

Research is a systematic process of gathering
information and making sense of it so that the
information can be applied purposefully. Of
course, research is not just limited to information gathering as often perceived. Nowadays,
information is quite ubiquitous. Research is
also about determining what information to
collect and whether collected information
makes any sense.

As an analogy, if we have to construct a building we have to understand the surrounding
ecosystem and the constraints offered by it.
Research helps us know and understand the
landscape, existing or past conditions, creatures
inhabiting the area, and ongoing social and environmental interactions. Essentially, research
helps us make sense of what is happening
around us so that we can better understand the
existing situation and future possibilities.

Research is about informing the past and the
present state, about what has existed or exists
and what has happened or is happening now.
Research prepares us for the future: it helps
us move from the present into the future with
a better understanding of the challenges we
face, possibilities ahead of us, expectations we
can have and, eventually, what can be done.

What is design?

Design has been defined, re-defined, and re-
re-defined so often that it is hard to answer
this question. Design has shifted from a more
tangible, artefact-based field of work to an
intangible, abstract and problem-solving discipline. To define it in simple terms, I would
say design is applied imagination. Imagination in this case is positively applied to solve
problems and is itself linked to creativity.
Design is a problem-solving process where
one alternately diverges and converges across
problem space based on past experience and
new found knowledge to uncover alternative solutions that might not be possible
otherwise.

The purpose of design is to improve and innovate to make every day human experiences
more desirable, memorable, and pleasurable
as a whole. Design, however, is very different
from art. Design is not done for its own sake
or for the sake of mere expression. Design is
done for others. The bigger purpose of design
is to serve humans. The value of design is in
translating abstract information into tangible
experiences in order to take things forward
from where they are now.

How are they different?

Research is about landscaping the existing
and/or past situations and scenarios; it is
about the present and the past. Design is
about creating future scenarios. It is about
the future. They work best in tandem: where
research ends, design begins and then feeds
back into research.

The job of research is to find existing gaps -economic, social, psychological, physical, etc.) or even to predict potential future gaps. Design creates solutions to fill existing gaps that eventually alter the future. Ultimately, this means that they deliver different outcomes. Research is more about 'the truth', about what 'is' now. Design is about alternatives generated by taking the present and making it better.

Research as such can be done in isolation to build knowledge. However, that knowledge might be useless if no one acts on it. Design, by its sheer nature creates possibilities for people and cannot remain isolated or disconnected.

How are they similar?

Both research and design make the intangible visible. Through research, you get to know or see something that you may not have known or seen before. Design makes the intangible visible in the form of interactions, experiences, and artefacts.

Research and design can therefore be used for value creation, which is critical for organizations. The contribution of design goes above and beyond that of research in this case: it delivers economic, social, and cultural value as it helps crafting experiences that are differentiated by the sheer act of designing. Design thus integrates value into business initiatives. But, of course, design is incomplete without research.

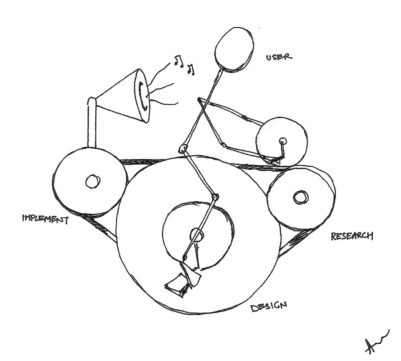

How do you envision the future of research and design within the business context?

I'll explain it in terms of music. Music is made by combining discreet elements in an aesthetically pleasing manner, which finally can be enjoyed by people using a simple interface such as a music player or a radio. As a musician, the kind of music you produce depends on the kind of audience you have as well as the kind of elements you choose.

Businesses are going to be similar. They will not only have to serve as an interface but also have to co-create and tailor the content to suit the user needs. Businesses will take discrete data from user research and combine it to build a simple, coherent, and an aesthetically pleasing output that surprises, engages, and delights. They will need to have focus, determination, and a sense of empathy so as to deliver what really matters to the listener/user. In simple terms, businesses have to connect research and design and act as an interface for people to access the values. They have to transform dreams and aspirations into reality.

Cycles of continuous learning

Michael Hohl
Professor of Design Theory
Anhalt University of
Applied Sciences
Dessau, Germany

Who is Michael?

Michael Hohl, Ph.D., is a designer, academic and researcher. He enjoys making things, thinking about things, how we do them, and how this changes us. He has a background in digital media. Michael's interests include research methods and methodologies in practice-based research and he regularly gives invited talks or conducts workshops about these. At present he is professor of design theory at Anhalt University of Applied Sciences.

What is research?

Within academia, research is mainly scientific research and about creating new knowledge and making it available, applying a rigorous methodological framework. But in a broader human context, research is what children do from a young age as they explore the world around them. Trying things out, experiencing them, crawling and walking around, putting things in their mouths, making distinctions, and discovering patterns. Through that process we humans construct and build the world around us together and are continuously developing theories. And when we feel we've discovered how things work, we can tell others and disseminate that knowledge. We invent words and by doing so, help others see what it is that we learned.

The subtlety is that knowledge and understanding are processes that take place in the bodies and minds of people. Research is the rigorous process of extracting that knowledge and some of this knowing becomes knowledge when we write it down. One could say there is no such things as knowledge; there only is knowing.

What is design?

Design is something deeply human, which we have all been doing for hundreds of thousands of years now. Designing is how humans solve problems. It involves 'playing around', recognizing a problem, inventing a solution, and creating steps to solve it.

I think everyone is a designer. We design all the time, even with the simplest things like how we organize our kitchen. Whenever we arrange or rearrange things to how it suits us in order to facilitate our processes, we are designing. There is no such thing as 'design' in an abstract sense because as design is an innate human ability, there are as many different ways to design as there are designers. One of these we call product design, another interaction design or sound design, and so on.

Nowadays we are in the middle of a revolution in the field of design, and I think this is an interesting challenge, also for design education. Just as we had the desktop publishing revolution we now have the desktop manufacturing revolution with things like 3-D printing, so suddenly everybody can be a designer. The question arises, What do designers contribute? So designers have to reflect upon what their actual expertise is and reinvent themselves, and keep reinventing themselves.

There are enough toasters and chairs in the world already. Designers need to focus on their essential skills, which involve listening with a true intent to understand and reading whether what the client wants is really the appropriate solution. I think design needs to be redefined in a more integrative and comprehensive way. Not as a science, but research related, as people who know how to look and ask the right questions, as comprehensive thinkers who can facilitate multi-disciplinary communication and that are expert learners in inventing solutions. I see designers like hubs in a wheel of interdisciplinary work or research. At the heart of designing is empathy, understanding the needs of people.

How are they different?

Designers and researchers make an observation, become curious, and try to understand the phenomena they observed. Whereas design is focused on inventing an appropriate solution to change the world, scientific research tries to understand the world as it is and to clearly describe these phenomena.

Designing also involves research. Research provides understanding through evidence. Scientific research comes with a very particular way of thinking and looking at the world. This however is only *one* possible way of looking at the world, among many other ways, which also have their strengths and weaknesses. Design can be seen as one such other way of thinking that involves acting.

Design is more about creating results, than it is about trying to understand. Designing is a reflective process; but apart from sketches, models, and the final result, there is no written record of this process. Designers are not encouraged to do systematic, thorough research, take notes, write, and reflect. I think this is something lacking in design.

"The design process is a research process, testing in different iterations whether an idea works."

This would make designers better thinkers, writers, and communicators.

How are they similar?

The design process is a research process, testing in different iterations whether an idea, a design, works. This process leads to a better understanding and learning, through intervention and exploration, often leading to new and better things. The academic researcher might emphasize as outcome the understanding and learning part, how we got there, whereas the designer puts emphasis on the new and better thing that is created as a result.

Scientific research and designing are similar in that they both begin with a hunch, an observation. Both require creativity and thinking out of the box. So the similarity is in the way of looking at problems, though the questions they ask come from different perspectives. If you put on your designer's hat you will try solving a concrete problem. If you put on your researcher hat you would reflect on how the solution emerged and consciously analyze the situation, how you got there, and possible outcomes based on what is happening. Then you steer towards the desired outcome. Both might be surprised by what they end up with.

How do you envision the future of research and design within the business context?

My drawing looks like a flower but it is really a cyclical process, a feedback process with different iterations. It symbolizes integrated, multiple-loop learning that adapts in a changing world as a never-ending process. Design changes the world and the world changes design.

People and teams go through this continuous learning together, in multiple layers as they generate ideas, test them, think about their implications, and generate again.

Designers in the future will be learners, not experts. Design will be research based. The days of the heroic designer who knows what is right are over. Co-design and participative design -design thinking- are among the research methods to explore what people want. Designers have to work bottom-up, top-down, outside-in, inside-out simultaneously. Prototype and test with real people to see if a design works.

I think this will also require to think about vision and values. How should our desirable future look like? How do we want to get there? The vision tells us where to go, our values why we are going there. Perhaps we need to design everything again, only this time learning from nature, in a sustainable manner. These changes will also need to be reflected in the curricula of design schools.

The future of business after how design and research have been integrated.

Michael hohl

Circular regeneration

Thomas Fischer
Director of the Design
Research Institute
Xi'an Jiaotong-Liverpool
University
Suzhou, China

Who is Thomas?

Thomas Fischer, Ph.D., is the Director of the Design Research Institute at Xi'an Jiaotong-Liverpool University in Suzhou, China. Thomas is a Fellow of the Design Research Society and a recipient of the American Society for Cybernetics' Warren McCulloch Award. Thomas's research is focused on design process studies, computer-aided architectural design, on cybernetics,and design education in Sino-foreign contexts.

What is research?

I see research as a forward-looking renegotiation of the constraints within which we act. It is a process of speculation through which we get to understand and change the world. Acting in the world, we identify patterns; relying on those patterns we get to act better; acting better we identify better patterns, and so on.

Scientific research is a constrained form of this process, which we assume has a beginning and an end, and which we subject to criteria like observability and repeatability.

What is design?

I see design as research, i.e. as a forward-looking renegotiation of the constraints within which we act. It is broader than scientific research, with a wider range of processes, formats, and criteria. The design process is a cyclical conversation between acting and understanding, between articulation and perception, and it needs no shortcuts to pretend otherwise.

Insisting in observability and repeatability makes little sense in design. I cannot observe your experience or your having an idea. If you give the same brief to two designers, you will get two different outcomes. We value design outcomes for resonating with our values and preferences, which may be shared amongst groups. This primarily personal form of evaluation has little need for objective truth.

Nonetheless, design has a bearing on our readiness to agree or not about how we see things because design outcomes are also symbols we exchange to assert and to challenge our meanings and values. It is a language through which we negotiate collective desires and constraints for stability and change.

How are they different?

Scientific research seeks to get a good match between the patterns it expresses and the world as it is, while design seeks a good match between patterns it expresses and our values and preferences.

Since scientific research and design are subject to different values and criteria, and since they tend to be done by different groups of people, they happen in different cultural ecosystems that speak different languages. So, ironically, these two modes of re-negotiating the constraints within which we act can have a hard time negotiating ways of acting together. The differences between both modes of inquiry are mainly differences in formats of presentation, while the experience of practically conducting them is more similar than most people would expect.

How are they similar?

Both are forward-looking ways of renegotiating the constraints within which we act, with scientific research being a constrained subset of design. While scientific research needs to

take a shortcut and tell stories about linear relationships to arrive at static conclusions about
an ongoing world, its process is more faithfully
described along the same lines of how design is
described increasingly often; as a cyclical conversation between acting and understanding,
between articulation and perception. And both
are ways of negotiating where we agree and
where we do not agree, and where we desire
stability and where we desire change.

How do you envision the future of research and design within the business context?

Business has a role to play in how we relate to
our world. So we have to ask whether short-term
profit motives, deregulated financial markets,
and corporate influence in politics, for example,
offer a sound basis to take on this responsibility.

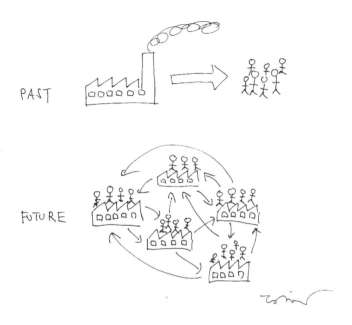

I see a crisis within the design professions.
Designers are on the one hand educated in the
intersection of human values, business and the
physical realities of the world to see systemic
relationships and to anticipate and recognize
consequences of actions. At the same time,
however, most designers serve industries,
which exploit human and natural resources,
ignore the long-term effects of their action in
favour of short-term gain, and thereby grossly
contradict human values. My sense is that
most designers are aware that they are stuck
in a serious contradiction. Society at large is
beginning to see this, too. Business and industry will hopefully evolve accordingly.

As a vision of a desirable future, I'd propose a
world in which our acting and understanding
has moved from a focus on linear input-output
relationships to a focus on circular processes
of regeneration –a shift from cause-and-ef-
fect transactions to equitable give-and-take
relationships. At the moment, we are not very
good yet at understanding such relationships,
how they interact, how they play out over
time, and how interventions set them onto
desirable paths. This is where research is
necessary, be it scientific or not. In this vision
we are moving from a past where big business
dominates the economic landscape, operating
centrally, between mining resources on the

one end and waste disposal at the other
end on large scales, towards a future in
which everyone can be both a producer
and a consumer, industrially, culturally,
educationally, and so on, in a network of
communities with a high level of interdependency, and at scales that are humanly
relatable. All this may not do much by
itself. But it may undermine our culture of
hiding consequences of actions and lead
to greater systemic honesty and a return
of effective individual ethics as a standard
in socio-economic development. I think
designers can relate to that, and have
much to contribute to such a shift.

Setting horizons

Marc Stickdorn
Co-Author, This is Service
Design Thinking
Speaker and Trainer,
This is Service Design Doing
Innsbruck, Austria

Who is Marc?

Marc Stickdorn is a trainer and consultant for service design. Marc guest lectures at various business and design schools and co-founded smaply, a software company developing web-based solutions to visualize customer experiences. More recently, he co-founded ExperienceFellow, a software start-up developing a tool to research customer experience through mobile ethnography. Beside various scholarly articles, Marc initiated and co-authored the book *This is Service Design Thinking*.

What is research?

Research is about empathy, about understanding people. There are some classic distinctions within research, like qualitative versus quantitative. Often research linearly follows one approach throughout data collection and data analysis. I believe in a broader scope for research, where you triangulate methods, types of data and even people. This delivers a richer understanding, which is what research is supposed to do. Good research allows you to get to good insights that are based on multifaceted human-centred data, insights that are e.g. formulated based on customer's point of view and what they want to achieve.

For both the planning and the actual research, iteration is key. This is because research centres on problems. So you start with what you think might be the problem, but you don't really know whether that is a real problem. Finding insight means understanding where the friction lies. Research shows that which is not working as it should be and helps understand the implications of that in the perspective of the user. Research is thus about problem identification and empathy.

What is design?

The design process is a process of changing a product or service system into a better state. It is a much broader process than research alone. I would say that design includes research at different stages of the process.

Design enables people to quickly create boundary objects. These help a team to know what they are talking about and what is not part of the discussion. This is the power of what we call the 'shitty first draft'. By creating simple objects and prototypes, design makes the strategy process manageable: it is not just trial and error, it is the ability to guide people through the process by giving them prototypes of a future solution that they can help shape.

How are they different?

Every good designer has at least a few research skills, though that does not necessarily work the other way around. Researchers, in particular those focusing only on linear quantitative methods, might be wizards in calculating and analyzing data but may not know what to do with that insight.

The purpose of research is to gather findings. Research is truly valuable when those findings are used to actually change something. But all too frequently scholarly research does not add to the existing body of knowledge; it merely rephrases existing knowledge. And the results are not necessarily used, other than to trigger a new research process.

Design goes beyond research findings, and helps to trigger discussions or even trigger change. Design knows at the explorative and prototyping levels of the process when

"There simply is no design without research."

How do you envision the future of research and design within the business context?

My drawing is a rip and mix collage of several concepts that to me are based on the same process anyway and are merging more and more. I have included the visualization of iterative loops which are crucial to any design process, merged that with a squiggle that shows that we don't know where our new understanding will lead us, merged with a visualization of the Agile process where people work towards a vision in a non-linear fashion.

Our future way of working within business will be one in which we will define direction and goals by setting a horizon, without going into detail of the steps because those will be design iterations. We will not go into the details in advance; we will explore again and again and again instead of defining milestones and planning years of a strategic process with Gantt charts.

enough research has been done. It follows the concept of 'theoretical saturation': getting more answers is not going to provide you any news. It is time to design more, adjust prototypes, or review ideas so that you can ask new questions.

Designers often use their gut feel for research in order to advance the design process. The disadvantage of this is that you may overlook things. The advantage, however, is that the purpose of design is to find out what the problems really are and to create solutions. This really takes things forward beyond mere discussions and into the creation of things -both objects as well as less tangible things like services, systems, interfaces or websites.

How are they similar?

By the same token, research is an integral part of the design process. Design is creating things, but also prototyping and testing them. As soon as we test, we are researching and this is fundamental to designing.

There simply is no design without research. Especially in the context of business, research gives you accuracy: measuring impact is the domain of research. Research also allows you to find the main issues that need to be tackled for whatever it is you are designing to be usable and valuable to the user. Whether methods emerge from research or from design. The similarity lies in that they are both about finding things out to be of benefit to the user.

MAKE

NEW

CONNECTIONS

The business designer hybrid

Alexander R. Wilcox Cheek
Assistant Teaching Professor,
Information Systems
Carnegie Mellon University
Doha, Qatar

Who is Alex?

Alexander R. Wilcox Cheek is a faculty member in Information Systems at Carnegie Mellon University. Alex is the co-founder of Macromicro, a data visualization company, and Classroom Salon, an interactive media platform. His research, teaching, and professional practice unite many areas of design, including interaction design, service design, and organization design.

What is research?

Design research, which is my area of focus, is actually quite similar to and borrows considerably from social science research. Many methods are ethnographic in nature, applied to the same context but with different goals in mind. Design research is research with the intent to make things and to gain deep insight in the making process.

If what you are making is relatively simple, 'posters and toasters design', I would suggest that your 'research' needn't be that rigorous. But as things get more complex you need to take into account people, products and whole ecosystems, lots of things conflict and overlap. This kind of complexity demands research.

Design research is a broad set of tools, from shadowing people, to competitive analysis, to prototyping. Prototyping, for instance, allows you to take your learnings back to people and gain further insight: 'I heard you say this, I interpreted it like that, and here's a possible solution, Now, what do you think? Does this seem right?' In short, you could argue that design research is what you do any time you are trying to gain understanding or feedback in order to advance.

What is design?

Design is everything human-made. Over and above the act of making, design is also the intent of making, the intellectual activity of having an idea, seeing an opportunity, and bringing high levels into concrete reality.

Design is one of the three primary fields of human inquiry. These fields are, science, the humanities, and design. Science helps us in understanding the natural world and its underlying mechanisms. The humanities help us to understand the human condition and make connections between ideas. And finally, design is concerned with the built world and helps us create the future.

The twenty-first Century designer is less about maker skills and more about thinking laterally, pluralistically, and engaging all the senses in ways to understand audience, context, and purpose. We are addressing more complex things, juggling more stakeholders and technologies than before and we are seeing that traditional skills in design arts don't necessarily scale. You cannot take the 'genius designer' approach and apply that to complex problems. These require a more holistic approach and a certain disposition for understanding the world in its entirety in order to move things forward.

How are they different?

Whereas research is about understanding the current state, design is about shaping the future state of people, things, and environments. There is a lot of overlap of course. Any good designer will want to look at what is being created and learn from it through a back-and-forth interaction through research.

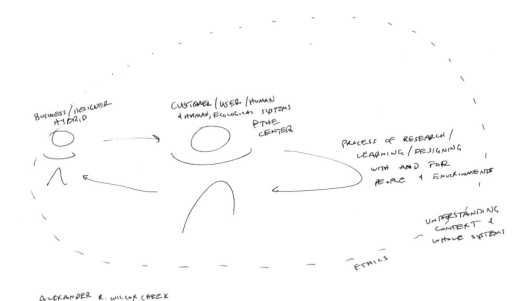

Business/Designer Hybrid

Customer/User/Human
↑ Human, Ecological Systems
@ the center

Process of research/
learning/designing
with and for
people & environment

Understanding
context &
whole systems

Ethics

ALEXANDER R. WILCOX CHEEK

Designers are the connecting point between now and the future. For a design researcher, the research side may involve data collection, interacting with people, prototyping, and in bringing the human-centred approach into the equation. Designer skills involve synthesis and the ability to decide what is valuable and not, what is going to inform us versus what is going to inform the product.

How are they similar?

The degree of similarity hugely depends on the purpose or desired outcome. If the research you are trying to do is about creating something new, then the overlap between research and design is almost complete. If you are only trying to gain understanding of, for example sociological conditions in a particular neighbourhood of a particular city, then it is less about design, more scientific in nature. But maybe later you, the scientist, become the designer and bring about change to that neighbourhood?

The value of design plus research is ultimately proven by the degree of success it brings. As I say to my students, it is perfectly possible to come up with brilliant ideas without leaving the classroom. But those ideas emerge in a vacuum that may or may not have anything to do with what is really happening around us. Approaching a problem as a design researcher allows you to really understand the context from a first person perspective. This is more grounded in reality, making the design step a more meaningful and connected one.

As we move from the simple to the complex, from static to dynamic, from parts to whole systems, the more designers become facilitators. This makes designers within a business context take on a fused role as business designers, understanding the context, considering the implications to the whole system while contributing to build future solutions.

How do you envision the future of research and design within the business context?

The future will be much more dialectic and cyclical. Designers will continue to put the human at the centre and I can see the business designer being very suited for a facilitator role in this cycle of research, learning, and designing for people and environments.

The business designer hybrid will allow businesses to hit the mark sooner, by integrating broader human ecology into the solution making. This involves ethical considerations, an articulated sense of purpose, and value-addition in more sustainable, relevant ways.

Collaborative future

Pieter Jan Stappers
Full professor, Design Techniques,
Industrial Design Engineering
(IDE)
Technical University Delft
Delft, The Netherlands

Who is Pieter Jan?

Pieter Jan Stappers is full professor of design techniques at the Technical University Delft IDE (Industrial Design Engineering). He coordinates the Faculty's Graduate School, being informal director of ID-StudioLab, and heading the research subprogramme on tools and techniques for the conceptual phase of design. Key elements in his work are research through design, experiential prototypes, and context mapping. Pieter Jan is co-author of *Convivial Toolbox: Generative Research for the Front End of Design*.

What is research?

Research is the generation of knowledge and the creation of insights. Knowledge that is explicit, and some of what is implicit and is brought to the surface, is abstracted in such a way that this knowledge can be applied by different people.

The aim of research is thus to generate knowledge with a purpose.

What is design?

Design is the generation of plans for desired future situations. Design is always specific and geared towards a solution. There may or may not have been a problem, but design aims to generate an improvement. Design is about new solutions, about something that has not been there yet. And finally, design is always about something that needs to be realized *in the world*.

Design was created as a service to business in the context of the Industrial Revolution. But 'design' has grown to mean so much more than products. The term refers not just to a profession or a trade; it also denotes a cognitive activity that is about development, all the way from the generation of an idea through to its implementation.

Nice to have ideas, but that is not all of it. Are those ideas achievable, makeable, realizable, desirable? You know, its nice to have an idea to make flying cars but if you can't put ideas into practice you might as well be a fiction writer. And when it comes to implementation, the same is true. Hobbies are nice to keep people busy, but in design you need to consider the bigger picture. What are you making, how will you make it, and what will people do with it? Good design combines the exploration, the ideas, and their fruitful implementation, and all the phases in between.

How are design and research different?

In contrast to design, research can feed from the world but does not need to act in it.

A lot of the way many business work, especially big corporations, is based on predictability and extrapolation, which would all be very well, were it not that the world keeps changing and that design is fundamentally about the not-yet-existing future. If you want certainty and safety, then you can use those for running existing operations. But for exploration? Really, it is a different space. Here in the Netherlands we live below sea level and in order to continue to do so we need dams and dikes. They help you control the situation and keep the sea at bay. However, if you want to extend the land mass then you have to be able to let a few of your experiments flood and disappear under water as you learn. Both skills are necessary, but they are not the same.

Professionals doing market research have been trained to ask predefined questions to pre-re-cruited respondents that fit into a box in terms of socio-demographic and attitudinal traits. Their aim is thus to provide companies with certainties and to inform decision-making to decrease the chance of making expensive mistakes. But in so doing, it overlooks the fact that organizations do not exist in a vacuum.

The thing is that corporations have become victims of their own routine when they just do surveys to acquire knowledge. And this produces dangerous knowledge. It's like the proverb, 'A little knowledge is a dangerous thing'. It is dangerous to become overconfident. Nice if you have a principle that guides you, a piece of data that informs you, but that is far from a certainty. The world changes several times before any idea reaches the market. So you need to keep your eyes and ears open; you need to keep questioning the data.

To put it in business context, for a recent project we supported a large corporate organization in understanding key drivers for their user. We carefully presented the information using direct quotes of what the users had said. And we also provided bullet points that summarized the themes. The quotes were quickly forgotten, because the organization was neither used to nor prepared to understand information directly from the user nor to empathize. The bullets made it to the annual

"Both design and research interact with the world in order to understand it."

operating plans, and even lived on for a few years. But in my perspective, all subtlety of meaning was lost in that process.

Design and research share the same challenge in those terms. They can both potentially bring value to business by working in a more connected way.

How are they similar?

Both design and research interact with the world in order to understand it. There is always an intervention, an action, or a probe to see how things act and react. What they have in common is knowledge creation. Like research, design is also a way of gathering knowledge. As you design, you find insights that can be generalized and applied to the product or service you are creating. That is,

if you are able to transfer that knowledge to other people and/or other situations.

These disciplines are both being affected by a changing business context. Business itself has changed. It used to be enough to create a product and sell it. Businesses could hire creative teams to help them make products and services for people. The lines are blurring now. It is not enough to put something out in the world. Businesses are realizing that that model is finite. Innovation fails; it is put into the market and people are not buying just anything anymore. Having a link, a relation, a connection with the end user is key to the survival and sustenance of business.

We all face the challenge that tools will be hollowed out by managers who think that connection with users is made through models, books, or indirect reports. It's not enough to draw a square and a circle to call yourself a designer. It is not acceptable to say you know for certain or that you can bring 'the' answer as a researcher. There is a risk that much lip service, and shallow action, is paid to the involvement of end users. And that affects both research and design. We need to bring these disciplines to life because it is not as simple as ticking items off a list: I've done my personas, my ethnography, my ideation, etc. It's not the process. With most of these tools, the value is in the experience and the insight you generate as a group. Once you've filled the template, it's obsolete.

How do you envision the future of research and design within the business context?

I envision a future in which the creation of products and services is a lot more collaborative. More people are 'sucked into' the process from different areas and all those people get a sense of participation and accomplishment and they extract value from the process as well themselves.

Design will emerge from this process as a more solid discipline, as it is well positioned to connect three different knowledge areas:
• the needs of people
• the possibilities of technology, and
• the organizational power of business.

People as connectors

Bruce Hanington
Associate Professor, Director
of Graduate Studies
Carnegie Mellon University,
School of Design
Pittsburgh, Pennsylvania, USA

Who is Bruce?

Bruce Hanington is an Associate Professor, the Director of Graduate Studies, and former Program Chair of Industrial Design in the School of Design at Carnegie Mellon University in Pittsburgh, Pennsylvania.. He has dedicated his teaching and research to methods and practices for human-centred design, with an emphasis on design ethnography, participatory design, and the meaning of form in context. Bruce is also co-author of the book *Universal Methods of Design*.

What is research?

In its most basic form, research is the collection of information in order to gather insight and move things forward. What defines research is the investigative process, which is targeted towards some ends.

Design research, as a particular form of research, is less focused on the ends or searching for any 'right' answers. You often don't know what the ends are so the process is open ended.

I usually refer to the Frayling Framework in order to separate the different levels of design research, namely
• Research for design
• Research about design
• Research through design

Research for design, which is the focus of my work, is about getting information from people and things in order to inform the thought process of design. The other two forms of research, about design and through design are respectively about understanding how design works and utilizing design as a potential research process in itself.

What is design?

While I subscribe to Herbert Simon's definition that 'design is transforming existing conditions into preferred ones', I think we need more nuance. With that definition, everyone is a designer: a school teacher or a fireman.

In truth, not everyone is a designer. Design is characterized by certain processes, methods, and practices, which include the following four notions
• The notion of interaction, which involves the concept of a 'user' by which design is a means to an end in the creation of value for the user.
• The notion of reflection and critique, which is something designers can do alone or as a group, weighing the validity and relevance of their progress within the design process.
• The notion of working collectively and sharing the process, with a highly visual component such as modelling, hand-sketching, prototyping, or digital tools.
• The notion of ambiguity, which involves not necessarily finding a 'correct' solution. This is a difficult threshold for many because it implies accepting the fact that there are millions of answers, which can be good or bad, but are ultimately one of many. It includes the realization that one can inspire behavioural change through anything and that no answer as such is correct. There is a spectrum of better or worse solutions.

These four elements constitute, in my opinion, hard hurdles, which are difficult for non-designers to cross because they are unfamiliar. And thus collectively they define design, making it a unique discipline. You might perhaps find some of these in other disciplines; however, the combination of these four notions is what defines design.

How are they different?

Research and design are perceived as different. Research, on the surface, is perceived as having more established methodologies. There's this belief that each method gives a certain type of information.

Research has the potential of giving quantitative information more than design does. In design, there is more value for qualitative methods that may not lead to quantifiable outcomes, although, of course, both research and design have explorative and measurable aspects.

The main contrast is in the way of working. Designers work contextually and visually. Particularly when you look at the use of ethnographic tools and anthropology-based approaches, you will see that designers want to work contextually, and in participatory design, visually, with participants.

I particularly like the contributions Liz Sanders has made to the field of design research. She has helped us understand that we need to clarify in our methods what the aim of our research is: looking for information or looking for inspiration.

Guiding inspiration is done via design practices, which is not the typical aim of research. So when one is simply collecting information to inform a design project, to guide and inspire

the project team, some would not consider this 'research' by standard definitions.

Collecting information via research practices does not always correspond to the aims of design. When we are looking to find things that are generalizable, we need to be systematic, thorough, and rigorous in our research approaches -processes that are sometimes at odds with the creative design process.

How are they similar?

Traditionally, the practices of research and design have been separate. This has led to the perception that research is not creative while design is. In its ideal form, research is actually very creative.

Creativity in research ranges from the selection of methods for a particular research purpose, the application of those methods and even how meaning is extracted.

Both research and design are ultimately solution-seeking endeavours. A separate process of research, research, research... then stop once you have sufficient information...then design, design, design is ultimately ineffective. Design and research can be similarly creative when they are integrated. The process is not rational, then creative.

At Carnegie Mellon we work with a cyclical and stepped process for design research, as follows:

• Phase 1: Scoping and Definition
The outcome of this step includes things like territory and stakeholder maps. The idea here is to put boundaries to the project and understand the people affected.
• Phase 2: Exploratory Research
Includes user/human and product studies with the purpose of gaining knowledge and empathy into the subject. The outcome includes the raw criteria for the project and implications for design.
• Phase 3: Generative Research
Includes creative exercises, co-design and participatory design. The outcome is the definition of potential design areas to investigate and first speculative/preliminary design concepts.
• Phase 4: Evaluative Research
Involves testing ideas and making final refinements, both via formal and informal feedback on the various components. It is the verification that this is responsible and responsive design. The outcome is a finished prototype, usually with a convincing visual, a compelling narrative and scenarios of use.

As we are not in business practice we acknowledge but don't typically carry out the phase of 'Launching and Monitoring' which would involve the commercial release and assessed success of the product.

This integrated process allows us to capture the most value out of the combination of research and design. Our Research Methods course, for example, is coupled with a studio project.

How do you envision the future of research and design within the business context?

I think we are in a transition so I have drawn two situations, depicting 'now' and 'the future'. What I still see as the dominant paradigm -the now- is a world in which business is quite dominant, followed by research, which is smaller than business but has some overlap as it is often fuelled by the resources of business. In this paradigm, design is smaller and tangential to both; it is not well integrated.

In the future I have drawn three large and overlapping boxes, all of equal size. These cascading boxes go in multiple directions. Each discipline has its own unique elements. Business can be in the lead, design can be in the lead, and research can be in the lead, too, depending on the context. What connects business, design and research is ultimately people.

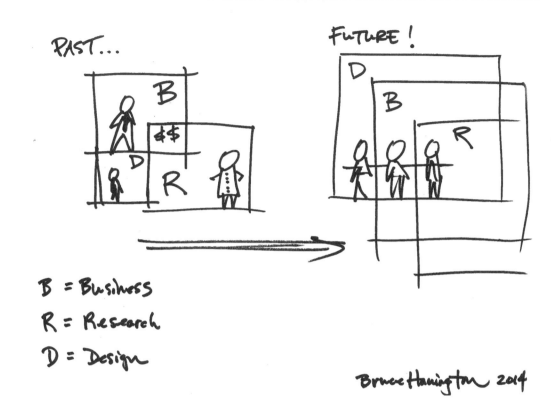

PAST... FUTURE!

B = Business
R = Research
D = Design

Bruce Hanington 2014

Cyclicality and transparency

Lauren Currie
Programme Manager
Hyper Island
Manchester, United Kingdom

Who is Lauren?

Lauren Currie is a designer and innovator and is often referred to as redjotter, which is also the name of her popular design blog. Management Today featured Lauren in 2014 as one of the UK's top thirty-five business women under thirty-five. Lauren co-founded the Service Design and Social Innovation agency, Snook. She is currently a Programme Manager at Hyper Island, and speaks and blogs on creativity, service design, and entrepreneurship.

What is research?

Research is a process of discovery. A big part of that process being valuable is mindset and attitude. A researcher should be open-minded and curious. Research is a way to explore what you want to be, see, and feel in the world.

Ideally, research should underpin and be the foundation for new markets, innovations, and business solutions. It should be the glue and the narrative that brings things together that aren't obviously together.

What is design?

What a difficult question! It's like, What is love? I would define design as the process of making something better, framing problems in new ways, and seeing the world from a different perspective.

At Hyper Island, my aim is produce students who are shapeshifters, practitioners who are surviving and thriving in a world of flux. The ability to understand context, whilst analyzing, to question and create ideas. I hope they will learn how to be comfortable with uncertainty and embrace emerging practices around disciplines such as systems thinking.

How are they different?

The primary difference is that research often informs design. Whereas design can also inform research, design is an act of creation and is not necessarily preoccupied with informing.

I suppose you could compare the design researcher with a researcher with a background in anthropology or psychology. One difference could be a design researcher is more likely to be more visual and more creative in their method and execution. A designer is also more likely to be more conscious of the audience, designing *with* the audience as opposed to *for* the audience.

Design and research can learn a lot from each other. Design needs to learn rigour and evaluation from research. Researchers need to learn the importance of participatory research methods from design and respond to the reality that many traditional research methods are dated.

How are they similar?

The human condition is at the core of both research and design.

A designer's process starts with a discovery phase. They will ask questions such as, What is the problem? Why is it a problem? And look into whether that really is the actual problem at hand. Designers then create a hypothesis as a starting point and are driven to understand. Researchers, on the other hand, are driven by a need to describe the problem and report it back because they are often not the ones in charge of crafting the solution.

How do you envision the future of research and design within the business context?

The main characteristic of the future I envision is cyclicality: continuously evolving with no beginning and no end. A second key characteristic is transparency: we will celebrate and live by people's openness and transparency. This will lead to companies looking up and outwards more, as opposed to inwards.

Businesses will involve people; they would be truly co-creative from the outset, owned and informed by people; members of the public and employees. This would invert the hierarchical pyramid as we now know it; the structure would become different: power would be something very different to what it is now.

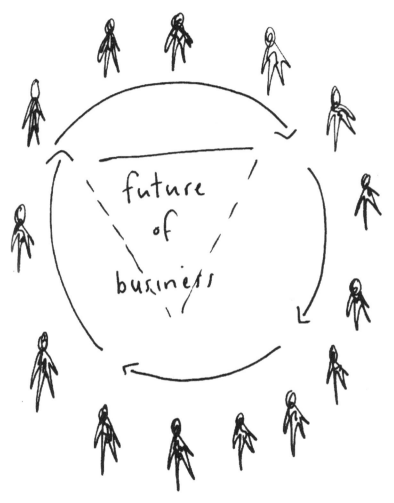

Transversal Lens

Roberta Tassi
Author of Service Design Tools
Milan, Italy

Who is Roberta?

Roberta Tassi has an eclectic background spanning Research, Communication and service design, combining a deep knowledge of user-centred design methodologies with an expertise in designing and facilitating collaborative sessions. She is author and editor of the Service Design Tools website, an online repository of tools used to design solutions for complex systems. She is currently working as Contract Professor at Politecnico di Milano, as Principal Design Researcher at frog, and as UX for GOOD design fellow.

What is research?

Research is mostly about understanding people. Based on my research practice as a designer, I would say it encompasses a mix of ethnographic activities to get in touch with people, their motivations, and their needs.

Research allows us to dig deep into the human aspect so that we can understand the full ecosystem, all its variables and forces. Not just the user, but also surrounding ecosystem, and the business side of it.

What is design?

Design is translating learnings and insights developed during the research phase into solutions that are meaningful, based on what you understood.

Design is not just driven by creativity and intuition. More than in the past, it needs to be driven by insights into human needs that become the real metrics to develop successful, useful, meaningful solutions.

The complexity of what we design has increased versus what it used to be: when you have to design a simple object, the process and tools can be simple. Now, the things we design are systems of connected objects orchestrated by an added layer of service -complex solutions based on different types of interactions with a heterogeneous set of touchpoints, taking place in different moments of time. To control all

these elements, the designer needs a strong reference point, which is represented by the human needs identified during research.

How are they different?

Research and design are not very different instances; they are part of the same process. Research builds small pieces of understanding that put you in the natural condition to start designing.

The way pure researchers do research and the way designers do research is slightly different. In the end, the designers want to discover things that lead to solutions, so they constantly and naturally look for 'hooks' -being either problems and/or opportunities -that trigger their thinking around what could be done. This attitude of going further can be seen also in the way designers set the stage to discover insights, which is often very visual and physical, leveraging the use of representation and prototyping skills to bring stimuli that push the conversation more in-depth.

Researchers are great systemic thinkers: they have the analytical capability to manage complexity at the conceptual level and enough confidence to deal with the uncertainty of not knowing. Great researchers are able to meaningfully synthesize the information they collect to explain key findings to others.

Designers focus on the tension between problems and solutions: their skills include curiosity, eagerness to learn, and flexibility. Their humbleness is essential to interpret research outcomes and, eventually, if they see they are framing the problem and the solution in the wrong way, change their focus.

At the end of the day there is a huge complementarity between the two lenses. I see research as the ability to learn transversally, across all the entities that are part of an experience system or journey. Design is more vertical: it digs deeper and deeper into the single touchpoints to create concrete and beautiful answers.

How are they similar?

The integrated design and research process is shaped through a number of progressive iterations. It starts broad with foundational research and slowly gets to a moment when assumptions can be formulated. At that point you usually start building something, see how it works through generative or evaluative research, and then return to your assumption to incorporate what you have learnt. The learnings help you start over again, formulating new assumptions, and so on, leading to the final solution through progressive refinements.

Both design and research are interpretative acts that involve communication. For researchers, interpretation -and translation- is essential

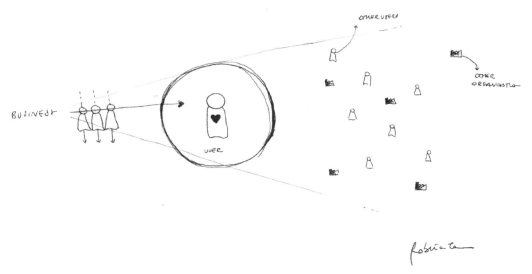

er interlocutors in the process, share information and stories to someone else. For designers, interpretation -and translation- is essential to make choices: design is oriented at obtaining a reaction, a feeling, or emotion in the user. This means designers have to choose what they want to transfer and how, as they shape and interpret possible solutions.

How do you envision the future of research and design within the business context?

We are already moving from a hierarchical and vertical model of business to smoother systems of collaboration grounded on a transversal perspective or lens. The user represents the focus of this transversal lens: putting people at the centre of business efforts to design things they would love and buy.

Additionally, in the background I drew a galaxy of other entities, people and organizations, to represent that there is also a second layer the transversal lens needs to consider: a larger evolving ecosystem that ultimately influences the human motivations and the business choices.

As I made the drawing I actually drew the person in the middle first, and then organized all the other elements around that person. I hope in the future this will be the natural way of thinking for a larger crowd of innovators, being the only path towards the creation of a better world.

A working ecosystem of people

Magda Malachowska
Associate Fellow Academy of Arts
Service Design Polska
Szczecin, Poland

Who is Magda?

Magda Małachowska, PhD, is an expert in innovation and service design. As cofounder of Service Design Polska, a think tank initiative, she increases awareness and spreads knowledge in the area of service design in Poland. Currently, Magda is associated fellow at the Academy of Arts and Westpomeranian University, both located in Szczecin.

What is research?

Research is a process that provides understanding of the needs of the people you are engaging with within a project. Research seeks to understand something based on a given requirement or need, whether it is in the context of a business project or a scientific project. By providing a methodology, research enables you to find the answers you need for your project.

Understanding people is central to research: defining who they are, deciding which methods will deliver the best result when approaching them, and linking this to the purpose of the study are all important aspects to help grasp the subject one is working on. There are many tools available from marketing research and sociological research which, when combined with design, deliver a lot of insight. In the context of design, research is mainly qualitative and involves asking the right people and building an understanding on how people decide and what they do, both as individuals and as communities.

What is design?

Design is the ability of communicating with people from different backgrounds. Design thinking gives you a process and tools to communicate with people and understand what each brings to the table, whether they are experts in marketing, technology, design, business, or anything else. Design makes their skills and the concepts they create visible to the people in the team.

This ability of designers has only developed recently. Designers all have different backgrounds: they may be visual/graphic designers, product designers, or other design-related disciplines. They all now need to understand a bigger perspective and not just master a skill. Because of this, 'design' has become a really broad term. Design now includes so many more things than just the basic design disciplines that it has become difficult to understand.

How are they different?

I believe research is a tool for the design process. It is the way designers search for insights. Design is much broader: it encompasses searching and looking for topics to define a problem, doing the research, building the prototype, and testing. Design gives you a framework of which research is a part that helps guide how to work and how to move from one step to another.

Design is gaining terrain in business because companies want a result and an outcome. Companies often know what they want to solve but they haven't always developed an awareness of how to address this. Design combines interdisciplinary tools in a framework so companies can feel 'safe' as the framework gives a sense that you know what you are doing. By providing that framework, design makes visible to the stakeholders *this* is how it is and *this* is what we might do about it.

And then design has the tools to fail quickly in order to get to the real problem that needs addressing. Design communicates: it gives you the means to explain why you choose a certain direction for developing solutions.

How are they similar?

Their similarity is that they are both about asking questions. They both have an attitude of searching for an answer that might lead to solving people's problems.

Research and design come together through the tools they use to ask questions: qualitative research, ethnography, observations, anthropology, meeting people and watching their lives, and being part of their lives.

Both research and design bring in different perspectives and generate conversations. Design tools allow us to take this further by drawing or putting post-its on walls and showing back to the team what is said, what has been learnt, and putting everyone on the same page so that issues can get unstuck and the team can move forward. Design enables that communication: it communicates back and translates the meaning back to the team so people can work together towards a solution, through a unified and shared view. Mostly in business teams, people speak of the same thing by using different wording and get stuck in the same conversation without realizing it. Design tools help to focus the energy on the real things that need addressing.

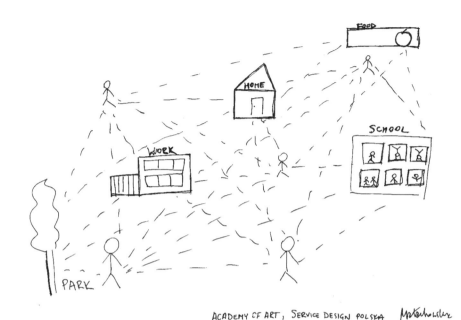

ACADEMY OF ART, SERVICE DESIGN POLSKA Mstaholsler

How do you envision the future of research and design within the business context?

I envision the future as a working ecosystem of people co-designing their world. The boundaries between the lives people lead with their family, school, and business will blur and we will begin to see that people design themselves and the environments they are in.

People are more engaged already nowadays. When they go to the grocery store they don't just pick fruit or vegetables. They are actually deciding what they want to support as a philosophy: do they buy fresh fruit from the local farmer or do they buy fruit flown in from a far away place? Increasingly, people will design their ecosystems through their decisions, creating their own lives and impacting business through those creative choices.

Through their decisions and their actions people will design their relationships with brands, products, services, and the businesses behind them. This will change business, and those who are not part of the change will be changed by it.

Working together

Jacques Lange
Lecturer in Information Design
and Visual Communication,
University of Pretoria
Pretoria, South Africa

Who is Jacques?

Jacques Lange is a partner and the Creative Director at Bluprint Design in Pretoria, South Africa, a lecturer in Information Design and Visual Communication at the University of Pretoria and consultant to various public and non-profit institutions. He is a member of the Mandela Poster Project Collective, and a design curator, writer and editor. He has published widely on topics related to design. He is a former president of the International Council of Design (Ico-D, formerly known as Icograda).

What is research?

Research relates to exploring, gathering, fact-finding, documenting, understanding, and synthesizing existing or new knowledge to enable creative and solutions-based outcomes. More simply put, it is the process of accessing knowledge and inspiration to spark solutions-based creative outcomes.

Research for design differs from other fields such as the traditional sciences, humanities, economics, management, and even market research because it is generalist, participatory, and cross-disciplinary. New dimensions of design-lead research are arising, as we want to understand the softer issues of a vast array of fields and how these relate to human behaviour. This has made broad, qualitative, and participatory investigation much more relevant to design practice, because we need to take a vast plethora of factors into account in any business undertaking if we are going to make a difference in any way that is relevant to people: clients and end-users.

The type of research I mostly engage in on a daily basis is applied practice-based research for design and as I see it, research cannot be isolated from the design process. The magic that happens at the intersection where life, research, and design is a constant and critical reflective process and structured as an integrated feedback loop. It is not possible to do effective design without having an inquiring mind.

What is design?

My definition of design is quite philosophical: Design humanizes and clarifies technology, information, spaces, processes and systems in order to enhance and improve the human and ecology's condition physically, materially, spiritually and sustainably.

The definition that I subscribe to implies that you can only achieve all or most aspects if you have a truly broad and critical understanding of what you're dealing with, what you're doing, how you're doing it, for who, and what the outcomes are. Just looking at design as a way for solving problems would be over-simplifying it, because solutions often create new problems. MOMA curator, Paola Antonelli, claims that design is not just about 'problem solving' but also about 'problem making' -for good and bad.

This is where research and design work together as a critical reflective process and an integrated feedback loop. Yet, it is an area that is fairly new to the design, business, and market research sectors and an area that remains in small pockets. The reason being that most designers are not sufficiently trained in research methodology and research practice since only a handful design schools provide rigorous research training as part of their curriculum. For many designers, a good reading of a client brief and Google searches are regarded as research. which is obviously not sufficient.

This means that the research knowledge and skills of many designers are seriously limited and that a solid culture of research is not commonly fostered in the sector. This also applies to the economic sciences and market research curricula because these hardly ever include the complexities involved in design practice and, therefore, the integrated feedback loop remains elusive.

The responsibilities taken on by designers in recent times are, however, encouraging and evolving. Increasingly, designers are focusing on doing good and serving end users, rather than immediate clients more efficiently by engaging actively and intelligently in research activities, instead of just delivering good-looking design. The result will make design and research evolve further: there are so many other kinds of things that people and our planet need than just good-looking design. More designers are now daring to ask what is really needed rather than just what is desired. Thus, great design takes on new dimensions. It is not just about promoting a brand or crafting an object, piece of information, or space. Today, design has to work a lot harder to achieve many more goals and outcomes that reach more expectations and criteria than ever before.

How are they different?

They're not so different when it comes down to it. I would say the only big difference is with market research, especially quantitative re-

"More designers are now daring to ask what is really needed rather than what is desired."

search, which is the furthest away from practice-based design research because it creates clinical, lab-like conditions whereas the real world is not a lab environment. In quantitative market research, the human factors are so often missing and not supportive or relevant to the work of designers.

Research for design requires methodologies and parameters that are flexible, broad, humanistic, and allow for alternative pathways and outcomes which don't always need to be systematic or statistically quantifiable. These

aspects often cause barriers between designers and traditional researchers because much of the design domain's work are interpretive and operate in the sphere of speculation. It is my opinion that this is exactly the space where design could really make a difference to research because it asks an awkward question: 'What if?' instead of 'What is?'.

Technology most certainly also plays a role. Market research used to work on hard and fast figures. Everybody is now realizing that there are seldom yes-or-no answers to questions.

Look at social media for example, which is highly integrated with design. Designers and design researchers are tech savvy and know how to use online platforms, especially social media, in order to access and understand ongoing conversations. This provides a source of continuous, ongoing interaction that provides a stream of ever-increasing feedback, which is in stark contrast to market research. Market research mostly happens seasonally or intermittently, is expensive and complex.

How are they similar?

Both research and design are about abstracting and simplifying. They aim to uncover knowledge and understand a landscape even though the outcomes might be different.

This common aim is similar to what happens with food preparation, which is a good analogy to describe the relationship. The research process is about going into the garden to pick fresh ingredients and/or going shopping for groceries. It is about figuring out the effects of the ingredients on one another. Design seeks to understand how the ingredients could infuse each other and what the potential end results could be. Design is about coming up with an idea for a recipe, cooking, the assembly and presentation of the dish. It involves the steps of putting it together, letting it rest, cooking it, and finally serving the dish. It's also a bit like alchemy.

How do you envision the future of research and design within the business context?

I have drawn a face to represent the human factor, with a world map that stands for the huge environment and ecosystems in which all interact. There are a series of thought bubbles, showing the steps of the process in which I envision businesses working together in the future: a question mark for the research process of asking questions; an exclamation mark for the moment in which we scrutinize our findings and our work choosing where to go next; a symbol for pausing to understand what the impact of those choices will be; and a symbol for play or move, indicating the dynamic of change caused by our intervention. I envision a future in which this process will be collaborative, cross- and meta-disciplinary, seamless and more human centred.

A new common language

Macrina Busato
Head of Design & Management
IE, Instituto de la Empresa
Business School
Madrid, Spain

Who is Macrina?

Macrina Busato is a design and anthropology researcher. With a formal education as Cultural Anthropologist, Art Conservator and Graphic Designer, Macrina's vision is to apply the innovations associated with the field of design and creativity into education, business and the management world. Since 2013 she has been designing content and managing the Area in Design & Management at the IE Business School.

What is research?

Research is about the search for answers and new questions. Yet traditionally defined 'market research' is research commissioned usually by the marketing departments in order to gain information or come to new insights or ideas. But everybody does the same, so chances are you will have the same information as your competitors.

Research has an important and valuable role in opening perspectives and improving our ability to observe. There are also many other interesting/insightful forms of obtaining information to add value to research in a broader sense. For example, lets say you want to explain to me what a forest is. You could give me a great description about a forest. You could provide me with lists of what is in the forest in terms of flora and fauna. You could give me a map with the exact dimensions of the forest. You could make an inventory of who walks through the forest, what it is used for, etcetera. That is helpful and interesting data that provides me a piece of a static vision of what this forest is. But, this information does not talk about the experience of the forest. There is nothing comparable to experiencing the forest oneself to gain creative insights: you experience the colours, the smells, the breeze and the temperature, the changing lights and shadows, the seasons, the falling leaves, the vegetation underneath the forest, the softness of the musk, the sound of the birds....And what about learning more about the life of the people who walk, work, observe, or live in the forest? What meanings does the forest have for them? This kind of holistic research will be crucial for me to make sense of all the data.

Data and information are not enough to make sense of things. You need to interpret, to understand the meaning behind that data. And that process needs some level of uncertainty, of randomness in the discovery. It may look random but it isn't really. It's like with scientific discoveries: chance favours the prepared mind. The element of chance is something you have to create space for. I wonder whether market research actually leaves any room for that.

What is design?

Design is about creating something -a process, an object, a service etc.- to be used for any user-defined purpose. It is a creative act of making something that wasn't there before in a way that is relevant to the user. Design sets energy in movement, which to me is fascinating. Design looks at the spaces and opportunities, which ask to be filled with meaning and creates a solution.

I think the beauty of design as a process is that it can be understood and it can be embraced also by people from other disciplines. Traditionally the design process has been seen as uncertain and unpredictable by non-designers. So we have tried to systematize and explain what, how, and why we do it. That's what design thinking is.

"It is the endless experience of discovery, reframing questions, and learning that defines design."

But here is a danger in just focusing on the 'design thinking' process as an A-B-C. It removes design from its soul. It is not just a matter of following steps. We may be creating confusion and even frustration if people come to think its just the process. Actually, it is the endless experience of discovery, reframing questions, and learning that define design. And that takes skill, but it also takes a lot of time.

Within innovation people often want to learn design skills. So they just go through the A-B-Cs, the tools, but never actually go through the iterations,. They miss the learning and insights that embracing uncertainty gives us: the opportunity to discover and explore. This process of learning and reflection is to me the essence of any creative endeavour.

Designers seek this experience because we have been trained to understand relevance within the real context in which things function. We cannot separate the two -context and object- because if we do, things crumble into meaninglessness.

How are they different?

First, let me say that to me research and design are inseparable. To me, research is not 'just' market research though. It is anything and everything you need to do in order to broaden and deepen your understanding. That said, I think there is a difference in the approach: design allows you to use anything you can find as a source of information because you want a rich understanding, you want to compare and contrast. Somewhere, you are bound to find

insights that will surprise you and that will deliver new combinations, new spaces of opportunity.

Market research is often directed at more particular, more defined, pre-framed topics or search areas. This is why in the ideal world as a designer I would want to have access to as many research reports as possible to add on top of those, other different forms and sources of research.

We live in a world in which everybody has access to information. This is why I feel just 'having' research insights is not enough to make a difference. Design goes beyond that. We put everything out on the table; we seek to visualize it, to see patterns, to understand layers. Designers are trained to do that, to create a corpus of knowledge through integrating different sources and different views. I think researchers are more specialists in the data gathering techniques, whereas designers understand that relevant data can be gathered in many different ways.

How are they similar?

Both research and design are ways of looking up from your own agenda and into the world of real people and users. In the eagerness with which business is seeking to adopt design thinking practices in recent years, there is also a danger. They may just want to check off boxes and state that they spent time understanding user perspective but that is not so. In their primary purpose, both research and design are about uncovering what matters to the user through empathy.

Another similarity is that their application to business stems from an industrial background. Yet in the twenty-first century we no longer live in an industrial model. We have evolved and things are much more fluid. Knowledge, communication, interaction, everything is more fluid. Both market research and design have an opportunity to add value in the emerging model of business.

How do you envision the future of research and design within the business context?

I think in the future we will see two disciplines, which have found a way to deliver value to business through a developed common language. This is the language of the user, but translated into business activities and actions. This will take time, but the time is ripe for this new language where the understanding the user and creating meaning will increasingly be the key to sustainable business growth and profitability.

Conscious collaboration

Beatriz Russo
Assistant Professor on
Design-Driven Innovation
and Emotional Design
ESPM
Rio de Janeiro, Brazil

Who is Beatriz?

Beatriz Russo works both in academy and industry. For over ten years she has lectured in design-related graduate and post-graduate courses (both in Brazil and The Netherlands) and has conducted workshops on the topic of emotional experiences and design research/innovation all over the world. She is currently Assistant Professor at the ESPM (*Escola Superior de Propaganda e Marketing*). She is also owner and lead consultant at IGPD – Design-Driven Innovation.

What is research?

Research is something that allows us to understand reality, so that we can negotiate over that understanding and come up with solutions that are not only effective, but that people resonate with.

As a designer, I see research as an intrinsic part of the creative process. Research is a basis for inspiration. It helps us guide a process that leads to a design. In business, too often research is used to prove a certain point or confirm preconceived ideas. However, if you do not take research as a first step in your projects, you are basically designing something for yourself, not your customers.

What is design?

Design is about solving problems no matter what kind of problem you need to solve. It is about following a process in which you basically look into a problem from many different angles in order to formulate interesting questions and, later, come up with useful answers that are able to provoke relevant experiences. The design method –or design thinking- provides a good path for solutions.

Only following the process does not make you a designer. It also takes the development of some skills and personal characteristics that, added to the process, help its flow, for example, long-term orientation. People who are long-term oriented are able to deal with 'today'

while also thinking about 'tomorrow'. This is a very good trait as it helps designers contemplate the whole scenario and make decisions that are more ecological, more useful to the whole picture The generation of ideas within the design process is really an outcome. In order to deliver innovation, there are things you have to have, things you have to be and things you have to do.

Through design thinking we may have over-emphasized what you need to do, which can be summed up in the process. But to put it in practice you have to have things, like courage. The courage to go against the flow, to experiment, and to try things out. Or persistence: if you don't have persistence you may give up too soon and not learn from mistakes. And then there are things you have to be: design is also a state of being; being open-minded, being passionate, being focused, being resilient, to name a few. All of these characteristics are what make a designer.

How are they different?

It seems that while business has traditionally used research to find answers, design uses research to formulate the right questions and guide themselves throughout the project they're engaged in. It helps us make better decisions along the way. Research is the only tool we have to dig really deep into people's lives and come up with a screenplay that allows us to shut down our own thinking process, our own ideas and understanding of the world, and act as if we actually are the final user or customer.

How are they similar?

If we look into the scientific process, it also relies on research to come up with good finding. I believe that, in essence, the scientific process and the design process are very similar. However, the scientific process has certain rules and rigour one must follow in order to generate knowledge. The design process is more flexible; it is not looking for purity but inspiration. Design deals with the social world and the social world does not have set rules. At most, you can see some patterns, but those are always changing as human activity and thinking provokes change over time. You cannot put out an experiment, repeat it over time, and expect to find the same results.

How do you envision the future of research and design within the business context?

I have drawn a pyramid to explain what would be in the hierarchies of the future of business: at the top of the pyramid are more feminine values, which are about inclusion and collaboration.

The second level is about the ability to look at things from a broader perspective; I have drawn someone climbing up a tree to get a panoramic view of what is happening.

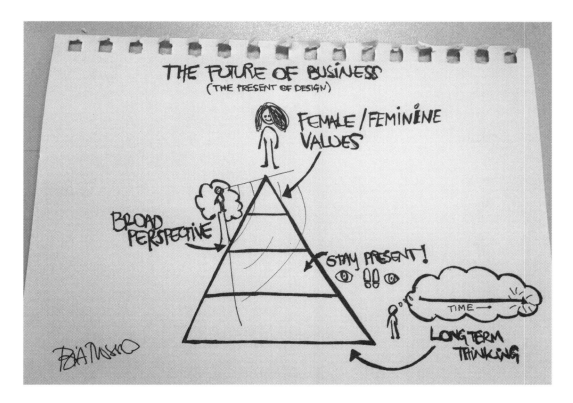

The third level is about the ability of staying present, It is about being mindful, not overly focused on the past, nor future obsessed, but about having both feet on the ground and looking at where we are in the 'here and now'. Dealing in the present which is the only moment in space-time in which we have the power to change things.

The base of the pyramid is about the ability to think long term, being aware that our actions today have long-term implications. We need to act consciously and ecologically.

My hope is that companies, in the near future, would have developed these abilities: working collaboratively, keeping the broader perspective in mind, and acting consciously to generate change that will impact our lives positively.

Interconnected and interdependent

Sue Biely

Post Graduate Fellow and Program Coach, OSR Master's Program at Seattle University
Vancouver, Canada

Who is Sue?

Sue Biely is an accomplished designer, facilitator, team coach, collaborator, innovator and public speaker. She is drawn to situations, people, groups, and organizations that are on the edge of an evolution. Her work bridges gaps between core strategy and implementation, often using rapid prototyping and experimentation to help an organization learn faster and take risks. She ignites adult professionals to strengthen their team dynamics, collaboration skills, and breakthrough thinking.

What is research?

Research is about seeing the whole system, sensing the culture, observing through multiple ways of knowing, deep listening, and inquiry. It involves a willingness to let go of assumptions yet follow hunches.

As a researcher knows, letting go of assumptions creates the opportunity to see beyond them. Any information or data in one's assumptions will block one's capacity and willingness to see anew and be surprised, which is crucial to openness as research ability.

So while in this state of suspension, you still need to allow yourself to follow hunches. When you get a hunch from an energy sense in your body, or you get hit with a deep curiosity and something about what you are researching becomes compelling, you need to be able to follow that clue. I would dare to say, follow that with abandon, at the risk of sounding too poetic. These 'clues' come into your field from the outside, rather than being sought out from an already existing assumption on your inside.

Research provides a protected piece of time in which you are engaging in a deep dive with 'what is', as I just described. Then, you come back to the surface and look again. It's like climbing and then reaching a threshold where you can take a snapshot of what you've discovered and start reflecting on that snapshot by asking: What is patterning? What is outlier information?

What is surprising me? What is attracting my curiosity? What is attracting my energy?

Ideally research is done in teams, so you share all of this, building a field from the deep dive snapshot that allows you to move forward by asking: What are some leverage points? What are probes or small experiments we could conduct? In this iterative process of learning, research blends into design.

What is design?

Design is a consciousness, an awareness and a process by which we sense, evoke, and interact with 'what is' to provoke what 'wants to be', even when we do not know what it might be.

As a consciousness it relies on the presence of 'what is' and taps into multiple forms of data points to move towards something that doesn't exist yet, that you don't quite know what it is but there is a sense that it's a compelling, better opportunity than 'what is' and you've started to find clues.

How are they different?

Research is a space where you're open and trying to take your meaning-making lens off, thus suspending your meaning-making capacity and so you can lead with curiosity. In essence, research is an inquiry. It focuses on the question not on the problem. The problem is just a symptom. Research sets out to engage with the question to be explored.

"Research and Design are in service to positive outcomes for the whole."

In the process of data collection, meaning-making and being informed by the data, there is a continuum, a cross-fade between research and design as you start understanding which actions to take. This is an iterative process. It starts from research and gathering information but then the iterative cycles accelerate as the meaning-making takes place and the sense of 'doing' rather than 'observing' starts to emerge. The design team needs to share their inner wisdom from the observing process so that it informs how they may move into doing.

In turn, in the first phases of design, one is hugely open to learning. During the open research phase, designers are rebuilding their internal information from the system so that they can work on behalf of the system later on. If you don't come in clean and open to pick up on the data from the system, you risk working from your own experience and bias, so you would not be in an actual dance with the system. Instead you would be putting yourself 'onto' the system. When this happens, interventions do not end up having long-term, positive impact of the system. It would be more along the lines of telling others you want them to change, and how, which doesn't work. Design is about evoking something together and it moves from just being logical idea in one's head to a fully sensed activation of energy of the whole system. It's a far more intimate process.

Research and design are companions, but there are times when one is leading more than the other. They both inform each other, like in a respectful collaboration.

How are they similar?

I would say that both research and design are in service to positive outcomes for the whole. They are both in service to finding and fuelling and ultimately making iterative 'leaps' for society. And I'd like to say here that it's my wish that these powers are used for good and the evolution of human kind.

Done well, it is almost like a wisdom practice. You have to really open yourself up, you have to have to have really clear intentions around being in service. Also, with both research and design you need to have strong ethics and awareness of the moral impact of their interventions, though this is something that is not talked about enough. Done well, they consider the total experience of being engaged from all parts of the system, whether as research, designer, or participant in the system.

How do you envision the future of research and design within the business context?

I have drawn an office building to represent business, but the windows are linked to other energetics and to each other by all these different lines, which go both ways. And this building has roots: it is organic, it is connected, and it is grounded. All these roots are feeding from this same nourishment. Anything that is above ground is supported by what is below ground, and vice-versa.

On the outside, there is this bounded circle with the word 'wholeness', to symbolize the ability to hold this sense of the whole respectfully, to see the interconnectedness and the interdependency and the 'inter-ethics' of it all. We are all contributing to this larger and shared phenomenon, not just at one point in time but also in the near future and in the far future. We need to remember that.

In my vision of the future of research and design within business we will have learnt not only to think laterally about what we impact but also temporally so that we are enhancing our ability to create a whole over a longer period of time.

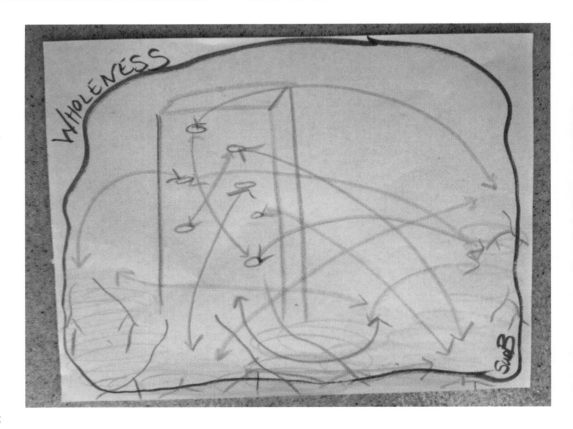

Aligned with life

Arne Van Oosterom
Founder DesignThinkers Group
and DesignThinkers Academy
Amsterdam, The Netherlands

Who is Arne?

Arne van Oosterom is the Founding Partner at DesignThinkers Group, and the co-founder of DesignThinkers Academy and the Design Thinkers Network. Arne is an innovation facilitator, and team and personal coach helping build people-centric innovation capabilities within organizations and has worked with many top 500 brands. He is also a frequent keynote speaker at various international universities and conferences.

What is research?

The reason for conducting research is wanting to find out things you don't know. I would define research as a journey. The research goal offers direction, but it is a journey of discovery.

The journey of research involves trespassing boundaries, as you move from what you know into what you don't know and want to learn more about. Research is a continuous effort; it doesn't stop once you found something that may be of interest. It is a continuous activity of looking at the context and understanding it.

What is design?

Design is connecting things that are not yet connected. It leads to either new or better connections and by doing so to the generation of value.

The value of design cannot be defined beforehand, as it is contextually dependent. The relevance and value of the connections that design makes may be good or bad depending on the context and the user.

Design is ultimately what connects the research with new answers, it is the creation of new solutions based on what we see happening.

How are they different?

Where research is about asking questions, design is an attempt to provide answers. Because of this, they provide different angles while both coming from a mindset of not knowing enough about something and opening up to what might be out there. They both start from a position of not having the answer to something and wanting to investigate.

Designers are not always design thinkers. Researchers do not always provide relevance. That's why we shouldn't look at people as 'designers' or 'researchers'. What we need is groups of people with complementary skills who can help the group find the tensions and contrasts that give insight into the issues at hand.

The difference between research and design skills is in their complementarity. You cannot research or design only from your own point of view: you need others to help you see the full system, to interpret what this might mean. and to apply the findings in relevant ways.

How are they similar?

Both research and design have the ability to question things in their aim to understand the context. The questions they raise range from *why* to *who* to *what*, in an attempt to understand what connects to what and what the triggers are that cause things to be as they are or work as they do.

Even a small project can lead to a thousand questions. Design involves a continuous process of research, iterations, options, and choices. The questions are important, because better questions lead to better design.

Research and design are also similar in that they recognize that other people are involved, not out of empathy, which may or may not be accurate however well intended, but from a deep understanding that you cannot be the other person. By acknowledging the user as different from yourself, they become the object of study, of inspiration, and of relevant understanding.

How do you envision the future of research and design within the business context?

I have drawn a small family, of parents with a child walking out in a park. This is my metaphor for the future of people and communities. The family represents human connections: friendships, families, neighbours, even colleagues. The people we care about. In my drawing they are where they want to be, with the people they want to be with.

My vision of the future of business is in one word: Life. Business will be more aligned with people's lives; we will no longer be juggling the work-life balance. That is a construct. There is no such thing. People are currently forcing themselves to work jobs they don't want, with people they don't like, in companies that do not represent their values. In the future we will be inspired by the capacities of research and design to understand and make new connections, and we will connect our work to our life. Going back to the essence of what matters most.

Emerging understanding

It is humbling to realize how much we do not know about what research, design and strategy actually involve. It is somehow relieving that there are no clear-cut definitions. This leaves a lot of space for discovery and experimentation and building a new future. To discover, through these dialogues, that the ways we understand the world and try to capture that understanding are somehow finite, providing only one angle of the total panorama. Each one of the experts interviewed shared their perspective, bridging cross-disciplinary gaps by comparing and contrasting how research and design are transforming the way we think and do. If there is one common element shared by the experts it is the realization that collaborative learning will help enrich our perspectives, enhance our understanding, and unite our efforts.

The human factor, beyond definitions, processes, and disciplines, is the common element of how the different experts look at the emerging understanding around how these disciplines are practiced and how they are evolving. As we have seen in these conversations with experts, mindset is crucial. It is the mindset that makes the designer able to look for new ways of solving problems and eager to understand the real framing of the problem to ensure that relevant solutions are created. It is the mindset that makes the researcher, able to do research for design, linking the efforts to an outcome, yet always putting the understanding of the context, the user, and the situation first (since solutions only work if they are relevant to this understanding). Being a researcher or being a designer are not just labels or qualifications. The new breed of researchers and designers constitutes a breed that goes over and above their own areas of expertise, sailing out into the world to co-shape better business. Better in the sense that it is more meaningful, more relevant, and ultimately more valuable through the integration of research and design skills.

The consensus is that research and design are inseparable. They need one another, they feed on one another, and they build on one another -just like great sailing teams who rely on each other's abilities and celebrate new discoveries.

7 THE NEXT FRONTIER

Creating a culture
that embraces
change.

'Individually, we are one drop. Together, we are an ocean.'

–Rynosuke Satoro

Continuous waves of renewal

We can be certain that, in a context of change, specific discipline-based skills are no longer a static asset one can rely on for life. While specific disciplinary skills are important, learning a trade or profession once in one's life and then exercising that discipline throughout one's career is no longer enough. As the context keeps changing, we must keep learning.

Today, people attending schools and universities are learning based on the premises of a system that served the industrial era well but which may not be equipping them with what they will need as they move into a future where they will be doing jobs we have not heard of yet and working with technologies that we don't know yet.

Learning is not an option anymore. It is a way of life we all need to adopt. Just like business moves into a new era of creative empowerment by embracing change, so should people on a human scale. A context of change in which continuous waves of renewal come and go like the tide is a context of opportunity for those who choose to dive into its fluidity with an open mind.

The ocean of context is as vast as it is filled with opportunity. Our attitude and openness is what makes a difference in how we appreciate the enormity and complexity of it.

Stanford professor Carol Dweck[1] explains this by contrasting a fixed mindset with a growth mindset. According to Dweck, people with a fixed mindset believe their basic qualities, such as intelligence or talent, are fixed traits that one either has or doesn't have. A fixed mindset assumes that these qualities are fixed and that they cannot be developed, whereas those with a growth mindset believe that their abilities can be developed through dedication and hard work. This view of oneself and the world creates an eagerness for learning and a resilience that is essential for great accomplishment.

At this time in the evolution of business, embracing a growth mindset has become crucially relevant. As Dweck states in her book *MindSet*: "Create an organization that prizes the development of ability -and watch the leaders emerge."

T-shaped professionals

As human beings, we have the innate advantage of communication, in order to share and exchange views with others and thus enrich our understanding. And we have imagination, in order to apply learnings to other situations and envision abstract alternatives which are not physically present.

These human skills of communication and imagination are what empower us beyond the mechanistic, industrialist paradigm as change enablers. Traditionally, we have praised experts and individual professionals and thinkers for the depth of their expertise. In the choppy waters of today's context, only having depth of knowledge is not enough. Broadening one's skills through learning and by teaming up with other people from other disciplines to complement one's perspective gives teams more flexibility and stability when facing the waves of change. This combination of depth and breadth is what defines so-called T-shaped professionals[2].

T-shaped people combine the ability to connect knowledge and apply it across situations with deep, specialized skills and expertise within a particular discipline or field of knowledge. T-shaped individuals working in teams are more likely to generate distinctive, valuable innovation and strategic renewal within organizations, by bridging worlds, interlinking perspectives and fostering the cross-fertilization of ideas.

As the 'arms' of the T-shaped professionals interlink within teams, they are better able to learn from one another, cope with changing conditions, and engage in problem solving in more effective ways by integrating abilities and perspectives. Most problems organizations face are not necessarily new nor more complicated. They are more complex, which means that there are more levels of issues to be addressed in order to understand and solve those problems and strategic issues. Problems have become more systemic in nature and require a more systemic and team-based approach to unlock new and relevant solutions.

There has been a lot of discussion about the development of T-shaped skills. Some people believe there is a risk of the T's becoming too 'shallow' by putting too much emphasis on the breadth, forgetting the importance of the depth in order to get things done skilfully. While this concern is understandable, my belief is that T-shaped professionals are like skilful sailors. No concessions need to be made to the individual skills, experience or contribution. Working together is a matter of attitude and good teamwork adds breadth, while every individual contributor brings in specific skills and abilities that enhance the intrinsic quality of the work being done. Engaging across disciplines strengthens the whole as it builds trust, enables teamwork, and fosters creativity.

Importantly, like the growth mindset, T-shaped skills can be developed and learnt. As business teams navigate the turbulent waters of a changing context, the kind of teamwork and attitudes needed become akin to that of a sailing team in an ocean regatta, combining self-reliance with team-reliance, using specific tools and methods from one's own discipline, and integrating those of others, ultimately pulling through the waves together in a sustained effort.

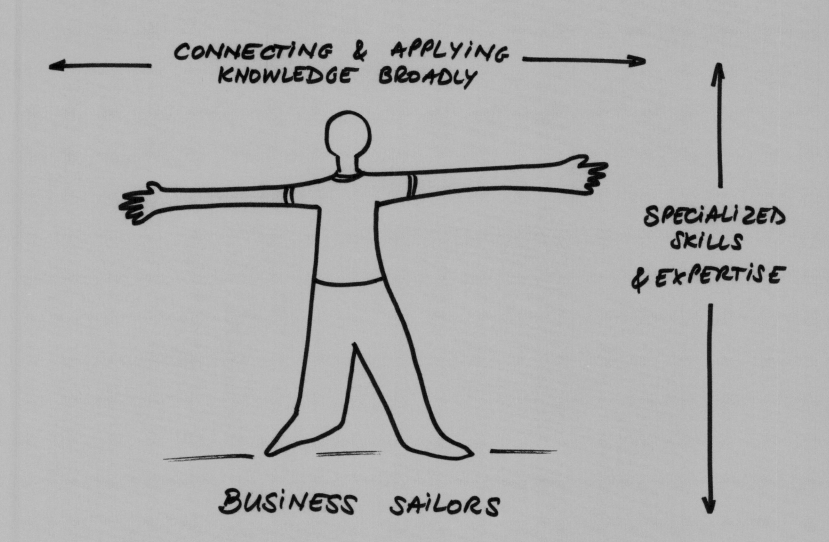

Enabling Change

As the functional separation of skills in business gives way to more blended skills, research and design are more relevant than ever in the co-development of strategy. Learning amidst ongoing change demands a curious and creative attitude -exactly what research and design bring to teams:

• Research skills provide the ability to look openly at the context and understand it without an agenda or interpretative lens in order to learn from it;

• Design skills provide the ability to interpret and develop the creative solutions that emerge from that curiosity-driven research and to integrate the different factors that come into play through the creation of valuable solutions

The reality of the business evolution cycle is that systems change more slowly than people. So we need change agents, change enablers, and change facilitators who will inspire through their attitudes, move ahead of the system, and co-shape it from within as they lead by example and help establish new practices.

A changing context and the overwhelming amount of information available demands that all team members produce, create, and synthesize information. It also means for everyone that we cannot really know whether things will work until we try, and that by doing we will learn what could be done differently in new iterations. Cycles thus get shorter, learning is a collaborative endeavour, and if businesses don't want to miss the boat then we need to engage in continuous processes of strategic inquiry by learning to learn together. Not offering resistance to the waves of context, but navigating and steering towards strategic intent.

Paradigm shift

In business practice, according to Philip Atkinson[3], "Eighty per cent of organisational cultures exist by accident or default, rather than design. Most are shaped by critical incidents or key events that have happened in the history of the organisation. Many are shaped by key personalities moving through the business. Generally, few organisations really have a clear understanding of identifying the core factors that shape culture and how to orchestrate them to best effect."

If we are going to transform business and make it more alive and adaptable to its environment, we will need more than only the mindset that research and design provide, and which involves accepting the cyclicality of business strategy with an open mind and a willingness to effectuate change. This is why this chapter goes beyond the realm of research and design as core skills and into a set of attitudes that can help shift the culture of organizations.

We are moving away from the super-hero, visionary, and individualistic approach to strategy. Today's strategic processes promote and require engagement: engaging the context, engaging the user, and engaging the teams. Engaging in these ways helps make things happen as the business navigates in order to manifest its strategic intent in ways that resonate with the context and create meaningful value.

For business to be sustainable in a changing world it is necessary that we understand its interdependency. As the African proverb goes "If you want to go quickly, go alone. If you want to go far, go together". The world of quick-wins is limited and the crises that businesses are facing are linked to that. The world of opportunity is one in which curiosity, experimentation, empathy, and co-creation are the norm. This requires a set of attitudes and a world-view that embraces change.

Modelling attitude is not applying models

Culture is not something that can be imposed on people. In order to build a work culture that can cope with change and a team that has the right set of attitudes to face it, one must enable change from the inside out.

As Satoro's quote at the beginning of this chapter implies, when people work together they can accomplish much more than they would alone. Importantly, people are models, too, a dynamic set of behavioural patterns can inspire us to act in better ways.

People are better at following other people's examples, than they are at following advice. Model attitudes allow us to learn experientially by interpreting the strategies of others necessary to get to their particular outcomes. Once we understand the strategies that lead to those outcomes, we can adopt them and apply them in our own ways in existing or new situations.

Enough modelling has been done with tools and templates to fill complete libraries. Let's now look at model attitudes: inspiring behaviours that demonstrate how a creative, curious, and determined approach can do to make a meaningful difference for business. As we have seen through the inspiring interviews with pioneers and experts, a lot of the skills and attitudes that make people and teams excellent stewards of change can be contagious through example.

Change agents

Changing necessarily means doing things differently. And while transformation and evolution are necessary for survival, they are uncomfortable. They pose a challenge, in that they require breaking patterns and redefining the game. In changing times, a positive attitude towards change is mandatory for survival and it involves learning as a mindset. In the words of Warren Bennis: "In a time of drastic change, it is the learners who inherit the future. The learned find themselves equipped to live in a world that no longer exists."[4]

The underlying principle behind change is progress. Once we understand that change leads to progress, it becomes easier to change as a way to break free from assumptions, break out of conditioned mindsets, and break open the mental boxes we are trapped in.

The ability to rethink assumptions, to reformulate goals, and to readjust the course for more relevance and meaningfulness is crucial in making the most of change. Seeing oneself as a change agent shifts the perspective from victim to co-creator, and in so doing changes the potential for seizing opportunities and helping change the world positively instead of becoming obsolete or irrelevant by ignoring it.

Attitude for growth

As we all sail together into the future, one which we cannot possibly fully prepare ourselves for, we need each other as a source of inspiration. This is why I want to emphasize the importance of a learning attitude, an open mind, and an adaptable stance to enable the success of any business. It is not just the tools matter; our attitude makes or breaks the thriving of these practices.

The twenty-first century company culture contains what I call the 14 Cs: a set of attitudes that will increasingly become an integral part of the business DNA. More and more, business teams will be made of people with different backgrounds, different skills, and different abilities. This is how businesses will stay adaptive and nimble while embracing the challenges of uncertainty and complexity in a changing context.

These 14 Cs are, in random order: collaboration, curiosity, contribution, connection, critical thinking, citizenship, character, celebration, caring, creativity, courage, communication, commitment to change and clarity of purpose. If we are to create 'ad-venturous' companies together, these are the essential attitudes that we will need to make it happen. The more of these a team practices, the more adaptable it will be to change, and thus, the better positioned it will be to sustain its business into the future and to reach the next frontier.

"As we all sail together into the future, one which we cannot possibly fully prepare ourselves for, we need each other as a source of inspiration."

The 14 Cs build further on existing business literature that I have read over the years and has inspired me to think in terms of attitudes and culture when supporting business teams. These are the attitudes that I feel make a difference. Arguably, the list could be longer, shorter, or slightly different, yet the essence of their message is timeless. It's the attitude that shapes the culture, and it's the culture that makes a company resilient, sustainable, and ultimately successful.

The context has gotten so complicated that it becomes difficult to model, so the way we take it in stride becomes vital to any company that is to thrive in our changing times. We don't necessarily need to model tasks or behaviours. We need to model attitude. In this chapter I will make an attempt to describe these attitudes, which will be crucial to companies pushing the new frontier and leading the way for all of us through what they do, how they do it, and how they view business strategy, research, and design as integrated disciplines.

Collaboration, Curiosity, Contribution, Connection, Critical thinking, Citizenship, Character, Celebration, Caring, Creativity, Courage, Communication, Commitment to change, Clarity of purpose.

Collaboration

A collaborative attitude starts with the realization that one person accounts for one perspective, while more people working together deliver more perspectives than the number of people in the room. Ideas multiply exponentially when shared because in the world of ideas there is no zero-sum game. Let me explain: in economic theory there is the understanding that there is only so much of anything to go around. Therefore, it is inevitable that when one person wins the other must lose, keeping the combined change at zero once you add the gains and subtract the losses. Thus the name zero-sum.

With ideas there is no such thing. If I have one idea and you have one idea, once we share them with each other, each of us both have two ideas. And then, maybe, we get inspired by each other's ideas and make new connections and benefit even further from the exchange.

That is the magic of collaboration. It is particularly interesting when the context leads us to realize that in an increasingly complex environment, we will benefit from sharing because collaboration will give us more coping strategies, more ideas, and more insights than we could have created on our own.

In this era of creative empowerment, interaction and collaboration have taken over from hierarchy as a way for proactively implementing strategy. When collaboration is effectively seen as an attitude for exchange rather than an excuse for endless meetings it becomes a propelling force. It links everything together into a more powerful whole: from strategizing, to cross-fertilizing ideas, to developing those idea through to implementing the ideas successfully.

Curiosity

As young children, we are innately curious. We engage with the world around us investigatively, wanting to understand and experience all kinds of things. Curiosity is an optimistic attitude and one that is crucial for growth and discovery.

In his book, *Curious?*, Todd Kashdan[5] succinctly describes the magical working of curiosity: "There is a simple story line for how curiosity is the engine of growth. By being curious, we explore. By exploring, we discover. When this is satisfying, we are more likely to repeat it. By repeating it, we develop competence and mastery. By developing competence and mastery, our knowledge and skills grow. As our knowledge and skills grow, we stretch and expand who we are and what our life is about. By dealing with novelty, we become more experienced and intelligent, and infuse our lives with meaning. Curiosity begets more curiosity because the more we know, the more details that we attend to, the more we realize what there is to learn. Why? When we embrace the unknown, our perspective hangs, and we begin to recognize gaps—literally and figurative—that weren't apparent before."

Curiosity is what links a business to its context, what leads it to self-reflect about what could be done differently, what allows it to originate new ideas, make new connections, and take in new perspectives.

A recent *Harvard Business Review* article[6] introduces the idea of a Curiosity Quotient, or CQ: "CQ stands for curiosity quotient and concerns having a hungry mind. People with higher CQ are more inquisitive and open to new experiences. They find novelty exciting and are quickly bored with routine. They tend to generate many original ideas and are counter-conformist. It has not been as deeply studied as EQ and IQ, but there's some evidence to suggest it is just as important when it comes to managing complexity in two major ways. First, individuals with higher CQ are generally more tolerant of ambiguity. This nuanced, sophisticated, subtle thinking style defines the very essence of complexity. Second, CQ leads to higher levels of intellectual investment and knowledge acquisition over time, especially in formal domains of education, such as science and art (note: this is of course different from IQ's measurement of raw intellectual horsepower). Knowledge and expertise, much like experience, translate complex situations into familiar ones, so CQ is the ultimate tool to produce simple solutions for complex problems."

Contribution

In the industrial model, contribution was linked to productivity. This was the essence of the transactional agreement of asking someone to do work, measuring the results of the work done and paying in accordance to the contribution or results. In the creative empowerment era, contribution takes on new meaning.

Contribution has less to do with key performance indicators, scorecards, and annual objectives. It has everything to do with being part of a team, collaborating with others, and interacting with others to think, frame, and work together, cooperating proactively and taking on the responsibility of helping to generate value, shifting from 'me' thinking to 'we' thinking, aiming for the success of the team rather than for individual saliency.

As the saying goes: 'Teamwork divides the task and multiplies success". A lot of the skills for contribution involve stepping out of the competitive mindset that might otherwise lead to personal reward and distinction. Understanding that, as I often quote, "the only place where success comes before work is in the dictionary". Contribution requires knowing one's strengths, being generous in applying them, openly sharing knowledge, pulling up one's sleeves to work cooperatively, being flexible, and communicating constructively. Success requires of contributors that they do not wait to be told what to do, but take initative and work together to

"Curiosity is an optimistic attitude, and one that is crucial for growth and discovery."

make things happen. Success demands hard work, but also provides high satisfaction.

Importantly, the way teams contribute is not only an attitude of the team, the right conditions need to exist for contribution to become the norm, for it to be inspiring and contagious. This relates to how others are contributing and also to the level of connection or connectedness in the company.

Connection

Business hierarchical models are shifting from a top-down, visionary and directional approach to management to a horizontal, collaborative and inclusive way of working in which empowered teams proactively shape the culture and build the business. And, reflecting the networked and interconnected world outside of the business realm, there is a need for connection and connectedness inside business teams, too. This is taking place in different

geographies, as a 2014 study[7] on inclusive leadership shows. And the findings from six different countries show that
- "The more included employees felt, the more innovative they reported being in their jobs.
- The more included employees felt, the more they reported engaging in team citizenship behaviours—going above and beyond the "call of duty" to help other team members and meet workgroup objectives.
- Perceiving similarities with co-workers engendered a feeling of belongingness while perceiving differences led to feelings of uniqueness."

As social animals, we seek connection. In fact, we thrive on it. It is the glue that holds systems together. Talented, forward-thinking people are inspired by being part of something larger than themselves, they seek interactions and connections with others, who are similar to them in talent, but different to them in interests and expertise. Such interactions foster a cross-fertilization of ideas, creativity, and innovative buzz.

If there is no connection, no inclusion, then there is no engagement with the overall purpose. Connection is key to motivation, as Daniel Pink[8] explains, "Human beings have an innate inner drive to be autonomous, self-determined, and connected to one another. And when that drive is liberated, people achieve more and live richer lives." As horizontal systems rise to the challenge of innovation, connection will drive resilience in teams and sustained learning within organizations. These are essential to coping with complexity.

Critical thinking

At the threshold between action and reflection is critical thinking. Critical thinking entails the ability to take a step back and observe theories, ideas, and actions from an outside position in order to assess their soundness. It involves conceptualizing, synthesizing, and evaluating information, objects and behaviours.

Critical thinking also involves the ability to question the question and reframe problems, which are skills that are intrinsically present in both research and design. At its core, critical thinking is the problem-solving ability that derives from appreciating a situation and seeing alternative solutions.

The amount of information and knowledge that circulates around us is greater than ever before. Thus, one's ability to separate wheat from chaff is key to preventing becoming overwhelmed.

Former Harvard University President Derek Bok[9] summarizes the effect of critical thinking and problem-solving abilities on economic growth: "Economists who have studied the relationship between education and economic growth confirm what common sense suggests: The number of college degrees is not nearly as important as how well students develop cognitive skills, such as critical thinking and problem-solving ability."

Citizenship

We are all citizens of the world. The internet, the impact of resource depletion and the rise of wicked problems are all pointing in the same direction: this is an interconnected world. So it has become plainly obvious and out in the open that with the privilege of being part of this world comes the responsibility of acting like citizens, not consumers.

Our world is finite and it's the only one we have. We need to behave accordingly. I think this quote from Carl Sagan says it all: "Look again at that dot. That's here. That's home. That's us. On it everyone you love, everyone you know, everyone you ever heard of, every human being who ever was, lived out their lives.

The aggregate of our joy and suffering, thousands of confident religions, ideologies, and economic doctrines, every hunter and forager, every hero and coward, every creator and destroyer of civilization, every king and peasant, every young couple in love, every mother and father, hopeful child, inventor and explorer, every teacher of morals, every corrupt politician, every 'superstar', every 'supreme leader', every saint and sinner in the history of our species lived there -on a mote of dust suspended in a sunbeam."[10]

Citizenship involves being part of the solution. Command and control systems within organizations have made people over-reliant on procedures. Citizenship requires a heightened sense of commitment and an awareness of the effect of our actions on the broader ecosystem of stakeholders. It means looking at the long term as well as the short term.

Character

If we are going to inspire one another, model our own behaviours from others, and get energized through our collaboration and interaction then we must open up to the world what we have to offer. Each person has a set of traits that define him or her. Character is how we show to the world what we believe in and what we stand for.

Character also includes our morals and our ethics, and as we are so interconnected and networked it becomes a crucial aspect of our reliability as people and as teams.

The etymology of the word character clearly conveys why this matters in business and in life: character stems from the Latin *character* and Greek *kharakter* which meant 'engraved mark'. Character is what defines a person, and by extension, a team or a business.

Celebration

In the industrialist era we have learnt to praise work as a goal of its own. Truly, work is a means to an outcome that is driven by purpose and belief and that happens through hard work. Once the work is done it is important to celebrate our achievements and recognize the results of our efforts.

Sailing involves resilience and hardship but also the huge satisfaction of accomplishment. Celebrating the journey and acknowledging its lessons should also be part of the process. It is necessary to make the team resilient in the face of new storms and changing tides. And it is important to look back on the journey and celebrate the results. This feeds the team with a renewed sense of adventure and passion, which is necessary to initiate new cycles with optimism and rolled sleeves.

Caring

Caring and business are terms that are not traditionally used in the same sentence. So-called 'soft' skills cannot always be directly linked to hard metrics. Yet in this post-industrialist business context they are becoming crucial to business performance because, in the end, business comprises people, and good business professionals need to understand people to be of service to them.

Empathy involves standing in someone else's shoes in order to understand what they experience, think and feel. Forbes magazine states: "There is growing evidence that organizations that have happy employees, strong organizational health, empathetic leaders, and maybe even a social mission, outperform their peers."[11]

In a systemic view of business, in which we understand that business is interrelated with its environment and interconnected with its stakeholders, caring is about being trustworthy, being connected, and being coherent in one's claims and actions. Business integrity manifests itself to the degree that business teams are able to consequently translate their strategic intent into actions while being considerate of the impact of these actions. Caring involves embracing the total system and taking responsibility for one's actions, whether by a business, interacting with the rest of the world, or by as a team interacting with others within the business itself.

Creativity

We live in an era of creative empowerment. This is not just by chance. It feels, to a degree like a return to the beginning of 'being' with all the gathered wisdom from the industrialist era in all its glory and all its shortcomings. Before us is a future that is filled with opportunity and change. This can be terrifying because it is new and it is unknown. Or it can be an invitation to engage, explore, and generate new value.

This is where creativity plays a key role in business. If we continue approaching strategic processes as we've always done in business, how can we expect a different result? We need creativity because the solutions are not just created out of data analysis and doing business as usual. As Sir Martin Sorrell points out: "Recently, some of the world's leading business brains have gone out of their way to highlight the role of more intuitive, subjective, creative thinking in driving corporate performance, and to warn that an excessive boardroom focus on number-crunching and cost management is coming at the expense of experimentation, innovation and top-line growth."[12]

At an individual level, I relate creativity to playfulness and the ability to let go of pre-conceptions and assumptions in order to co-shape new possibilities. If this is done at the team level, the power is exponential. When we are creative as teams, venturing into the unknown becomes less terrifying and the playfulness becomes contagious, leading to new alternative futures we may not have seen otherwise.

Courage

Breaking convention and daring to disrupt take courage. Obviously, you might fail. Yet chances of success only manifest if you have the courage to try things out. Seth Godin[13] brilliantly states, "If failure is not an option, then neither is success."

Traditionally, sailors have always been seen as courageous people who showed fortitude and resilience in the face of weather, wind and the hardships of a seafarer's life. Such a life, demonstrates the zealous pursuit of goals. But also, etymologically, courage derives from the Latin *cor* which means heart. This emphasizes the importance of convictions and beliefs in applying courage.

In the context of business, it takes bravery to change things. A large part of management practice in large organizations is linked to maintaining the status quo and increasing efficiency. It is not geared towards questioning the strategic course or introducing new ways of doing things. But not doing so might mean losing relevance. So innovation and strategic renewal take courage -the courage to question what is being done, how it's being done and why it's being done. The courage to stay relevant and defy the inertia of continuing to sail without adjusting the course.

Communication

Our world has become more networked and cross-cultural, and chances for miscommunication have risen exponentially. This puts new demands on our communication skills, especially within business. Leaders must engage their teams through communication, to inspire them and encourage proactive action based on shared beliefs. It means that we have to get better at listening, to tune in to what matters, and better at storytelling, to make our ideas travel in compelling ways.

Active listening is the key to good communication. Too often we think communication is about conveying messages persuasively. In reality, people are so overwhelmed by the sheer number of messages they are getting that sending out more messages probably won't even get through the clutter, let alone achieve the desired effect. So we must learn to listen to understand, not listen to reply. We must use dialogue to open perspectives and take us in new directions.

Story telling is on the rise in business. And it can be very effective if used well. "Research on the human brain has shown it is predisposed to think in the terms of a story. This predisposition is continuously reinforced and strengthened throughout the life of your brain. Imaging studies have shown only a small, quarter-sized region of your brain lights up when someone tells you a series of facts. However, when someone tells you a story laced with those facts, or those facts in action, your entire brain lights up."[14] Stories are ownable; this is why they travel well. They are empowering because they allow us to envision a world that is possible and inspire us to co-shape it. And. also, stories create engagement and connection which are at the core of great communication. As we evolve in our post-industrialist mindset we will begin to engage differently: using both facts and stories to understand and interpret the world.

Commitment to change

To quote social entrepreneur Bill Drayton: "Every successful organization has to make the transition from a world defined primarily by repetition to one primarily defined by change. This is the biggest transformation in the structure of how humans work together since the Agricultural Revolution."[15] We are immersed in this transformation and are an integral part of it.

Change is not something that can be accomplished half-heartedly. Change is about realization. It is about crossing a threshold and getting things done to give shape to a new reality. This involves a transformation and a shift. Being committed to change is being committed to achieving those results effectively. It involves putting in effort and time and resources to make it happen. It involves cheering others on and continuing to pursue the end goal even when conditions are adverse. It means being resourceful and predisposed to solving any challenges that present themselves along the way.

Clarity of purpose

In his famous book *Alice in Wonderland*[16], Lewis Carroll relates an encounter between Alice and the Cheshire Cat:
"Would you tell me, please, which way I ought to go from here?"
"That depends a good deal on where you want to get to," said the Cat.
"I don't much care where-" said Alice.
"Then it doesn't matter which way you go," said the Cat.
"-so long as I get somewhere," Alice added as an explanation.
"Oh, you're sure to do that," said the Cat, "if you only walk long enough."

Venturing out into open waters is not what is difficult. Much like the challenge of strategy is not just in stating an intent. Nor is the challenge of innovation, only in getting ideas. Once you set out an ambition, it is as important to work on developing it as it is to be reminded of what the purpose was in the first place. Because conditions change, navigation is never linear and the journey can be long. Being clear on one's purpose allows for flexibility on how to get there so that it is ultimately possible to do so. Not having a purpose in mind makes any journey equally relevant and none really effective, like in Alice's story.

LeaderShip

Leadership is no longer an individual trait. It is no longer a heroic position, mandated by hierarchy. Leadership is an attitude that unifies efforts. In our sailboat analogy it is something that the total team embodies, by doing. Leader-Ship.

LeaderShip is characterized by these fourteen attitudes, working together and complementary to one another. It is not enough to have just one attitude; they work organically and situationally depending on what is best and what is needed. Collaboration, curiosity, contribution, connection, critical thinking, citizenship, character, celebration, caring, creativity, courage, communication, commitment to change. and clarity of purpose, are all aspects of what it takes to lead and inspire in the twenty-first century. All empower the teams that form the business of the future.

There are no rules carved in stone and these attitudes are not static. They guide us and remind us of what matters -that we are in this together, that we must be able to inspire and rely on each other to make it a pleasurable, successful journey in which we can all rightfully share in a sense of accomplishment and progress.

It takes both attitudes and skills. The attitudes we have discussed in this chapter are essential to all business sailors of the twenty-first century. The skills needed for strategic renewal are the skills of research and design, and they can potentially empower non-researchers and non-designers to engage with the world with curiosity and creativity as we sail into a new paradigm.

LeaderShip entails both an outward-facing connection with the market, customers, and stakeholders and an inward-facing strengthening of the teams and their sense of purpose. It is not enough to integrate the skills of research and design into processes and structures to make a company more resilient. The belief

in and ownability of the strategy is crucial to see it through and it is something that cannot be imposed on people. It is something that is driven by passion from within the teams. Achieving that level of teamwork takes a unifying sense of purpose, a flexible organization of project-based initiatives, and a collaborative approach to bring in all of the 14 Cs into play.

8 CHANGE AHEAD

'The ocean stirs the heart, inspires the imagination and brings eternal joy to the soul.'

–Wyland

Value creation

Change in the context of business means reinventing the company and designing new business models that allow a company's strategic intent to manifest in the future.

Business is aimed at creating value, and as the context changes, business becomes part of a dynamic system in which value creation is achieved through engagement and vision. Business becomes interconnected to the whole ecosystem and plays into the opportunities that come with complexity and change in iterative and experimental ways while linked to a clear strategic aim.

There are many ways to look at the context around us. Within this book I have chosen the analogy of the sea. It works for several reasons. First, the sea is where we came from, the origin of life on earth as we know it, and a critical element for our sustenance and survival. Business rises from within the market context, when ideas and needs connect. Second, it fascinates us beyond our ability to fully understand it. We are able to accept that it is complex, untameable, and erratic. Third, it changes us: it turns us into avid explorers seeking to dive into its depths, and travel its breadth, and whenever we take the plunge and venture into its immense vastness, it changes us. We each re-emerge a different person than we were when we engaged in the dance of the waves.

"Research and design are uniquely positioned as facilitators of change."

Value creation is the result of businesses being connected, meaningful, and relevant to their context. At the front end of the value creation process, design and research are blending in. The reason why they are more relevant now than ever before is that both research and design thrive in the face of complexity by reaching out and generating involvement, which is especially relevant in situations in which the outcome is unclear and the context is turbulent.

Involvement is key in this era of creative empowerment. Everyone wants to be involved. Clients want to be involved by agencies, not just brief them about what needs to be done. They know, that if you can brief what the desired outcome is, you are repeating patterns from the past. There is a need for reinventing and learning.

Senior management wants to be involved by the project teams, and not just dictate strategy top-down and waiting for results to be reported back. They want to co-develop and learn from the process.

Users want to be involved and proactively co-create the brands and businesses they interact with. They are no longer subjects of research and design. They are co-creators of strategy as partners in a process by co-defining the 'why' and the 'what' and co-participating in the 'how'.

This need for involvement means businesses need both people skills and creative skills to bring stakeholders together and navigate through the different stages of value creation -particularly the initial stages of strategic planning and strategy development.

In this way, value creation is increasingly taking on collaborative forms. Strategy is teamwork: contributors co-create the future by bringing in different skills and perspectives, creating together, sharing the learning process, running different scenarios, and making them explicit through prototyping.

Facilitators of change

As we've seen, research and design were both originally functional roles within business. They have changed, alongside the changes that business has undergone, through their ability to add value throughout the process, by their iterative interaction of research, design, research, design cycles, and choreographed curiosity and creativity. They are not independent from one another and they are not isolated areas of expertise within business. Nor are they a set of tools. They are a way of thinking and doing, a way of integrating analytical thinking and intuitive thinking with a sense of purpose and a process of generating what could work and of testing what doesn't work to learn again.

The creative endeavour of infusing meaning into products and services is the direct result of truly understanding and distilling what matters to others. This requires empathy and facilitation, while also having the vision to shape the business in ways that are unique and that imbue it with a sense of direction and purpose. This does not happen in a vacuum.

We need both responsive research and adaptive design to help facilitate the process.

Liz Sanders[1] sees promise in the abilities that transformative agents in research and design have, to facilitate change: *"In the future, designers and researchers will be the creators of scaffolds upon which everyday people will express their creativity".*

Research and design are uniquely positioned as facilitators of change. They are excellent conduits to enabling creativity. Thanks to their intrinsic skills of understanding and creating, learning and applying, thinking and doing. They rise above their functional expertise areas, reconnecting teams with their primary, human abilities of experiencing the world and co-shaping it.

Any sailor venturing out into waters knows nothing remains stable for very long. When you go out sailing there some things you know:
• The journey is not linear,
• You will be affected by the environmental factors including waves, weather, changing conditions,
• Sailing as a team makes the group more resilient because more eyes see more things; more skills and abilities can intervene more flexibly and adaptively
• It involves a certain level of risk, letting go of the shore and venturing into the unknown

In the current context we really do not know what might happen next. It is possible to have a smooth sail with clear conditions as much as it is likely that conditions change and we need to contribute all of our skills and abilities to adapt to those conditions. We need facilitators to guide us through this process, to be alert for the context, and to be aware of what to do to steer business in the right direction.

Wandering and wondering

Little is said about research in the context of design because it is assumed to be part of the design repertoire. But that does a disservice to research. Though research is an integral part of the design process, it is slightly different. Where design is creative and wonders what could be, I find that research is explorative and wanders out into the world to reveal things that had not been noticed before. Research makes new connections by looking at what is hidden in plain sight, either because it is taken for granted, because consumers cannot or have not articulated it, or because it is only just emerging.

There is a belief in the business world that consumers cannot tell you what they want. Often, business people refer to the words of Henry Ford, that if he had asked people what they wanted they would have said they wanted a faster horse. That is, of course,, like Henry Ford himself, at the basis of industrialist thinking.

But discovery is oblique, not linear. Of course you can ask direct questions to people, but they might only give you answers. Engaging in conversations and dialogues enables learning, which comes from discovering new questions.

In reality, consumers truly know a lot about what happens in their lives and their contexts. They are experts of their own experience. The ability to wander through that context and know how to ask and what to ask is essential to creating meaning for consumers and customers. Consumers will not provide all the answers and they certainly will not design the solutions all by themselves. But they are the source of great insights, based on what they currently do, what works for them, what doesn't work and what might be missing. As business solutions are designed, context-based research is the best possible source of feedback, it goes into the environment to study solutions in the world, to understand what is real and behaviourally based. It is an interaction-based dialogue that helps teams understand what works, what they might have overlooked and what is less relevant.

Due to the increasing complexity of the challenges faced by businesses, identifying the right problem becomes the extended territory of finding great solutions. You need to both wander and wonder. The eagerness to scope out the problem, to learn what might really be happening, is essential to solution making.

"Alive organizations are vehicles to solution-making."

Business sailors are the linking-pin between understanding the context and making a business come alive through its products and services. They are not only designers, nor only researchers. These business sailors are a new breed of professionals that are changing business through new methods that are design based and with a mindset that is curious, explorative and adaptive. Wired[2] magazine reflects on the adoption of this mindset in the context of business, signalling that there is a change towards "Understanding people in the context and culture they live in to develop genuine empathy, and testing and iterating solutions with customers to explore the validity of decisions. Often this means relying on intuition to guide decision-making when the data isn't clear, a skill that the principles and methods inherent in design have a uniquely positive impact on."

Alive organizations

Business ultimately creates value through the dynamic interaction with its context and users. Such dynamic interaction requires of businesses a high level of adaptability, and that they add layers of meaning to their core values, seamlessly integrating the business with its context, yet maintaining the unique attributes that define it.

Alive organizations live and breathe in their contexts. They are the vehicles of solution making through which users access solutions to their problems. This demands that companies be
• Meaningful and relevant, addressing problems that matter, and doing so in ongoing and collective ways that enable them to understand, organize and prioritize the problems that need addressing;

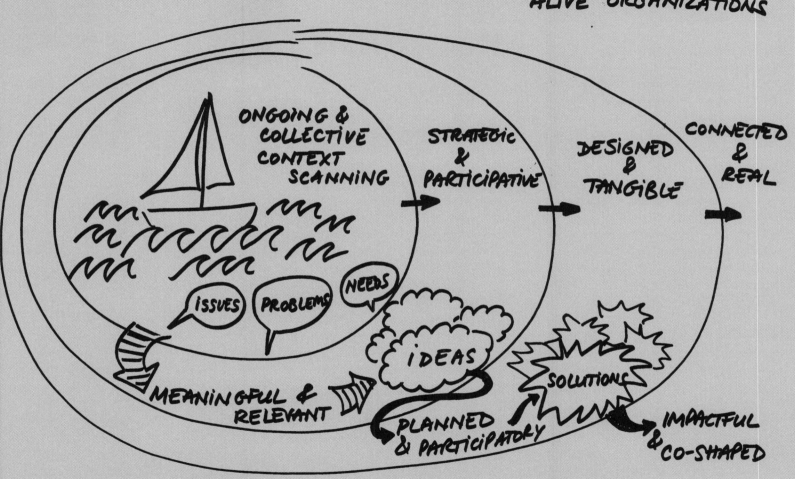

ALIVE ORGANIZATIONS

ONGOING & COLLECTIVE CONTEXT SCANNING

STRATEGIC & PARTICIPATIVE

DESIGNED & TANGIBLE

CONNECTED & REAL

ISSUES   PROBLEMS   NEEDS

IDEAS

SOLUTIONS

MEANINGFUL & RELEVANT

PLANNED & PARTICIPATORY

IMPACTFUL & CO-SHAPED

- Planned and anticipatory, identifying ideas and opportunities. And doing so in ways that are strategic and participative in order to create future scenarios which they play with, experiment with and imagine in a process of strategic renewal.
- Impactful and co-shaping, creating solutions that deliver value. And doing so in designed and tangible ways that give shape to the context by applying, integrating and forming solutions that are co-designed with the users.

This aliveness is symbolized by the sailing journey. Sailing requires being fit and knowing oneself, trusting the team and discovering one's instinctive abilities, building confidence and resilience. It requires an enhanced appreciation of the context: whether to enjoy a peaceful summer day or to excel in regatta racing, to weather a storm together or to the exhilarating discovery of new shores.

Collaborative learning

Business sailors look out into the ocean and understand that conditions will change constantly throughout the journey. Sailing is less about planning and more about interaction and a fluid sense of purpose. It is about adventure and teamwork. Successful business navigation entails integrating perspectives and skills collaboratively. Businesses that are able to revisit how they integrate these disciplines will not only have a competitive advantage. It is my conviction that they will gain entirely

new vantage points that will enrich their value-creation process. They will transform and be transformed by the process.

These processes are complex and messy. They require LeaderShip as we've seen in the previous chapter. Business sailors, while taking into account the context, navigate in order to serve a strategic purpose. Within alive organizations there is less structured planning and more free-form navigation in order to achieve the desired outcomes. This, in turn, means that functionalities and departments as they were defined within the industrialist paradigm start to interact and overlap one another as they reshape business towards a goal. They rise above the functional mandates towards co-shaping, co-inventing and co-designing the future.

The very functions themselves are changing. It is not just design that has a different mission. Research and strategy have different missions, too. As businesses enact more project-based methods, and as they connect thinking and doing, the different orders of design, research, and strategy will need to integrate themselves into a collaborative learning adventure that ultimately creates value.

The pioneers and experts interviewed for this book show us that there is not a one-size-fits-all model. They also showed us that the synchronicity between research, design, and strategy is emerging.

A ripple of curiosity initiates the discovery of new shores, and as these three disciplines venture out into the sea of collaborative navigation they are able to move forward in a state of perpetual creative tension and learning.

The result is that the whole becomes so much more than the sum of its parts. Initially separated, tactical initiatives grow outwards in a more anticipatory, proactive orientation and grow towards each other in a more systemic orientation.

Research has evolved from a hypothesis based, scientific approaches to a more designerly, requirement-based approach, from investigation (as a means to confirm), to knowledge generation (as a means to understand) into insight generation (as a means to empathize) and finally to foresight (as a means to anticipate).

Design, as we have seen through Richard Buchanan's *Four Orders of Design* model, evolves from visual design to product design into experience design and systems design.

Strategy, in turn, evolves from operational strategy and the management of organizations into revenue-driven strategy, and then more outwardly into growth-driven strategy, and finally into a mindset of change in which culture is leading the delivery of the strategic intent.

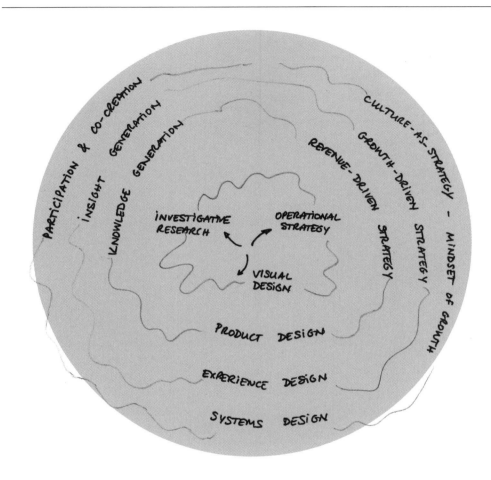

The diagram contains the following labels (from outer ring inward):

PARTICIPATION & CO-CREATION
INSIGHT GENERATION
KNOWLEDGE GENERATION
CULTURE-AS-STRATEGY — MINDSET OF GROWTH
GROWTH-DRIVEN STRATEGY
REVENUE-DRIVEN STRATEGY

INVESTIGATIVE RESEARCH
OPERATIONAL STRATEGY
VISUAL DESIGN

PRODUCT DESIGN
EXPERIENCE DESIGN
SYSTEMS DESIGN

Each of these disciplines has seen in their own ways that the processes are not what make the difference. It is the people. Organizing teams flexibly to collaborate by bringing people together is the most powerful change lever on any sailboat in the sea of business.

Humanizing our efforts

Systems of control, speed, and efficiency take out the human aspect of organic growth, openness to change, cyclical learning and connection. The complexity of our systems, the problems we face, the contextual turbu-

lence and the speed of change all demand a kind of intelligence and skills that are beyond the individual scale. Each individual needs to go through his or her own learning cycles, and within teams, we need to work together to access that kind of multi-layered intelligence.

People are not machines and systems are not just structures. At the heart of everything we do are our human abilities. Without them we lose touch, lose connection, and ultimately lose engagement. The complementarity of skills that emerges from teamwork actually increases the resilience of the whole system, not through structure but through human interaction. The interaction helps contain the fear of failure because no one is going it alone: it becomes a generative, constructionist engagement in which we build on each other's talents and skills.

Sailing into the unknown and crafting the future together entices passion and the belief in our abilities, and it has the powerful lure of adventure -which has been missing at the heart of most large businesses. The sailing metaphor is about putting the adventure back into venturing, re-dynamizing the strategic process to link it with the speed and complexity of the process, and recognizing the multiplicity of skills and attitudes that can add value to the whole, ultimately situating 'company' back on the human level by linking the interaction of people's efforts and the overarching network intelligence of the teams at the heart of business growth.

Everything is a project

The process is iterative and the cycles are shorter. Everything is a project in which businesses put people at the centre, learn progressively, and act on that learning.

The continuous iteration of projects, unified by a strategic intent, is the powerful unifying force that enables companies to pull across the water. It is what helps align resources towards a new destination, even when you do not know what the path looks like that will get you there.

This way of approaching value creation necessitates its own form of empowerment. It cannot be dictated by a hierarchical leader, or a 'sage on the stage'. It can only flourish in the presence of 'a guide by your side, as the project teams co-develop the world we all want to live in.

Trying to control such a system is futile. The iterations within the projects are endless. Therein lies the creative power of business navigation, just like with the international maritime flag system, which was developed more than 150 years ago as a means of communication. The combinations of flags signify different messages and more than twelve thousand combinations are possible. This system is a symbol of communication and understanding because it aids communication even at moments of radio silences to ensure everyone is on the same page.

New business leaders should not aim for control but for empowerment. This creative empowerment is achieved through a contagious attitude of openness and learning, by considering things like

- Availability of information, the freedom to connect and interrelate ideas through shared, visual and interactive processes.
- Cross functionality and mixed teams to allow for new perspectives, new questions, and empowerment to make new combinations.
- Parallel streams to allow room for failure. Some things will inevitably fail. But by not over-committing to any one thing, the risk of failure becomes acceptable, generating room to learn.
- Embracing ambiguity and paradoxes, and daring to see obstacles as questions that can help reframe the problems that arise along the way.
- Making room to play, create random combinations and see new things that may seemingly have no connection and yet can be repurposed to create user value.

One cannot fully prepare for change. But one can make sure that the sailboat is in top condition, the team is ready, and the processes are flexible leaving, which leaves room for creative solutions.

Fluidity

In the twentieth century, we didn't have the internet as we do now. Nor did we have technology with the level of accessibility we do now. Nor did we have maker-movements on a massive scale. Information is ubiquitous; makeability is within hand's reach.

The combination of information overload, tools, technologies, and platforms for making, and a complex environment require discerning skills. Providing more of the same or offering resistance to this fluidity of torrential speed will not make a difference. There is more than ever a need to understand (as opposed to know), to design (as opposed to make) and to dynamically shape strategy (as opposed to plan it). These abilities will best equip organizations and businesses in the face of change.

However, they are neither separate nor exchangeable. Like the multi-layered intelligence of teams, they are all necessary and they are complementary. The beauty of it is that they come from different paradigms -from different areas of expertise- but they converge in a new space. Fast business and fast gains are individualistic and separatist. Lasting prosperity is dependent on our readiness and openness to work together towards solution making, on strategic goals that envision value creation for everyone, and on striving for long-lasting results through excellent, coordinated, and collaborative efforts. This may well have been what early industrialists had envisioned, except that we got lost along the way by putting our too much of our attention on processes, efficiency, control, and speed.

It is time to reconnect with what research, design, and strategy are and what they signify. We can rise above the individual scope by bundling strengths. Business allows people to integrate these talents and skills, providing synergistic, collaborative, and proactive opportunities for engagement. Delivering business's ultimate purpose: value generation.

By bringing in research's ability to get to the heart of matters by putting people at the centre; design's ability to shape solutions by generating user value and strategy's reflective ability to rethink what can be evolved -as well as its anticipatory ability to envision what comes next- we can bring business strategy-making and strategic renewal to new levels. Business and management are intrinsically good at coordinating efforts towards a common goal. By making that goal meaningful through a human lens, relevant through a design lens, and lasting through a strategic lens, we will be ready for all kinds of change ahead.

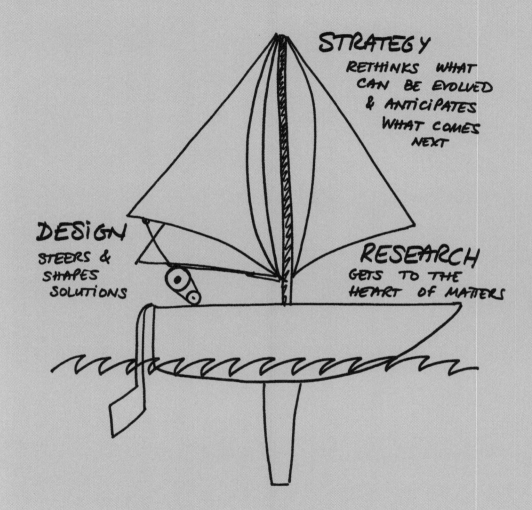

STRATEGY
RETHINKS WHAT CAN BE EVOLVED & ANTICIPATES WHAT COMES NEXT

DESIGN
STEERS & SHAPES SOLUTIONS

RESEARCH
GETS TO THE HEART OF MATTERS

"If you wan't to build a ship, don't gather people together to collect wood and don't assign them tasks and work, but rather teach them to long for the endless immensity of the sea."

- Antoine de Saint Exupéry

ENDNOTES

1 STRATEGY IN MOTION

1 http://www.businessdictionary.com/definition/rational.html
2 *The Opposable Mind, Winning Through Integrative Thinking.* Roger L Martin. Harvard Business Review Press. July 13, 2009.
3 FastCompany, *Design Thursday: Roger Martin on The Opposable Mind*, article by Bill Green. September 6 2007 (http://www.fastcompany.com/679333/design-thursday-roger-martin-opposable-mind)
4 *Fixing the Game: Bubbles, Crashes, and What Capitalism Can Learn from the NFL.* Roger L. Martin. Harvard Business Review Press, May 2011.
5 http://www.oxforddictionaries.com/definition/english/research
6 ESOMAR is the international association for market research, with more than five thousand members in one hundred thirty countries (www.esomar.org).
7 *Sciences of the Artificial.* Herbert Simon. MIT Press, 1969.
8 Stated by William Gibson in *Talk of the Nation* (NPR), November 30th, 1999 during a radio show on 'The Science of Science Fiction".
9 This quote is attributed to Peter Ferdinand Drucker (1909-2005), a renowned business consultant and management author.

2 REDESIGNING RESEARCH

1 David Snowden (1954) is a Welsh academic who researches complexity theory and knowledge management. He is the founder of the Cognitive Edge network.
2 Gary Klein, Ph.D. (1944), is a Senior Scientist at MacroCognition LLC. He has authoreed several books on cognition and knowledge management: *Sources of Power: How People Make Decisions* (1998); *The Power of Intuition* (2004); *Working Minds: A practitioner's guide to Cognitive Task Analysis* (Crandall, Klein, & Hoffman, 2006); *Streetlights and Shadows: Searching for the keys to adaptive decision making* (2009); *Seeing what others don't: The Remarkable Ways We Gain Insights* (2013).
3 http://www.oxforddictionaries.com, listed definition for 'research'
4 Page 28 of the slideshare presentation by Umar Ghumman titled *What is an insight?* http://www.slideshare.net/umarghumman/what-is-an-insight-34449790
5 *InGenius- A Crash Course on Creativity*, Tina Seelig, 2012 Hay House.

3 ▷ RESEARCHING DESIGN

1 Herbert Simon (1916-2001) was an American psychologist and sociologist. Simon was a researcher and professor at Carnegie Mellon University and an highly regarded expert in the areas of artificial intelligence and cognitive psychology. In 1978 he won the Nobel Prize for economics.

2 Source: *The Economic Effects of Design*, National Agency for Enterprise, Copenhagen, Denmark, September 2003 and *Design Creates Value*, National Agency for Enterprise, Copenhagen, Denmark, September 2007

3 Dave Gray is the founder of XPLANE. He is also the author of two books: *Gamestorming* and *The Connected Company* His website is: http://www.davegrayinfo.com

4 Rob Curedale is CEO of Curedale Inc., a boutique product design and design research firm based in Los Angeles, California. www.curedale.com

5 Wikipedia, http://en.wikipedia.org/wiki/Iteration

6 The *Double Diamond of Design* is a model developed by the British Design Council in 2005 through an in-house research study. Source: designcouncil.org.uk

7 *Eleven lessons: Managing Design in Eleven Global Brands.* British Design Council.

Publication date: 20/01/2007

8 *Change by Design*, Tim Brown, 2009 Harper Collins

9 This quote is attributed to Lee Iacocca, former president and CEO of Chrysler.

10 Richard Buchanan , Ph.D. Professor and Department Chair, Design & Innovation, Weatherhead School of Management, Case Western Reserve University

11 Antonio Damasio, Ph.D. *Descartes' Error: Emotion, Reason and the Human Brain*, Penguin Books 2005

12 Daniel Kahneman, *Thinking, Fast and Slow* Penguin Books, 2012

13 http://www.businessdictionary.com/definition/dynamic-equilibrium.html

14 *The End of Competitive Advantage: How to Keep Your Strategy Moving as Fast as Your Business* Rita Gunther McGrath, Harvard Business Review Press, 2013

15 *A Means-End Model Based on Consumer Categorization Processes.* Jonathan Gutman, Journal of Marketing, Spring 1982.

16 *Marketing Malpractice: The Cause and the Cure*, Clayton M. Christensen, Scott Cook and Taddy Hall. Harvard Business Review, Vol. 83, No. 12, December 2005

17 http://www.christenseninstitute.org/key-concepts/jobs-to-be-done

18 http://www.ideo.com/images/uploads/hcd_toolkit/IDEO_HCD_ToolKit.pdf

19 Charles Burnette, Ph.D. is a design educator and the initiator of Design Based Education. He was the Dean, School of Architecture, University of Texas at Austin, Director of the Graduate Program in Industrial Design at the University of theArts in Philadelphia, PA, and Chairman of its Industrial Design Department.

20 Jeanne Liedtka and Tim Ogilvie. *Designing for Growth*. Columbia Business School, 2011

21 *This is Service Design Thinking*. Marc Stickdorn and Jakob Schneider. BIS Publishers, 2011. Page 34.

22 *Creativity-based Research: the Process of Co-designing with Users*. Catalina Naranjo-Bok. UX Magazine, Article nr 820. April 24, 2012

23 *Convivial Toolbox: Generative Research at the Front-end of Design*. Liz Sanders and Pieter Jan Stappers, BIS Publishers 2012.

24 From Carnegie Mellon's School of Design website (February 2015): http://design.cmu.edu/content/doctoral-research-foci

25 IBM's *2010 Global CEO study*: http://www-935.ibm.com/services/us/ceo/ceostudy2010/

26 Wolff Olins 2015 report, *Impossible and Now: How Leaders are Creating the Uncorporation*. http://woreport.wolffolins.com

27 Marty Neumeier is an author and speaker on topics of innovation, strategy, and design. He has authored several books including: *The Brand Gap: How to Bridge the Distance Between Business Strategy and Design* (2003); *Zag: The #1 Strategy of High-Performance Brands* (2006) and *The 46 Rules of Genius: An Innovator's Guide to Creativity* (2014)

4 ◆ SETTING SAIL

1 *The Customer Experience Outlook, A Collection of Ideas for the Year Ahead.* By Kerry Bodine & Doberman, January 2015: http://kerrybodine.com/blog/eb-ook-the-2015-customer-experience-out-look/

2 Alain de Botton is a contemporary philosopher and author: http://alaindebot-ton.com

3 *Diffusion of Innovations,* Everett Rogers, 5th edition 2003, Free Press.

4 *What Do We Mean By "Innovation," "Collaboration," or "Design"?* Paddy Harrington, in FastCoDesign, February 18, 2011. http://www.fastcodesign.com/1663265/what-do-we-mean-by-innovation-collaboration-or-design

5 http://en.wikipedia.org/wiki/Sailing

6 Professor Ranulph Glanville (1946-2014) former Professor Emeritus of Architecture and Cybernetics at University College London. He also was Research Senior Tutor and Professor in Innovation Design Engineering at Royal College of Art in London, Professor of Architecture at the University of Newcastle in Australia, and Senior Professor of Research Design at the Catholic University of Leuven in Belgium.

7 *The Lean Startup: How Constant Innovation Creates Radically Successful Businesses.* Eric Ries, Penguin Books Ltd, 2011

8 http://www.merriam-webster.com/dictionary/bisociation

9 *Scamper: Creative Games and Activities for Imagination Development,* Bob Eberle. Prufrock Press Inc., new edition 2008.

10 For background information on this diagram developed by Kaoru Ishikawa as a quality management tool you can read the Wikipedia entry on the Ishikawa diagram: http://en.wikipedia.org/wiki/Ishikawa_diagram

11 *Zen Mind, Beginner's Mind: Informal Talks on Zen Meditation and Practice.* Shunryu Suzuki, Shambhala, 2011.

12 *The Lean Startup: How Today's Entrepreneurs Use Continuous Innovation to Create Radically Successful Businesses.* Eric Ries, Crown Business, 2011.

5 ◇ EMERGING PRACTICES

1 The drawings featured in the interviews were made by the each of interviewees and are printed with their permission.

6 ◧ CONVERGING TOWARDS COLLABORATION

1 The illustrations featured in the interviews were made by the each of interviewees and are printed with their permission.

7 ▣ THE NEXT FRONTIER

1 *Mindset: The New Psychology of Success*. Carol Dweck. Ballantine Books, 2007.

2 The term T-shaped is broadly used in education and recruitment. Its origin is attributed to McKinsey & Co as part of their recruitment policy for new consultants.

3 *Creating Cultural Change: The Key to Succesful Total Quality Management*. Philips Atkinson, IFS Publications, 1990.

4 *On Becoming a Leader,* revised edition. Warren Bennis. Perseus books, 1994.

5 *Curious? Discover the Missing Ingredient for a Fulfilling Life.* Todd Kashdan. Harper Perennial, 2010.

6 *Curiosity is as Important as Intelligence.* Thomas Chamorro-Premuzic. Harvard Business Review, August 27, 2014.

7 *Inclusive Leadership: The View from Six Countries..* Jeanine Prime and Elizabeth Salib. Catalyst, May 2014.

8 *Drive: The Surprising Truth About What Motivates Us.* Daniel Pink. Riverhead Books. 2011.

9 Derek Bok is a lawyer and author of several books on higher education. He was President of Harvard University for the periods 1971-1991 and 2006-2007.

10 *Pale Blue Dot: A Vision of the Human Future in Space.* Carl Sagan. Ballantine Books, 1997.

11 *Empathy in Business: Indulgence or Invaluable?* Ashoka for Forbes Magazine, March 22nd 2013.

12 *Creativity Makes a Vast Contribution to Business: We Ignore It at our Peril.* Sir Martin Sorrell, founder and chief executive of WPP, City A.M. March 1st, 2015.

13 Seth Godin is an American best selling management book author. He is an international speaker and regularly publishes his thinking on his online blog.

14 *Black Hole Focus: How Intelligent People Can Create a Powerful Purpose for Their Lives.* Isaiah Hankel. Capstone, 2014.

15 Bill Drayton is an American social entrepreneur and founder of the non-profit organization Ashoka. He has co-authored several books on the topics of innovation and change.

16 *Alice in Wonderland.* Lewis Carroll. Templar, 2009

8 ☰ CHANGE AHEAD

1 Liz Sanders at the IIT Design Research conference in 2008, during her presentation titled '*Co-creation and the New Landscapes of Design*'.

2 '*Design Led Companies work, But not Without Designers*'. Wired Magazine, March 2015: http://www.wired.com/2015/03/design-led-companies-work-not-without-designers/

Photography credits

All photography by Shutterstock, except:
p. 95 by Boris Rijksen
p. 142 by Carola Verschoor
p. 282 by NASA Goddard Space Flight Center, Norman Kuring, NASA Ocean Color Group via Flickr Creative Commons 2.0